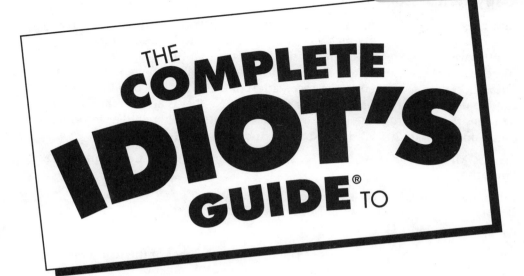

THE **COMPLETE IDIOT'S GUIDE®** TO

# World Religions

## Second Edition

*by Brandon Toropov
and Father Luke Buckles*

**ALPHA**

A Pearson Education Company

**Publisher**
*Marie Butler-Knight*

**Product Manager**
*Phil Kitchel*

**Managing Editor**
*Jennifer Chisholm*

**Senior Acquisitions Editor**
*Renee Wilmeth*

**Development Editor**
*Nancy D. Warner*

**Production Editor**
*Katherin Bidwell*

**Copy Editor**
*Cari Luna*

**Illustrator**
*Brian Moyer*

**Cover Designers**
*Mike Freeland*
*Kevin Spear*

**Book Designers**
*Scott Cook and Amy Adams of DesignLab*

**Indexer**
*Angie Bess*

**Layout/Proofreading**
*Angela Calvert*
*Mary Hunt*
*Kimberly Tucker*

# Contents at a Glance

# Contents

ix

## xiii

## Appendixes

# Foreword

With the close of the twentieth century and the dawn of the twenty-first, as one millennium has passed into another, spirituality and religion are on the ascent.

Having been compartmentalized, segregated, secularized, persecuted, and prohibited in various times and places around the world, religion still possesses a vitality that not only endures, but intensifies. It makes sense of that which science cannot explain, puts order into chaos, and spirit into matter. In short, religion feeds the soul.

Religion is important for the majority of people living on this planet. And in our technological age, with its instant communication, that planet has become smaller. Knowing more about each other, and about the belief systems that guide us, is a useful tool in gaining understandings that can break down barriers of suspicion and prejudice.

What commonalities emerge can be both surprising and edifying. For instance, all the major religions of the world agree on the existence of angels. Furthermore, this belief has been made manifest for centuries in the art and literature of many traditions. Yet not until recently has this trend emerged in a noticeable way in popular culture. (Today, of course, angels are the focus of a level of intense interest, an interest that would have surprised observers of, say, two decades ago.)

A spiritual bond—a bond that can tie the diverse human family together in a way that economics and politics cannot—is surely something to strive for. What culture or civilization can be said to exist without some spiritual or religious root feeding it? To fully understand the visible and material world around us, it is necessary to approach the invisible Spirit that motivates and drives that world.

But where does one begin?

This useful handbook is one place to start. While many tomes have been written about the theology or ecclesiology of a particular faith, there are not many books that have been written with the intention of bringing the reader an inter-religious, cross-cultural understanding.

All the faiths, institutions, and belief systems detailed in this book reflect the attempt to reach out to something eternal. And that search for the eternal never ends.

This book outlines the basic features and guiding ideas of religions you may encounter as an outsider. It is a significant and valuable aid to the basic understanding of people who are different from you. If you are looking for a tool that will help you reduce parallel tensions, gather information, and deepen insights about both the similarities and the differences of the world's faiths, you've found it here.

And you don't have to be an idiot to use it!

—Michael Morris

Father Michael Morris, O.P., is a Catholic priest and Dominican friar with a Ph.D. in the history of art. He teaches in the area of Religion and Art at the Graduate Theological Union in Berkeley, and is the author of many popular and scholarly works dealing with art, religion, and culture.

# Introduction

We started working on this book with the hope that it would help build bridges.

Our aim was to increase mutual understanding, in an entertaining and informative way, among believers of a wide variety of backgrounds. Now that we've concluded the project, we find ourselves taken aback, not by the many differences the world's religions presented (although these certainly exist), but by the many similarities we've come across in the world's systems of faith.

Discussing unfamiliar religious matters has a way of making people feel tense and uncertain, perhaps because of the natural human tendency to withdraw from subjects they feel uniformed about. Sometimes this instinct can be a valuable one. When it comes to making contact with people of other religious backgrounds, though, it has its limitations. A lot of people, on encountering someone who holds to a different belief system, simply "shut down." It seems safer not to inquire, not to examine, not to explore—and not to learn. As a result, old, often degrading preconceptions recirculate, along with the assumption that "they" approach spiritual and religious matters fundamentally different than "we" do. Walls rise between communities of believers—and not always just figuratively!

We believe that when followers within religious system A stop listening and arbitrarily decide that people operating within system B don't revere life as a gift, or that their terminology for describing the Divine is flawed, or that they mislead others regarding true salvation, something tragic happens. The followers within system B are no longer representatives of a unique tradition with its own distinctive history, goals, and worldview; instead they are now proponents of a competing ideology. Too many needless conflicts have arisen from this familiar process of "drafting" religious adversaries. We offer this book as a tool for sidestepping this process and opening up to the world's faith systems. We hope to help you understand their idiosyncrasies and differing emphases, and penetrate to the common themes of grace, compassion, and transcendent purpose. We've tried to make the book interesting and of value to people who probably won't ever get an advanced degree in comparative religion, but we have also tried to make our assessments thorough, responsible, and consistent.

Remember, though, the book you're holding in your hands is only the beginning. There is a lot to learn—more than we could possibly set down in one book—so don't stop here. Use this book as a starting point for your own explorations of the world's great faiths. Use it to make your contacts with other traditions more fulfilling for both sides of the discussion. Use it to support and enhance your own spiritual journey. Use it to find new sources of insight. Use it to open up new doors. Use it to build new bridges.

For us, the discovery that the world's religions share much in common is a joyful one. To paraphrase an observation made during the Second Vatican Council:

*The problems that weigh heavily on human hearts are the same today as in ages past. What is the human person? What is the meaning and purpose of life? What is upright behavior, and what is sinful? Where does suffering originate, and what end does it serve? How can genuine happiness be found? What happens at death? What is judgment?*

*What reward follows death? And finally, what is the ultimate mystery, beyond human explanation, which embraces our entire existence, from which we take our origin and towards which we tend?* (Nostra Aetate—*Declaration on the Relation of the Church to Non-Christian Religions*)

The authors of this book, both of whom have their own faith commitments, have, in writing it, come to understand not only the religions of the world but also each other. Both of us remember and celebrate another important message from the same publication of the Second Vatican Council: "The Church urges her children to enter with prudence and charity into discussion and collaboration with members of other religions. Let Christians, while witnessing to their own faith and way of life, acknowledge, preserve, and encourage the spiritual and moral truths found among non-Christians, (and) also their social life and culture." Our prayer and our hope is that this book may serve all of us in the attainment of our true selves and that our extraordinary potential as communities of human beings will allow us to use the gift of life on this good earth and be blessed in journeying together with others while embraced by the Ultimate Mystery.

# What You'll Learn in This Book

This book is divided into eight sections that will help you understand the world's religions.

**Part 1, "Opening Up to Other Traditions,"** shows you why you should bother to learn about other faiths in the first place, which basic ideas support virtually all of the world's religious systems, and how to approach people from religious backgrounds that are unfamiliar to you.

**Part 2, "Judaism,"** offers an introduction to the world's first great monotheistic religion.

**Part 3, "Christianity,"** explores the rise and development of this diverse faith, whose influence in Europe and the Americas has been so profound, and which has become, in modern times, a truly global religion.

**Part 4, "Islam,"** helps you understand the history, principles, and practice of the religion founded by the prophet Muhammed.

**Part 5, "Hinduism,"** examines the prehistoric origins of the dominant religion of India, and its development over thousands of years.

**Part 6, "Buddhism,"** traces the growth and development of a faith whose originator abandoned his life of luxury in favor of true self-realization.

**Part 7, "Nature, Man, and Society in Asia,"** introduces you to the Confucian, Taoist, and Shinto systems.

**Part 8, "Old Paths, New Paths,"** explores some traditional patterns of indigenous worship, as well as some exciting new religious forms that have emerged in the United States in the twentieth century. This part of the book also shows that many of the thorniest questions of human existence are answered in strikingly similar ways by the world's religious scriptures.

Last, there's a glossary of key words and definitions.

# Extras

You will probably want to take advantage of the little nuggets of information distributed throughout the text. They will help you gain an immediate understanding of some aspect of the topic under discussion. Here's how you can recognize them:

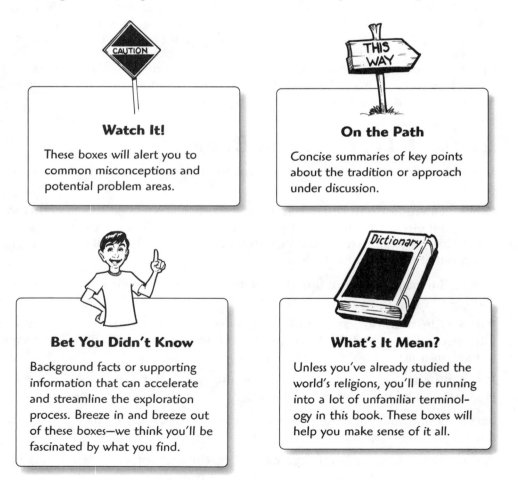

**Watch It!**

These boxes will alert you to common misconceptions and potential problem areas.

**On the Path**

Concise summaries of key points about the tradition or approach under discussion.

**Bet You Didn't Know**

Background facts or supporting information that can accelerate and streamline the exploration process. Breeze in and breeze out of these boxes—we think you'll be fascinated by what you find.

**What's It Mean?**

Unless you've already studied the world's religions, you'll be running into a lot of unfamiliar terminology in this book. These boxes will help you make sense of it all.

# Acknowledgments

We thank the team at Alpha, and our technical reviewer, for all their help and support.

Thanks are also due to a friend of many years, Kate Layzer, who served as an editor on this project, and to Gretchen Henderson and Robyn Burnett, for whose unfailing patience and skill we are, as always, deeply grateful.

Two more individuals made outstanding contributions to this book. Judith Burros supplied invaluable research assistance and textual help, and her contributions are much appreciated. Leslie Hamilton-Tragert helped with research and illustrations. Without the efforts, insights, review, and encouragement of these two women, this book could not have been completed.

# Trademarks

All terms mentioned in this book that are known to be or are suspected of being trademarks or service marks have been appropriately capitalized. Alpha Books and Pearson Education cannot attest to the accuracy of this information. Use of a term in this book should not be regarded as affecting the validity of any trademark or service mark.

# Part 1

# Opening Up to Other Traditions

*Each of the world's religions may seem foreign to "outsiders," but to an "insider," each represents a means by which both a particular society and creation as a whole can be understood more completely. So, what happens when the representative of one religious tradition comes in contact with the representative of another tradition? Will the contact bring about conflict, accusation, insensitivity, and misunderstanding—as it often has in human history—or will it lead to a renewed understanding of the worthiest aims of the various religious forms?*

*The simple fact that you're reading this book suggests that you would prefer the second outcome. If you're looking for ways to make mutual understanding more of a reality in today's diverse world, read on.*

# Chapter 1

# Why Learn About Other Faiths?

---

**In This Chapter**

➤ The growth of non–Western religions

➤ Why approaches to "different" religions have changed

➤ How this book can help you

---

If there was ever a time in human history when a nonjudgmental, curious, and open-minded approach to the religions of other people was an advantage, this is that time. In this chapter, you learn about the ways this book can help you adapt to an exciting new period of religious diversity.

## "I Read the News Today, Oh Boy"

Interest in "alternative" (that is to say, non-Western) traditions and patterns of devotion is seemingly at an all-time high. A recent wave of newspaper and television stories focused on an apparent increase in Buddhist practice in the United States—just one example of non-Christian religions winning new adherents in today's culture.

A similar series of stories pointed out the significant growth taking place among the various branches of the Islamic tradition. And for more than a decade, a broad wave of new religions focusing on exciting variations of existing Eastern, Western, and Native American traditions has been winning surprisingly large numbers of ardent adherents. (In fact, some scholars believe the followers of these new religions make up the fastest-growing category of religious observance on the planet.)

### Bet You Didn't Know

"Religious tolerance" now means much more than simply acknowledging differences within the Judeo–Christian tradition. If you live in the U.S. today, you live in a nation in which there are about as many Hindu practitioners as Orthodox Jews, more Buddhists than Seventh-Day Adventists, and more followers of Islam than Episcopalians. (Source: 1997 World Almanac)

The *ecumenical* tradition among "established" faiths, too, has been gaining strength. Constructive dialogues among members of the various Christian denominations have become much more common, and overt discrimination based on religious or secular differences, while still with us, has been rejected more often, more forthrightly, and far more energetically than in years past.

### What's It Mean?

The **ecumenical** movement promotes greater understanding and tolerance among the various branches of the Christian churches. In a broader sense, ecumenism sometimes refers to the process of attaining greater cooperation and understanding among widely differing faiths. Another, and perhaps more appropriate, term for this second sense is "interreligious dialogue."

In many settings, long-standing rifts between Christians and Jews are finally beginning to ease. In part, this may be because of greater social accommodation; it may also be related to a keen new interest on the part of many Christians in the "historical" Jesus; a Jesus whose life and teachings were, after all, a product of the Jewish tradition.

# Catching Up with the Constitution

Not so very long ago, the various denominations of Christianity served as the guiding religious force in this nation, a nation whose Constitution forbade a single official religion. The Christian tradition, in its rich diversity, exercised the single most important influence on religious life in the United States.

Other faiths existed, of course, but with a clear "outsider" status. Notwithstanding their *legal and First Amendment Right* right to worship in any church, few

Americans could envision a diverse religious tradition that placed Christianity on more or less equal social footing with other schools.

Those days, it appears, are over.

As we enter the twenty-first century, and as communication and economic barriers between members of various traditions fall away, the amazing diversity of the human religious experience becomes more and more exciting and more and more of a reality in our daily life. For most of us, the ideal of a truly pluralistic religious environment is no longer a distant target, but an undeniable (and occasionally chaotic) fact of life.

### What's It Mean?

**First Amendment rights** aren't just about freedom of speech and an unregulated press. The United States Constitution also guarantees the right to worship in any tradition, or none at all. In the words of the First Amendment: *"Congress shall make no law respecting an establishment of religion, or prohibiting the free exercise thereof."*

## Then and Now

*If you lived in the United States of America 50 years ago,* you could conceivably have moved from the beginning of the year to its end without encountering someone whose religious tradition differed markedly from the one that was most familiar to you.

*If you live in the United States of America today,* you are likely to supervise, be supervised by, meet on a social basis, or even suddenly find yourself related to someone who pursues a religious tradition that seems bewilderingly different from your own. What's more, you're likely to have little or no time to prepare for the new information that's coming your way.

In an earlier era, unfamiliar religious systems could be dismissed as "foreign" and left for the scholars to explore. In this era, that is usually not a realistic option.

## How This Book Can Help

This book is meant as a roadmap for a religiously pluralistic society—the society in which we all have found ourselves after the turn of the millennium. This book does *not* offer the final word on any of the rich traditions it discusses. Instead, it's meant to help you learn more about some of the most important aspects of each of the systems and disciplines we will be exploring. It's meant to pass along information that's likely to help everyone—not just people with advanced degrees—make sense of the various religions under discussion. And it's meant to continue the (welcome) recent trend of *building bridges* between faiths and celebrating their commonalties, rather than highlighting opportunities for division, discord, and misunderstanding among the members of the various faiths.

This book will help you if …

➤ You're a supervisor who must determine whether, when, and how to accommodate an employee who asks for time off to observe the Islamic holy period of Ramadan.

➤ You're a student who's supposed to develop a report on the history of the Church of Jesus Christ of Latter-Day Saints.

➤ You're an in-law who hopes to avoid awkward silences or unintended antagonism with a new member of the family whose faith is unfamiliar (or even a little intimidating) to you.

This book will also help you if …

➤ You're comfortable with your own religious practice or tradition and want to learn more about where and how it connects with other faiths.

➤ You're experiencing doubts about your current religious practice and wish to learn about other faiths.

➤ You have deep doubts about religious structures as a whole, but are eager to discover the points of contact among the various traditions of the world and to learn how these commonalties may support your own personal search for meaning and coherence.

➤ You're curious.

## What's It Mean?

An **agnostic** is a person who believes that the existence of God, or a primal cause, can be neither proven nor disproven. The word comes from the Greek for "unknown" or "unknowable." An **atheist** is one who believes that there is no such reality as God or a primal cause.

# "I Don't Have to Bother with This! I'm an Agnostic (or: an Atheist)!"

Whether we like it or not, the religious traditions and structures of the people we meet *can* have a strong influence on our relationships with those people. This book is meant to help anyone—even someone who is undecided about the existence of God or convinced that there is no such entity—to understand and respond intelligently to religious and cultural conventions and beliefs.

Not long ago, the world-famous astronomer Carl Sagan died. As part of its memorial service for Sagan, a radio talk-show broadcast an old interview with the scientist in which he was asked whether or not he believed in God. Sagan responded that, while he rejected certain images of the Deity that had been presented to him as a child—the bearded man in the heavens dispensing lightning bolts—he did, as a scientist, have to acknowledge the possibility of a principle, or set of principles, that governed the universe. He also noted that there were any number of religious traditions, Buddhism, for instance, that explicitly discounted the notion of God as a separate and distinct entity from the rest of creation.

Sagan politely declined the opportunity to set the world of rationality and the world of spirituality into opposition with one another. He also left open the possibility that the various religious traditions could offer important insights into the human condition.

Like the good scientist he was, Sagan was capable of keeping an open mind about big questions, and that definitely included questions of a religious nature. I like to think that this book would have stimulated and intrigued him. Certainly, the need to "build bridges" to initially unfamiliar traditions is shared by many nonbelievers who may be inspired to follow Sagan's example as well as by members of particular religious groups.

**Watch It!**

Tactlessly forcing another person (especially a family member) to come to terms with your decision to hold to a philosophy of atheism or agnosticism can cause just as many sparks as tactlessly forcing that person to deal with a differing religious faith. When the name of the game is harmonious accommodation, everybody needs to play by the same rules of respect and understanding.

# Mixing It Up

Another reason to study the various faiths of the world is that the ways they influence, mirror, and support one another are, quite simply, fascinating. Sometimes, the true nature of a particular religious tradition can come into clearest focus when a seeker within that faith examines *another* tradition with a nonjudgmental approach.

Can contemplative Christianity and Zen Buddhism be seen as variations on the same religious approach? The writings of the great Trappist monk Thomas Merton suggest that they are. This influence of Buddhist thought on Merton's own Christian spiritual practice gave rise to some of the most compelling writing of this century in either tradition.

Learning about the ways in which the world's faiths reinforce one another can be very fulfilling indeed, even if you don't have an advanced degree in comparative religion. Why leave all the excitement to the academics?

## "Hey, This Sounds Familiar!"

Anyone who seeks in the writings of "unrelated" faiths for "contrary" opinions on such fundamental issues as, say, the attributes of a sage or a saint will often find surprising agreement. In the Islamic faith, the Qur'an (25.63-76) speaks of those patient "servants of the all-merciful" who "are neither prodigal nor parsimonious" and who dwell permanently in the high heaven, a heaven whose chief attribute is "Peace." A comparable Taoist scripture (Chuang Tzu 6) speaks of those sages who do not "rebel against want" or "grow proud in plenty."

Such parallels abound in the various scriptures. For all their doctrinal diversity, the major religions of the world appear to have much in common. Discovering and celebrating these life-affirming similarities is part of what has driven us to write this book, and we hope the same motivations encourage you to read it. (In the next chapter, you'll find a summary of some of the most important "cornerstone" principles shared by virtually all the world's major religions.)

## The Academic Obstacle

Religious practices that seem unfamiliar to us often seem unfamiliar *because* they've been introduced to us surrounded with a thick layer of "expert" academic explanation. There is a place for scholarship, of course, and we've certainly done our best to assemble the material in this book in a responsible and thorough manner. But we've also attempted to make certain that the information we're passing along doesn't require advanced study to assimilate.

This book is meant as a beginning point, an *initial* introduction to the many and varied faiths of the world. It is not an academic treatise but a guide to the lay reader. At various points throughout the text, you'll be pointed toward more comprehensive works that will help you to gain further insight on the practices and history of the tradition(s) under discussion.

## Beyond Fear

Perhaps the most important reason to study faiths beyond one's own is that it's a marvelous way to replace fear with experience and insight. It's hard to be frightened of something you really understand.

A full study of religious intolerance over the centuries is beyond the scope of this book. It's fair to say, though, that fear has all too often been a driving force behind acts that are hard to justify in any religious tradition.

Fear kills, in both the spiritual and physical senses of the word. And no one who has studied history will dispute that fear and mistrust of the unknown, and especially misunderstanding of the religious practices of others, has led to innumerable bloody

conflicts. All too often, those conflicts accomplished nothing, except to demonstrate the futility
of violently opposing what you don't really understand.

## The Other

When we know little or nothing about the religious beliefs of our neighbor, it can be easy to clas-
sify our neighbor as the *Other,* the misguided (or
worse) victim of alien and possibly immoral practices. Once we define another tradition as Other,
it's a short step to devaluing it unfairly. Is there
room in the cosmos for more than one conception
of the Divine? If we are to build workable bridges
between one believer and another, there is probably going to have to be, at least for a while.

The Other is usually the enemy, or at least a com-
petitor. And when we make this designation, regardless of what words we use, we move from the
world of spirituality to the world of military conquest, whether or not a blow is struck or a shot
fired.

### What's It Mean?

When a member of another religious tradition is relegated to the
status of the **Other,** he or she is
often seen as somehow less
human or less worthy than we
are. (Consider, for instance, the
dehumanizing stereotypes associated with anti-Semitism over the
centuries, or the current media
bias against practitioners of
Islam.) This denigrating process
runs counter to the nearly-
universal injunction of most
major religious traditions to
honor and respect all human life.

## Words, Words, Words

Words like "pagan," "heretic," "heathen," and "savage" have typically marked this
Other identification in the Western tradition. These words were frequently served up
as justifications for acts of unspeakable violence and cruelty; they saw even more
common service as markers of (supposedly) permanent division between "competing"
traditions. Whatever their effect, these words, and their many companions, came
about because of a single cause: fear of that which was unknown.

There is only one cure for this type of fear: *Learning* about that which is unfamiliar.

It's much harder to designate a particular religious tradition as the Other when you've
taken the time to understand it. In recent years, our culture has finally begun to
adopt a more inclusive, questioning, and open attitude about the countless ways humankind has found to attempt to return to that which is enduring about us. If this
book hastens the process of knowledge and learning and helps to reduce the needless
fear that arises when members of one tradition encounter members of another, it will
have done its job.

## The Least You Need to Know

➤ We live in a society in which true religious diversity, guaranteed by the Constitution of the United States, is finally becoming a reality.

➤ Building bridges to practitioners of other faiths is essential, because we often find ourselves in social or family relationships with those whose traditions are unfamiliar to us.

➤ Learning how the various religious traditions reinforce and support one another can be rewarding in and of itself.

➤ The more you know about other faiths, the less fear will be a factor in your dealings with people who practice those faiths.

# Chapter 2

# Lots of Different Names, Some Familiar Ideas

**In This Chapter**

➤ How most religions regard the ancient truths (as inherited, rather than invented from scratch)

➤ What virtually all faiths have in common

➤ Why an unfamiliar faith may be more accessible than it first appears

There are countless schools of religious thought, and yet a few common strands seem to run through them all. In this chapter, you learn about some of the key beliefs and spiritual principles shared by nearly all of the faiths discussed in this book.

## This Just In ...

A Shi'ite Muslim pursues a very different belief system than a member of the Greek Orthodox church, who in turn pursues a very different belief system than a Zen Buddhist practitioner. All the same, these believers all follow a spiritual path, and as such, embrace certain ideas that, when expressed openly and without preconception, illuminate and clarify that path.

## Ancient Truths

What's more, the vast majority of the traditions *acknowledge* that the fundamental message being passed along to believers is not new and unique at all, but ancient and impervious to change.

## Bet You Didn't Know

The longer you study the great religions of the world, the more you realize that each celebrates and refines concepts that reflect the same elemental truths. As the editors of *World Scripture: A Comparative Anthology of Ancient Texts* (Paragon House, 1991) put it, "Interfaith dialogue in our time is going beyond the first step of appreciating other religions to a growing recognition that the religions of the world have much in common. The common ground between religions becomes more apparent as the dialogue partners penetrate beneath superficial disagreements."

This is not to say that all religions are identical. Far from it! But it's important to remember, as you begin your "tour" of the world's religions, that the great faiths did not spring into existence without preparation. A people's culture and traditional wisdom provide a context for a prophet's message, a sage's advice.

Voices: The Timelessness of the Founding Ideas Behind the World's Great Religions

*Christianity:* God, who at sundry times and in divers manners spake in time past unto the fathers by the prophets, hath in these last days spoken unto us by his Son, whom he hath appointed heir of all things, by whom also he made the worlds. (Hebrews, 1.1–2)

*Confucianism:* The Master said, "I have transmitted what was taught to me without making up anything of my own. I have been faithful to and loved the ancient ones." (Analects of Confucius, 7.1)

*Baha'i Faith:* (I)f you call them all by one name, and ascribe to them the same attribute, you have not erred from the truth. Even as He has revealed, "No distinction do We make between any of His Messengers!" For they one and all summon the people of the earth to acknowledge the unity of God. (Book of Certitude [Baha'i Faith], 152)

*Islam:* Nothing is said to you (Muhammad) except what was said to the messengers who came before you. (The Qur'an, 41.43)

*Buddhism:* All Buddhas of the ten parts of the universe enter the one road of Nirvana. Where does that road begin? (Zen Buddhist *koan*)

*Hinduism:* I am born in every age to protect the good, to destroy evil, and to reestablish the law. (Bhagavad Gita 4.7–8)

*Judaism:* And Moses said unto God, "Behold, when I come unto the children of Israel, and shall say unto them, The God of your fathers hath sent me unto you; and they shall say to me, What is his name? What shall I say unto them?" And God said unto Moses, "I AM THAT I AM;" and he said, "Thus shalt thou say unto the children of Israel, 'I AM hath sent me unto you.'" (Exodus 3:13–14)

Make no mistake. Each of the world's faiths must be understood and respected within its own context, of course. But it's important to note that the "we're-not-passing-along-anything-new-here-folks" message tends to be a consistent theme among the faiths you'll be examining.

That's not the only common note, either. There are three additional points on which the world's best-known religions (as well as the vast majority of the lesser-known ones) all agree. Let's look at them in detail now.

# Humanity and the Eternal

In his play *Our Town,* Thornton Wilder has his Stage Manager point out what may be the single most important unifying concept shared by the great religions of the world. "I don't care what they say with their mouths," the Stage Manager says, "everybody knows in their bones that something is eternal, and that something has to do with human beings."

The Stage Manager's moving speech goes on to note that the "something" that is *eternal* is "way down deep" in each and every one of us, and that the wisest souls have been repeating this simple message to their fellow humans for 5,000 years or so. ("You'd be surprised," he notes dryly, "how people are always losing hold of it.")

The idea that there is some aspect of the human identity involving contact with something change-less and beyond time is one that extends across all doctrinal and dogmatic barriers. Here are some scriptural examples of its expression.

**What's It Mean?**

A **koan** is a teaching riddle within Zen (or Ch'an) Buddhist tradition.

Voices: Humanity's Relationship with the Eternal

*Christianity:* I am the Alpha and the Omega, the beginning and the end, the first and the last. (Revelation 22:13)

*Confucianism:* The exemplary person is not deceived by that which is transitory, but rather focuses on the ultimate. (I Ching, Hexagram 54)

*Judaism:* Hark! One saith: "Proclaim!" And he saith: "What shall I proclaim?" "All flesh is grass, and the goodliness thereof is as the flower of the field; the grass withereth, the flower fadeth; because the breath of the Lord bloweth upon it; surely the people is grass. The grass withereth, the flower fadeth, but the word of God shall stand forever." (Isaiah 40.6–8)

*Buddhism:* Coming empty-handed, going empty-handed: that is human. When you are born, where do you come from?

When you die, where do you go? Life is like a floating cloud which appears. Death is like a floating cloud which disappears. The floating cloud itself originally does not exist. Life and death, coming and going, are also like that.

But there is one thing which always remains clear. It is pure and clear, not depending on life and death. Then what is that one pure and clear thing? (Cambridge Zen Center publication, "The Human Route")

*Hinduism:* The great and unborn Self is undecaying, immortal, undying, without fear, and without end. (Brihardaranyaka Upanishad 4.4.25)

*Taoism:* Without sound and without form, (the Tao) depends on nothing and does not change. (Tao te Ching, 25)

*Islam:* There is no changing the words of God. (Qur'an 10.64)

### What's It Mean?

A common understanding of the word **eternal** is "enduring forever," which is certainly one aspect of its meaning. But this definition is not complete. The primary sense of the word reflects a reality that is *beyond* time, that is, *without* beginning, end, or division. When the great religions of the world speak of a divine presence that exists eternally, they are speaking, as Einstein did, of the transcendence of time as human beings generally perceive it.

Our contact with and connection to the eternal, despite the seemingly transitory nature of human existence, is a consistent notion within the faiths of the world. Even those who reject organized religion or the "existence of God" may find themselves agreeing instinctively with the proposition that there is something deep within us that endures despite the fact that our physical bodies and the world around us obviously do not.

## Interconnectedness with All Creation

Are you the same as, or different from, the book you're reading right now? The question may be trickier than it sounds. Another "big idea" embraced virtually unanimously by the world's faiths is that of an intimate connection—and, yes, a shared identity—with all created entities in the universe. God, the great faiths assure us, is everywhere, and that really does mean *everywhere*.

Most faiths also acknowledge the difficulty of reconciling this "connected" divine reality with our own perceived, and presumably legitimate, day-to-day experience, in which we see ourselves as separate and autonomous entities. Even "acknowledging" some form of common identity with the book you're holding in your hands may reinforce separate notions of "book" and "reader." All the same, the primal cause is held to permeate every conceivable aspect of creation.

The joint message of the world's great religions is clear and unmistakable: All of creation is linked together in a fundamental and unalterable way, and the journey of the sincere seeker can be said to trace and illuminate the reality of that linkage.

Here are just a few of the (numerous) passages, scriptural and otherwise, that embody this idea as it is expressed in a variety of faiths.

> **On the Path**
>
> Despite massive cultural differences, despite innumerable doctrinal disputes, despite the occasional heated conflict with representatives of other factions and traditions, virtually every organized faith honors the notion of the individual believer's contact with something eternal.

---

Voices: The Divine Presence in All Creation

*Hinduism:* Our existence as embodied beings is purely momentary; what are a hundred years in eternity? But if we shatter the chains of egotism, and melt into the ocean of humanity, we share its dignity. To feel that we are something is to set up a barrier between God and ourselves; to cease feeling that we are something is to become one with God. (Mahatma Gandhi, quoted in *Be Here Now,* by Ram Dass (Lama Foundation))

*Buddhism:* Why should I be unable to regard the bodies of others as "I?" It is not difficult to see that my body is also that of others. (Shantideva, Guide to the Bodhisattva's Way of Life, 8.112)

*Islam:* His (God's) throne comprises the heavens and the earth. (Qur'an, 2.255)

*Taoism:* All things in the world came from being; and being comes from non-being. (Tao Te Ching, 40)

*Buddhism:* Banzan once walked through the marketplace and heard a butcher talking to one of his customers.

> "I want the very best piece of meat you have in the shop," the customer demanded.
>
> "Every piece of meat in this shop is the best," the butcher responded. "You will never find a piece of meat here that is not the best."
>
> Upon hearing this, Banzan attained enlightenment. (Zen story)

*Hinduism:* The Self is everywhere. (Isha Upanishad 4–8)

*Judaism:* Holy, holy, holy is the Lord of hosts: the whole earth is full of His glory. (Isaiah 6:3)

*Christianity:* In the beginning was the Word, and the Word was with God, and the Word was God. The same was in the beginning with God. All things were made by him; and without him was not any thing made that was made. (John 1:1–3)

So, just about *every* religion makes a point of emphasizing the all-reaching presence of the Divine in anything and everything, including you, this book, and that cup of coffee you're planning to have once you're finished reading. Admittedly, the logical basis of this contention is sometimes hard to grasp, but the notion of total interconnectedness is nevertheless an important common theme.

And speaking of the limits of logic …

**On the Path**

In many faiths, a human being's perception of himself or herself as fundamentally separate from the people, things, and obstacles he or she encounters—separate, in fact, from the Divine—is seen as one of the primary hindrances to spiritual growth.

# Beyond Words, Beyond Mind

Yet another oft-repeated message of the great religions of the world—one echoed by certain lay observers whose work points them toward what might be called "ultimate" conclusions about the universe—concerns the inherent limitations of the human intellect. Ultimately, the great faiths counsel, childlike simplicity, rather than overbearing intellect or rigorous logic, is required for true union with the divine.

Variations on this observation appear countless times, and in countless ways, in the religious practices, writings, and commentaries that have come down to us through history. A representative sampling follows.

Voices: The Limits of the Logical Mind

I didn't arrive at my understanding of the fundamental laws of the universe through my rational mind. (Albert Einstein)

*Buddhism:* The true path is only difficult for those who make distinctions. Do not like, do not dislike. Then everything will become clear. *("On Trust in the Heart,"* Master Seng Ts'an)

*Christianity:* Eye hath not seen, nor ear heard, neither have entered into the heart of man, the things which God hath prepared for them that love him. (1 Corinthians 2:9)

*An African traditional faith:* There is no need to point out God to a child. (Ghanian proverb)

*Islam:* He is far above the conceptions of those who refuse His existence, and also of those who imagine His attributes in various expressions of nature. (Nahjul Balagha, Sermon 54)

*Confucianism:* The presence of the Spirit: It cannot be surmised. How may it be ignored! (Doctrine of the Mean 16)

*Christianity:* All that the imagination can imagine and the reason conceive and understand in this life is not, and cannot be, a proximate means of union with God. (St. John of the Cross)

*Judaism:* Behold, I go forward, but He is not there; and backward, but I cannot perceive Him; on the left hand, when he doth work, but I cannot behold Him; he turneth himself to the right hand, but I cannot see him. (Job 23:8,9)

*Taoism:* The True Man of ancient times knew nothing of loving life, knew nothing of hating death. He emerged without delight; he went back in without a fuss. He came briskly, he went briskly, and that was all. He did not forget where he began; he did not try to find out where he would end. He received something and took pleasure in it; he forgot about it and handed it back again. (Chuang Tzu 6)

*Hinduism:* Eye cannot see him, nor words reveal him; by senses, austerity, or works he is not known. (Mundaka Upanishad 3.1.8)

# One More Thing

Let's touch on one more important commonality before moving on. The tradition you're eager to learn about may be more flexible than you imagine, regardless of what it looks like at first from the outside.

There are a number of reasons for this. For one thing, the process of developing a personal spirituality—a meaningful relationship, if you will, with one's true self—is an ongoing one. Lessons have a way of appearing when one is ready to receive them. (A pertinent saying in one tradition points out that "You can't rip the skin off the snake.") Odds are that the tradition you're interested in has *some* mechanism for dealing with people of a variety of interests and levels of experience, including yours.

**On the Path**

At some point in its scripture or philosophy, each of the faiths we will be discussing makes reference to the limited power of human reason as a final vehicle for contact with the infinite. Something simpler and more innocent is required for true realization; something beyond logic.

For another thing, religions that are *completely* inaccessible tend not to spread very far or adapt well to cultural changes over the years. While it's certainly true that religious institutions typically emphasize fixed rituals and sets of references that are likely to confuse an outsider, it's also true that there is usually *some* point of entry into the tradition likely to make sense to those who are unfamiliar with the faith.

In other words, there is one Roman Catholic church, operating under a distinctive set of rituals and principles; there are thousands upon thousands of local emphases and accommodations to local Catholic practitioners. The same principle operates, to a greater or lesser degree, for many other faiths that have become widely dispersed over the years.

Of course, it's not exactly *impossible* to find a particular faith that is completely rigid, inaccessible, and non-inclusive, one that makes no attempt to adjust to the evolving spiritual needs of its practitioners, one that briskly rejects those who have honest questions about how and why its followers do what they do. But it's not exactly common, either.

In the next chapter, you'll find specific advice for approaching and communicating with someone whose religious traditions are unfamiliar to you.

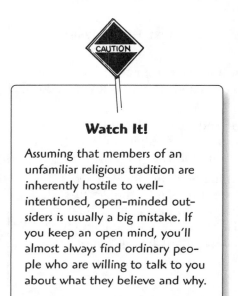

**Watch It!**

Assuming that members of an unfamiliar religious tradition are inherently hostile to well-intentioned, open-minded outsiders is usually a big mistake. If you keep an open mind, you'll almost always find ordinary people who are willing to talk to you about what they believe and why.

---

### The Least You Need to Know

➤ The vast majority of religions acknowledge that their core precepts are timeless, rather than new and unrelated to any existing tradition.

➤ The notion of humanity's connection to something that is eternal is a common one among the great religions of the world.

➤ The notion that all of Creation is somehow interconnected is a common one among the great religions of the world.

➤ The notion that rigorous, adult logic alone is not a sufficient tool for apprehending divine truths is a common one among the great religions of the world.

➤ An unfamiliar faith may be more accessible than it first seems.

# Chapter 3

# Speaking Softly and Dropping the Stick

## In This Chapter

➤ Learn why external differences are less imposing than they may seem

➤ Learn about the most common barriers to interfaith communication

➤ Find out how to ask the kinds of questions that make contact with people of different belief systems easy

So, you're interested in approaching someone to learn more about his or her faith, but you're a little perplexed about exactly *how* you should go about this. After all, most of us are counseled from an early age to avoid two topics with those who aren't family members or close friends: religion and politics. Why? People get so touchy!

Truth be told, they sometimes do. While this chapter won't be of much help to you if your aim is to reach out to a member of an opposing political faction, it *will* offer you some pragmatic strategies for reaching out to find out more about someone's religious practices.

## Non-Sectarian Knees

Not long ago, a Catholic priest teamed up with a Zen Buddhist teacher to conduct a Christian/Buddhist meditation retreat. After the retreat ended, the priest found himself in a discussion with a Buddhist practitioner who wanted to know "why" mainstream Christians didn't take greater notice of certain elements of Buddhist theology and practice.

For a while the priest tried to deflect the questions tactfully, but when his questioner persisted, it was clear the priest had to respond directly somehow. Finally, the priest told his companion, "I'm not very big on 'why,' and I'm not very big on labels, either. You and I just spent a whole day sitting in meditation together. As long as it was just knees and legs and pillows we were sitting on, we had no problem. The minute we start sitting on Christian knees and legs and pillows or Buddhist knees and legs and pillows, though, things start to get complicated."

The same wisdom can easily be extended to Islamic knees, Quaker knees, Jewish knees, or any number of knees of other denominations. All of them bow in reverence or sit in meditation with about the same level of efficiency. To the extent that people fixate on labels, on explanations, on differences that really ought to be reconciled, interfaith contact is difficult. To the extent that people focus on a sincere spiritual commitment that can take many expressions, interfaith contact is easy.

### Bet You Didn't Know

Showing a willingness to look beyond externals and penetrate to the core concerns of a person's faith is a great way to build bridges.

In discussions with those whose faith is less than familiar to you, remember that most of the objectives behind the religion are almost certainly similar (or identical) to the tradition you are comfortable with.

There's an old joke about a rabbi who upbraided a young man named Isaac, a member of his congregation. Isaac loved to ridicule the Christians he encountered regularly at his print shop. Isaac's jokes with his friends about the "goys" nearby invariably painted all of Christianity as an ill-informed, logically absurd religion that routinely went out of its way to persecute Jews.

One day, after hearing the latest of these jokes, the rabbi decided to share a joke of his own with Isaac. He took the young man aside, winked at him conspiratorially, and said, "Isaac, do you know why Christians make a habit of hitting the salt-shaker on the side, while Jews always tap it on the bottom?"

Isaac smiled, expecting a good joke at the expense of the "goys" he dealt with every day. "No, rabbi," he replied. "Why is that?"

"To get the salt out," the young man's spiritual guide answered quietly.

# Six Ways to Alienate Someone Whose Faith Is Unfamiliar to You (and What to Do Instead)

Here are six common traps even well-meaning "outsiders" fall into when dealing with practitioners of an unfamiliar faith. Following each, you'll find some advice on taking a more constructive approach.

## 1. Fixate on "Why"

"Why do you people dress like that?"

As the priest at the Christian/Buddhist retreat knew, "why" questions are often loaded questions. It's quite possible that the person you're talking to really has no clear fix on the *ultimate* reasons behind a particular practice. It's also quite possible that he or she will presume your question has some unfriendly intent.

Instead of focusing on "why," ask questions that will encourage your acquaintance to open up and start discussing nonthreatening aspects of his or her practice. ("It's wonderful to see you here. Are you a member of Temple Beth-Israel?")

## 2. Follow the (Unflattering) Lead of the Media

In other words, hold the person responsible for the most recent bad press generated by some representative of his or her faith.

**Watch It!**

Just a reminder: It is completely inappropriate (and usually illegal) to question someone who reports to you about the whys and wherefores of his or her religion as it relates to workplace performance. Stay on the right side of the law; do not give even the barest impression that you are judging someone's performance, or potential as a candidate for a job opening, on his or her religious beliefs.

Media coverage of religious figures is often sensational and irresponsible. (For that matter, media coverage of the very idea of personal or group spirituality is often sensational and irresponsible.)

Not infrequently, biased newspaper, magazine, and television reports about a particular religious group leave its adherents feeling as though they are under siege. "Current events" may *seem* like a harmless enough way to begin the conversation, but it won't be if your conversational partner perceives you as "one of the attackers." A fundamentalist Christian probably won't take kindly to your assumption that he or she is willing to defend, or even discuss, a publicly disgraced member of the clergy within that denomination. A member of the Nation of Islam may not appreciate being interrogated about yesterday's unflattering news coverage about that faith.

Play it safe. Assume the best, and use *neutral* conversation-starters.

# 3. Stare

There's not much that makes someone feel more like an outsider than being gawked at. Maintain appropriate, friendly, *intermittent* eye contact, but don't use your gaze to burrow through the person.

# 4. Talk About What's "Normal"

"Would you say you're a typical Catholic?"

How can a question like this be answered without polarizing a conversation? Overuse of words like "normal" and "typical" can sabotage otherwise promising exchanges. How would you feel if someone asked you whether or not close friends or relatives who worshipped within a particular tradition dressed "normally," or acted as "typical" members of that faith would?

The implication behind such language, of course, is that the practices of the person you're talking to *aren't* "normal," whatever that means. Acknowledge the validity of the other person's experience and traditions and stay away from language that implies there is one and only one way to categorize religious or cultural issues.

# 5. Use Attack Language to Describe Someone's Faith

There are any number of loaded words you can use to describe someone else's religious practices, words that will serve only to convince your conversational partner that you're not interested in learning anything more about the tradition under discussion.

Stay away from phrases like "sect," "cult," "recruit," "programming," "alien," or "variant" in reference to the person's beliefs—even if you're reporting what *others* have to say. The person with whom you're speaking may assume that you're eager to polarize the conversation, just like those you're quoting.

# 6. Stomp on Toes That Are Already Bruised

That is to say, ask the most obvious, and most sensitive, question right out of the gate. The point here is to avoid asking questions or raising issues that will cause the person you're talking to sigh (audibly or internally) and think, "Oh, great. *Another* one who has to talk about so-and-so."

A Christian Science practitioner may *eventually* be interested in discussing his or her beliefs concerning faith as a counterpart to contemporary medical treatment. A member of the Church of Jesus Christ of Latter-Day Saints (the Mormons) may *eventually* take part in a stimulating discussion with you about that tradition's history and initial acceptance of polygamy. But why try to initiate a dialogue by raising such issues?

At the beginning of your relationship with someone whose religious background differs from your own, your best approach is probably to avoid sensitive—and over-played—issues. Establish contact with the person first, and make it clear that you're interested in human-to-human contact, not sparring and preconceptions.

# Ask Questions!

Appropriate questions, questions that focus on "how" and "what" rather than "why," may be your most powerful tools when it comes to building bridges with people of other faiths. Intelligent questions, unlike statements or aggressive pronouncements, let others know your mind is open and ready for business.

Why work on developing questions? Because the right questions work to develop relationships! Questions that don't threaten, intimidate, or cross-examine let everyone know you're interested in *gathering* information, rather than dispensing judgment.

Questions that show you have a genuine curiosity about the other person's faith and practices will make it easier for you to develop a person-to-person, rather than proselytizer-to-proselytizer relationship.

Questions allow you to explore and celebrate commonalties, rather than highlight divisions. Here are some examples of nonintrusive, non-threatening questions and their more abrasive counterparts. One group will help you encourage the person with whom you're talking to open up. One group will ensure plenty of furtive looks and granite silences.

Whenever you can, choose *open* questions rather than *closed* questions.

### What's It Mean?

To **proselytize** is to make an effort to convince another to convert, typically to another faith or sect. Initial encounters between those of different faiths are sometimes needlessly polarized when one or the other parties believes that proselytizing is taking place or about to take place. You'll be likeliest to keep communication open if you make it clear you're engaged, not in proselytizing, but in its opposite: open-minded, nonjudgmental discussion and curiosity.

Open and Closed Questions About an Unfamiliar Faith

➤ *Open:* Where are you planning to celebrate such-and-such a holiday this year?

*Closed:* So, you really believe such-and-such, huh?

➤ *Open:* I'm curious: When do children in your tradition begin wearing such-and-such a garment?

*Closed:* I'll bet you have a heck of a time trying to talk your kids into wearing that kind of clothing to school, don't you?

➤ Open: Is there anything I should know about dietary restrictions in setting the menu for our get-together?

*Closed:* Why don't you eat meat?

Open-minded questions—posed intelligently and early—can also help you develop appropriate behavior patterns during the various rituals or ceremonies in which you may be taking part. *Don't* assume that a particular level of participation or response will be accepted simply because that standard represents what works in your own tradition!

Can you take photographs during a particular service? Is the type of clothing you have in mind suitable for the ceremony? Are there some parts of a ritual you'll be expected to participate in? If so, which?

Don't put off questions like these. Ask for help!

## The Best Advice: Don't Pretend to Have All the Answers

The simplest and most reliable principle to bear in mind during your initial encounters with representatives of other traditions is easy to remember: *When you listen, you can't make a mistake.*

Adopting a humble, open-minded attitude toward the practices of others *does not* represent a betrayal of your own faith. On the contrary, taking this approach allows you to deepen your understanding about other outlooks and will very likely result in a more profound appreciation of your own tradition's distinctive features.

> ### Watch It!
>
> If you're unfamiliar with the protocol around a particular religious issue, by all means ask someone (either an officiant or a member of the group) what should happen and how you should respond in a certain situation. That beats improvising your way through the ceremony and drawing unhappy stares from others. And remember: The earlier you ask, the better off you'll probably be.

## When in Doubt, Repeat: "We're All in the Same Boat"

Remember that religious traditions of all varieties represent, at the end of the day, a profoundly human attempt to address fundamental questions about life, growth, maturity, and death. In the final analysis, regardless of the undeniable differences among the believers who pursue the innumerable different faiths, every religious practitioner faces precisely the same basic human obstacles and dilemmas.

If you come in contact with a tradition that seems utterly foreign to you, remember that each and every person within that tradition shares *with you* the following challenges, simply by virtue of his or her membership in the human race:

➤ The common heritage of physical birth.

➤ The common destiny of physical death.

➤ The common desire to find meaning and purpose within the daily activities of life.

No matter your background, no matter your religious upbringing, no matter your past experience with members of this group, you already have much more in common with these people than you probably imagine. You, like each of the members of the faith you have encountered, are a participant in the dance of life—someone who delights in the birth and growth of children, someone who gazes through the vast and forbidding distances of a cold starry night and wonders at the immensity of creation, someone whose relationships with friends, family, and daily acquaintances are sometimes good and sometimes bad.

You, like each of the members of the tradition you now wish to understand more fully, have your good days and your bad days. You can recall choices from your past that make you proud and choices that have separated you from others and filled your heart with remorse. You, like each of the members of the religious group you now find yourself interacting with, realize that you have been born, that you will someday die, and that a pattern or series of patterns sometimes arises that convinces you that these events have taken place, and will continue to take place, for a very definite reason, a reason that transcends both your triumphs and your failings.

All of this is true for you. And it is also true for each and every member of the group you are studying now. If you can bear these points in mind as you interact with the representatives of that group, you will learn more about them—and, in all likelihood, learn more about yourself as well.

---

### The Least You Need to Know

➤ Showing a willingness to look beyond externals and penetrate to the core concerns of a person's faith is a great way to build bridges.

➤ "Why" questions may be more provocative than you realize.

➤ The unintentional use of loaded questions and "attack" terminology can undermine even a sincere effort to reach out to someone of another faith.

➤ Open-ended questions that don't threaten your conversational partner probably represent your best opportunity for contact.

➤ When in doubt, remember: We're all in the same boat.

# Part 2

# Judaism

*The notion of a single, true God is a powerful and enduring one. For millions of believers everywhere, this "single-God" principle is acknowledged as arising from the religion of the ancient Hebrews.*

*Within Judaism, there are stories about God's active and ongoing presence in human affairs: the patriarch Abraham, the great prophet Moses, the story of the Torah—the laws that have exerted authority from biblical times onward—and the people whose social and religious codes developed in response to the requirements of the single God.*

*Practicing Jews believe that, in return for their love and obedience, God promised to establish and sustain them as His people. In this section of the book, you learn the basics of this rich, and varied, Covenant faith.*

# Chapter 4

# The Roots of Judaism

**In This Chapter**

➤ Learn about the history of the world's oldest monotheistic faith

➤ Find out how Judaism has influenced other traditions

➤ Discover some of the most distinctive elements of this enduring faith

Like Christianity and Islam—two traditions that explicitly trace their lineage to the patriarch Abraham—Judaism is a faith that has encompassed many historical adaptations, factions, movements, and countermovements. In this chapter, you learn about the history and development of this diverse Covenant faith.

## The Hebrews

The Torah (the Five Books of Moses that begin both the Hebrew and Christian Bibles) teaches that the Hebrew people are descended from Abraham, the patriarch with whom God formed the Covenant.

The Torah also tells how, long after Abraham's time, the descendants of Abraham and his son Isaac moved to Egypt, where they were eventually enslaved. After centuries of persecution, the Hebrews were released from the Pharaoh's power and led back to Canaan (or Palestine) by Moses—with the help of the same single true God who had spoken to Abraham. On Mt. Sinai, the book of Exodus reports, God gave Moses ten commandments meant to guide the conduct of God's people, and initiated a solemn Covenant with this people.

*The Star of David.*

## Ten Enduring Rules

The Ten Commandments (or *Decalogue*), which also appear in the Hebrew Bible's book of Deuteronomy, now serve as the moral compass for the entire Judeo-Christian tradition. In fact, these 10 rules also served as profound influences on the *Islamic* faith, which regards Moses' delivery of the Ten Commandments as an instance of divine revelation.

It's fair to say, then, that the Ten Commandments set forth in the books of Exodus and Deuteronomy and ascribed directly to God speaking to Moses, occupy a position of unparalleled importance in our religious tradition. They are revered by *all three* of human-kind's major monotheistic traditions. That's a pretty impressive display of unanimity!

**What's It Mean?**

The **Decalogue** is another word for the Ten Commandments.

## Close-Up on the Decalogue

There won't be very many points in this book where you'll be asked to review extended scriptural passages word-for-word, but omitting the text of the Ten Commandments seems an oversight that would be hard to justify in any account of the spiritual pillars of Judaism. Even though, for most westerners, the Ten Commandments are pretty familiar material, not many of us today can recite them all by heart. Given the immense influence of these principles on religious practice around the world, they're worth reviewing in their entirety. Let's look now at all 10 of these rules, which represent the very heart of the Law in the Jewish tradition and have profoundly influenced religious practice and social interaction in so many other religions, as well.

### What's It Mean?

As recounted in the Bible, God made **covenants,** or agreements, not only with Abraham, but with Noah and Moses as well. The covenant with Abraham, as described in the book of Genesis, was an agreement under which God would establish a chosen people, a "great nation," from Abraham's descendants. In return, Abraham and those who followed would offer the one true God complete obedience. According to scripture, the covenant has been restated and renewed at various times in Jewish history.

## The Ten Commandments

*(Note: The division points between the commandments vary between Jewish and non-Jewish observance. The Jewish divisions of the text—Exodus 20:2-17—are used here.)*

1. I am the Lord thy God, who brought thee out of the land of Egypt, out of the house of bondage.

2. Thou shalt have no other gods before Me. Thou shalt not make unto thee a graven image, nor any manner of likeness, of any thing that is in heaven above, or that is in the earth beneath, or that is in the water under the earth; thou shalt not bow down unto them, nor serve them: for I the Lord thy God am a jealous God, visiting the iniquity of the fathers upon the children unto the third and fourth generation of them that hate Me; and showing mercy unto the thousandth generation of them that love Me and keep My commandments.

3. Thou shalt not take the name of the Lord thy God in vain, for the Lord will not hold him guiltless that taketh His name in vain.

4. Remember the sabbath day, to keep it holy. Six days shalt thou labor, and do all thy work; but the seventh day is a sabbath unto the Lord thy God, in it thou shalt not do any manner of work, thou, nor thy son, nor thy daughter, nor thy man-servant, nor thy maid-servant, nor thy cattle, nor thy stranger that is within thy gates; for in six days the Lord made heaven and earth, the

sea, and all that in them is, and rested the seventh day, wherefore the Lord blessed the sabbath day, and hallowed it.

5. Honor thy father and mother, that thy days may be long upon the land which the Lord thy God giveth thee.

6. Thou shalt not kill.

7. Thou shalt not commit adultery.

8. Thou shalt not steal.

9. Thou shalt not bear false witness against thy neighbor.

10. Thou shalt not covet thy neighbor's house; thou shalt not covet thy neighbor's wife, nor his man-servant, nor his maid-servant, nor his ox, nor his ass, nor any thing that is thy neighbor's.

# The Kingdom and the Dispersion

The Israelites established a stable kingdom. A period of political continuity and self-determination, under the kings Saul, David, and Solomon, followed.

But division of the kingdom, and domination by Assyrian and Babylonian forces in the sixth and eighth centuries B.C.E., respectively, led eventually to a dispersion of the Hebrews beyond the borders of their former nation. When the Hebrews finally returned to their homeland, Israel was a political power no more. A period of Roman domination led to a dispersal (known as the Exile) of large numbers of Hebrews beyond the borders of their former nation and the destruction of their sacred Temple in Jerusalem. A new Temple was built in Jerusalem, but under Roman rule, believers suffered the destruction of this sacred edifice (in 70 C.E.) and the eventual neutralization of all organized Jewish opposition.

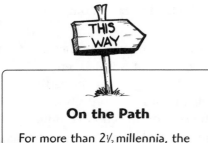

**On the Path**

For more than 2½ millennia, the traditions and observances ascribed to Abraham and his people have continued to thrive in societies around the globe, many of them distinctly hostile to Jewish practice and belief.

Despite the dissolution of their country as a political entity, however, the faith of the Israelites in their destiny as a "chosen people," and their commitment to the idea of a single true God, endured. That faith supported, and probably reinvigorated, a set of core traditions and observances that have remained in place from the Diaspora (the "scattering" that followed the Babylonian captivity) to the current time.

## Bet You Didn't Know

The ideas that guide Judaism are animated by a belief that God directs all aspects of human activity, public and private, individual and collective. A "religion," understood as a limited set of beliefs, or as a separate entity from a kingdom or a tribe, was not the point.

At issue instead was unswerving devotion to the will of God in any and every aspect of one's life. This single-minded devotion to a single all-powerful Deity may well have been one of the features that enabled the Hebrews to perpetuate and extend their faith even after the disappearance of what a modern observer would consider to be a "political" structure.

# The Prophets

Within the Jewish tradition, the revelation of the *Law*—the first five books of the Hebrew Bible—was reinforced and supported by the revelation of the Prophets. According to scripture, certain people were chosen by God to remind the people of the Creator's love for them, and of the necessity of their obedience to the Law.

# Fundamental Precepts

Regardless of denomination or sect, practicing Jews believe that ...

➤ There is one and only one God, with Whom each individual has direct personal experience, and to Whom prayers may be addressed.

➤ God is the ultimate authority and possesses final dominion over the universe.

➤ Life is holy.

➤ The Torah (a term that usually means the scroll containing the Five Books of Moses, but may also refer to accumulated sacred writings through the centuries) is a guide to

## What's It Mean?

In the Jewish tradition, the *Law* is the Torah, the five books of Moses. These represent the written account of the revelation of God, who is regarded as having been active in every aspect of human development and history, and as being active in the same way today.

correct and upright living and a source of continued revelation of the word of God. The act of studying the Torah is the practical equivalent of prayer.

➤ Group worship and prayer are indispensable elements of a righteous life.

➤ Jews around the world, regardless of nationality, share a broad common destiny and a sense of collective purpose and responsibility to one another.

Despite these common bonds, the truth is that Judaism has been in the past, and is today, a remarkably diverse faith; a faith that accommodates a wide variety of beliefs expressed by practitioners the world round. Beyond the major points laid out above, there really is no single unifying dogma or briefly stated summary of principles that is embraced by all practicing Jews.

There are, however, some broad and universally accepted ideas that arise from the principles just outlined, ideas worth reviewing in detail now.

# In Depth: Some Key Aspects of Judaism

The first timeless dimension of Jewish spirituality is the appreciation of the proclamation known as the Sh'ma: "Hear, O Israel, the Lord is God, the Lord is One." (Deuteronomy 6:4-9) Amidst many neighbors with different beliefs, the ancient Hebrews proclaimed that their God was one. The absolute primacy of this one God was a distinctive component of this tradition, the world's oldest monotheistic faith.

The prohibitions against idolatry in the Hebrew Bible reflect a deep and abiding concern that no limited entity or belief be mistaken for the one true God by God's chosen people. In their fullest sense, these warnings serve as injunctions against pursuing *anything* other than the Lord, who had been divinely revealed to Abraham in the desert, to Moses at Mount Sinai, and again and again through the prophets. This single transcendent God's demands were (and are)

### On the Path

Over time, writings reflecting the message of the prophets—a phrase that usually refers both to a specific prophet and his accompanying school—were received and celebrated within the community of believers. Their messages were diverse and sometimes included, as in the book of Isaiah, the promise of a national reawakening under the righteous leadership of a Messiah who would redeem Israel and all human beings. But throughout this diverse scriptural heritage, the final emphasis has been on the single nature of the divine entity.

### What's It Mean?

A **rabbi** is a respected teacher and leader of worship, usually connected to a particular **synagogue** (house of learning and prayer).

simple and nonnegotiable: Obey the laws and commandments I have set down for the good of all my chosen ones.

## The Covenant

Another key idea in Judaism is to be found in the notion of the Covenant. This one God called forth a people, a community, who received God's revelation both through the sign of the Covenant and through the Law.

In the Jewish tradition, the notion that God acted to bestow the Covenant and the Law upon a particular nation and that these gifts represent examples of divine intervention for and blessings to that people, are vitally important. A believer's ability to keep the Law demonstrates his or her conformity with the will of God and serves as a sign of belonging as a member of the community.

## A Community Gathered

Yet another distinctive aspect of Judaism has to do with the emphasis on the *group* identity assumed by believers regarded as the descendants of Abraham and Isaac. This tradition emphasizes community-based experience and worship in a truly remarkable way.

The constantly reinforced sense of *belonging*, not just to a happenstance social arrangement but to a people of the Lord, takes on great significance within the Jewish faith. This tradition does not, of course, *reject* the idea of a single individual's relationship with the Deity, but it does place a profound emphasis on the social phenomena that encompasses (and often regulates) both daily worship *and* daily social interaction among believers.

In other words, Judaism nourishes a community-based form of religious practice. Distinctive social customs (such as circumcision among male members of the community) reinforce this sense of belonging. The individual operates not merely within a set of precepts, admonitions, or philosophical

### What's It Mean?

The **Mishna** is the recorded assemblage of (originally) oral legal interpretation within Judaism. When taken together with some important commentaries, the Mishna constitutes the **Talmud,** a vitally important collection of studies, commentary, anecdote, allegory, and elaboration that forms a fundamental guide influencing day-to-day Jewish observance and thought.

### What's It Mean?

**Monotheism** is the belief in a single personal God, usually a figure seen as unifying the entire universe. It is not to be confused with the practice of identifying or worshipping a chief god within a group. The worship of many gods simultaneously is known as **polytheism.** Although many polytheistic traditions elevate a single god to a position of dominance, the Hebrew Bible's early emphasis on a single true God is distinctive.

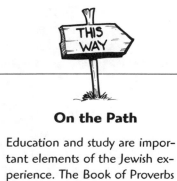

### On the Path

Education and study are important elements of the Jewish experience. The Book of Proverbs counsels believers to "Train up a child in the way he should go."(Proverbs 22.6.)

principles, but as part of a coherent, constantly reinforced community of fellow believers. In that community, the written account of the divine revelation is proclaimed and seen.

Of vital importance in Judaism is the sense of being called into the community to make appropriate contributions on a number of levels: in the synagogue or temple, as part of a family, and as a member of a Jewish citizenry. Prayer life in the Jewish tradition takes place both in formal settings, such as at synagogue, and also at home. The idea of attentive worship through predetermined, and usually written, prayer is also a distinctive and important one in this faith. This practice supports Judaism's emphasis upon a specific written liturgy to celebrate the community's ongoing relationship with the one true God.

### The Least You Need to Know

➤ The history of Judaism is intimately related to, but not synonymous with, the history of the ancient kingdom of Israel.

➤ The lineage of Judaism can be traced back to the patriarch Abraham.

➤ Both Christianity and Islam have been profoundly influenced by the Jewish tradition.

➤ The Torah teaches about Abraham and the Covenant he formed with God.

➤ Judaism's tireless emphasis on a single true God represents a significant turning point in the history of religious observance, and the keystone of the faith itself.

➤ The importance of the Covenant (God's agreement with the chosen people of Israel) and the Law (the written account of God's revelation) cannot be overstated within this faith.

➤ The Ten Commandments—the core of Jewish Law—have profoundly influenced not only Judaism, but Christianity and Islam as well. These 10 injunctions can be seen as central elements not only of the Jewish tradition, but of the entire monotheistic tradition.

➤ According to the Hebrew Bible, prophets were chosen by God to remind the people of the love of God and of the necessity of their obedience to the Law.

➤ Judaism is a distinctively community-based tradition.

# Modern Jewish Experience

Over the centuries, Judaism has proven itself to be a remarkably resilient and enduring tradition. It has united believers through good times and bad, in hostile surroundings, and in times of peace, plenty, and harmony. Yet the question of how much non-Jewish surroundings should be allowed to influence Judaism's distinctive practices has been a complicated one—a question that has resulted in a many-layered set of answers.

In contemporary times, the faith has evolved into a number of branches, each of which has taken a different approach to the difficult matter of whether, and how, to accommodate the various influences of the outside world. These influences, of course, were and are incredibly varied, since Jewish observance takes place in a bewildering array of social and cultural settings. In this chapter, you can read about the major contemporary movements within the faith, and how modern Judaism has defined itself.

### Watch It!

Judaism is an incredibly diverse faith, and the labels we apply to that faith are of limited use. The movements we'll be discussing in this chapter do carry out certain basic ideas and principles as part of modern Jewish practice, but making broad generalizations about these schools is dangerous. Other schools of thought also exist within the Jewish faith, and none of the major branches can claim complete accord among those who pursue the faith within it.

*Hebrew characters representing the Ten Commandments.*

# Reactions to the Modern World

European Jews of the nineteenth century encountered cultural, scientific, and technological influences that profoundly influenced their daily lifestyles. The European Enlightenment, among many other factors, led a number of believers to press leaders within the faith to take up a sensitive issue: whether a practicing Jew must always strive to live within the dictates of the vast and complex religious code laid out in the Hebrew Bible.

Not surprisingly, a strong set of voices within the Jewish tradition answered that question with a resounding "yes."

# The Orthodox Tradition

Members of the *Orthodox* movement, which remains strong to this day, maintain that they are bound to preserve ritual, tradition, and doctrine as received from rabbis of the past, all the way back to the very beginnings of the faith. These practitioners are willing and eager to preserve the faith exactly as revealed to the people of God in antiquity.

The core of the Orthodox experience can be found in its emphasis on complete, uncompromising conformity to the dictates of God. This branch of the faith tends not to recognize any possibility of accommodation to social changes or influences in what others might refer to as "the outside world." For Orthodox Jews, Judaism *is* the world, inside and out. The emphasis on complete observance of God's will within all aspects of the community, and not merely a supposed "religious sphere," is an ancient idea in this faith.

### What's It Mean?

**Orthodox** Jews take what might be called a "literalist" or "fundamental" approach to issues of faith The notions of unswerving faith to the written word of god, and to established religious tradition, with no alteration, are important ones within the Orthodox branch of Judaism.

### Bet You Didn't Know

The Orthodox approach can be summed up as a desire to live according to the faith, tradition, and liturgy associated with the Law and to pass those conventions on to the next generations. There is no interest in conforming with new social conventions. For the Orthodox Jew, the rest of the world is, one might say, its own problem. Like the Amish, Orthodox Jews are content to pursue the "old ways" not because they are easy or accessible to others (they are neither), but because these traditions, in their view, reflect God's will and are not subject to debate or revision.

The Reform movement, with its rejection of the notion that a faithful Jew must live within the entirety of the Law as revealed in the Scriptures and interpreted in Rabbinic tradition can be seen as providing a countervailing viewpoint. There is also a Conservative movement, which does not observe Orthodox standards completely, but nevertheless strives to retain a significant number of the traditions of historic Judaism. It can be seen as representing the "middle ground" in the reform debate that initially took place in the nineteenth century.

Within the Orthodox community, obedience to the will of God—and complete conformity to God's revealed commands—*is* the world. The primary and overriding influence is to the Law and the traditions that have grown up around it.

The Orthodox tradition reflects a reverence for custom, a deep concern with the word of God, a profound obligation to carry out God's dictates to the letter, and a further obligation to pass on, without alteration, the rituals that have been in place for centuries within the tradition. Distinctive clothing and firmly established social and family structures are expressions of this reverence for custom.

Within the Orthodox Jewish tradition, strong and unalterable gender roles prevail. Certain roles and activities are reserved exclusively for males; others are open only to women. During public religious ceremonies, segregation of the sexes into two groups is the rule. And in both home and synagogue worship, there are liturgical roles based strictly on gender.

# Conservative Judaism

In *Conservative* Judaism, the notion of *absolute* adherence to past traditions is not the guiding principle, as it is in the Orthodox branch of the faith. But a strong sense of tradition and continuity still prevails.

Here, the emphasis is on preserving and honoring appropriate traditions from the past, with favor always given to retaining as much as possible of the "old ways"—but not *all* the "old ways."

Like Orthodox Jews, Conservative adherents affirm the primacy of tradition within their religious experience. They are, however, willing to acknowledge the importance of *judiciously chosen* adjustments to the world in which they live, and they are not as interested as those within the Orthodox tradition in building a "closed" socioreligious system.

Jews in the Conservative tradition truly are "conservative" in the sense that they aim to hold on to as much as possible, while still making some accommodation with social realities that appear to have nothing contrary to Judaism.

Conservative Jews have also been known as adherents of the "historical school" of Judaism. They acknowledge the role of history and contemporary social development and are willing to make adjustments to important trends and practices that appear in contemporary life. At the same time, they are keenly aware of Judaism's own history and its demands upon its followers. They argue that tradition and change have been intimately connected throughout the development of the faith.

### What's It Mean?

**Conservative** Jews have rejected the principle that there can be *no* contact with the new societies and cultural systems Jews encounter in their daily lives, but they nevertheless try to retain as much continuity as possible with the ancient traditions of Judaism.

# Reform Judaism

*Reform* Judaism is the most pragmatic of the three major strands of the Jewish faith today and is the most open to dialogue and interaction with contemporary society. If the Orthodox tradition is focused upon absolute, unwavering adherence to the many dictates of the Law and the Conservative tradition is concerned with retaining as much as possible of the ancient traditions, the Reform approach can be described as an attempt to retain those essential elements of Judaism that *make the most sense in a contemporary setting.*

Of course, Reform Jews do not *reject* the Law as embodied in the Hebrew scriptures and commentaries. They do not, however, take a narrow approach to these injunctions, choosing instead to accept them in a larger ethical sense that permits each individual believer a greater degree of autonomy than in the Orthodox and Conservative traditions. Followers of Reform Judaism are also the most likely to adapt traditions to current social circumstances and values.

Reform Judaism arose in mid-nineteenth century Europe, but it experienced its most explosive growth in the United States, where immigrants from Europe helped to propagate it. The Reform branch's forthright acceptance of the notion that Jews were citizens of the nations where they lived and its rejection of the idea that practitioners must be bound by the narrowly interpreted laws of historic Israel, were probably important factors in the growing popularity of the movement.

### What's It Mean?

Within **Reform** Judaism, the entire Torah is accepted as inspired by God, but it is also seen as open to the study and interpretation of the individual. Reform Jews see God's relationship with the Jews as an ongoing process, and emphasize the broad moral messages of the Jewish tradition.

# The Pressures of the Outside World

Reform, Conservative, and Orthodox Jews take strikingly different approaches to the specific social questions that arise in contemporary life. The issue of gender-based roles within religious worship itself, for instance, can provide some interesting insights into the varying approaches each of the three wings of contemporary Jewry take to matters of "social accommodation."

Suppose a woman has great faith and sincere purpose, is as knowledgeable as her male counterparts on spiritual and scriptural issues, and is eager to become a teacher. The question arises: Why can't such a woman become a rabbi? And perhaps just as important: How will practitioners of each branch of Judaism address such a challenge?

The debate would be an easy one to resolve in the Orthodox tradition. An Orthodox Jew would probably address this issue by pointing out that "outside" notions of sexual equality in contemporary society simply don't matter in God's community. What has worked in the past, such a believer would point out, can be counted on to work in the future, and believers have an obligation not only to reinforce but to pass along existing patterns of worship, regardless of what outsiders have to say about who should be permitted to become a rabbi.

"Centuries of tradition," an Orthodox believer of either sex might argue, "have established certain distinct roles for men and women, roles that are not open to debate or alteration. Within the community of Jews that has been established and supported by God's intervention, women have never become rabbis, and so long as that tradition is maintained and faithfully passed along, women probably never will become rabbis. After all, if the word of God is represented within our tradition—and we certainly believe that it is—then tinkering with any aspect of the tradition in order to accommodate modern notions is foolish and unthinkable."

### On the Path

*Some* elements of the culture in which Reform Jews live are seen as part and parcel of their own identities as people of God. Reform Jews, then, attempt to take a pragmatic approach by balancing modern viewpoints and social conclusions more or less equally against established tradition, all the while hoping to honor, illuminate, and reinforce the *fundamental* truths of the faith. Their focus is on engaging in contemporary realities as they present themselves, rather than on pre-written prayers and rituals for every conceivable situation.

A Conservative Jew would be more willing to make "judgment calls" arising from outside influences when it comes to the larger issue of the relative social roles of men and women, but would nevertheless insist upon a firm base of tradition as the best means of making these decisions. Thus, strict gender stereotyping is less pronounced within the Conservative tradition than within Orthodox Jewry, since scriptural arguments can be made that these accommodations are, at some level, in keeping with the teachings of the Prophets.

A member of the Conservative tradition, then, would be likely to approach this issue as follows: "Yes, I live in Boston at the dawn of the twenty-first century, and yes, I am aware of the fact that I live in a society that places great importance on the fundamental equality of men and women. In evaluating issues such as this one, I also take into account the Lord's injunction to love my neighbors as myself." (Leviticus 19.18)

A member of the Reform wing, however, would be far more likely to ask about the *purpose* a given tradition is serving (or perhaps failing to serve). He or she would be more inclined to emphasize that religious traditions do not exist in a cultural vacuum and that the most essential aspects of the Jewish tradition are still served when adjustments and revisions are made in the interests of conformity to contemporary values, conclusions, and beliefs.

A Reform Jew, in addressing the question of whether women rabbis are appropriate, would not *ignore* the centuries of tradition that point toward male rabbis and only male rabbis. By the same token, the Reform movement does not allow the fact that "things have always been done that way" to assume fundamental importance when it comes to meeting the spiritual needs of contemporary Jews.

Reform Jews reject the claim that they are "tampering" with the scriptures or with doctrine and argue instead that they are allowing the scriptures to be lived more fully and more deeply by not erecting barriers likely to prove intimidating to modern-day practitioners. Reform Judaism makes far fewer social demands on its practitioners than the Orthodox and Conservative branches do. Very few Reform practitioners attempt to encompass every aspect of daily life in their customs and traditions as so many members of the Orthodox school do.

A Reform practitioner might reason the female rabbis issue in this way: "Is the possibility of a radical revision in gender roles, such as female rabbis, really in opposition to the fundamental ideas and values of my faith? Or does such a change instead have a chance to make that faith more accessible to me and to others in the community in which I live? If I can answer affirmatively to the second question, then there is probably no good reason not to alter tradition and practice in this area."

In the end, Reform Jews are likely to ask themselves some variation on the following question: How can those of us who live life in contemporary society best be *brought into contact* with the ancient truths? It's not surprising, then, that it is this group within Judaism that has formally accepted the notion of women as religious teachers.

There are many, many forms of observance within Judaism. Only a few have been touched on here. To try to define and isolate the "essence" of Jewish practice in its many diverse disciplines and innumerable social settings is to miss something fundamental about the faith; certainly it cannot be done with oversimplifying and perhaps seriously misreading the ancient traditions. Indeed, the very words "Jew" and "Judaism" appear nowhere in the Torah! The effort to refine, expand, and perpetuate this Covenant faith, however, despite obstacles and persecutions, extends in an unbroken chain from the mists of antiquity to the dawn of the new century.

### On the Path

The role of the rabbi has evolved over the many centuries of Judaism's development. In ancient times, rabbis were fundamentally instructors in, and explainers of, the Law. In later years, important responsibilities connected to the spiritual life of the community as a whole became important. Although preaching and administrative work have assumed greater prominence for rabbis in modern times within many communities (including Orthodox ones), Orthodox rabbis have always historically emphasized their roles as interpreters and instructors of the Torah.

**Bet You Didn't Know**

In addition to the well-known Orthodox, Conservative, and Reform traditions, there are a number of other currents within the Jewish faith that claim significant numbers of followers. The Reconstructionist school, a movement of the twentieth century, holds that Judaism is a fundamentally social (rather than God-centered) religious civilization. Reconstructionists, in other words, see Judaism as a cultural phenomenon, and boldly reject some core ideas about God embraced by other Jews. Reconstructionists do not, for instance, accept the contention that the Hebrew Bible is the word of God.

Other important traditions include those of the *Sephardic* Jews, whose distinctive traditions and practices evolved centuries ago in Spain and Portugal, and the *Hasidic* Jews, members of a sect that originated in Poland in the eighteenth century, who continue to emphasize religious mysticism and joy in prayer.

# Two Extraordinary Modern Events

Two twentieth-century occurrences have profoundly affected contemporary Judaism.

The first was the rise of *Zionism,* a philosophy that made its first appearance in the nineteenth century and gained dramatically in influence after the turn of the century. Zionism embraced without apology the goal of the re-establishment of the state of Israel. This goal was realized a few years after the conclusion of the Second World War.

The second influence, of course, and one that, like Zionism, can probably never be fully separated from the origins of the modern state of Israel, was the Holocaust. Hitler's virulently anti-Semitic Nazi German state pursued and perpetuated across Europe a brutal policy of systematic murder. The Nazis' assembly-line brand of genocide resulted in the deaths of millions of Jews, along with a significant number of non-Jews. After the defeat of the Germans, Jews around the world vowed never to forget, or permit a repetition of, the unspeakable horrors of the concentration camps.

### The Least You Need to Know

➤ Judaism is a vibrant and diverse faith with many strands, a tradition that is continually rediscovering itself in both new and old expressions.

➤ Orthodox Jews take a fundamental approach to the dictates of the Law, seek to pass along existing traditions without changing them, and strive to incorporate the dictates of their faith into a wide range of daily activities and social interactions.

➤ Conservative Jews acknowledge the need to make some accommodations to external society, but nevertheless grant an important, and usually dominant, role to the traditions of the past.

➤ Reform Jews do not see the dictates of the Hebrew Bible as specific, binding regulations on daily contact with others, but rather seek to honor tradition and faith by making religious observance accessible to contemporary practitioners.

# Chapter 6

# Jewish Ritual and Celebration

---

### In This Chapter

➤ Life itself as a ceremony within the Jewish tradition

➤ Jewish rituals and observances

➤ Jewish holidays

---

In this chapter, you learn about the specifics of religious observance within the Jewish tradition; about holidays such as Passover, Rosh Hashanah, and Yom Kippur; and about the rituals that mark important landmarks in the life of practicing Jews.

## Life: The Ultimate Religious Ceremony

As you've seen, one distinctive aspect of Judaism is its emphasis on a detailed code of conduct, a code rooted in the survival of the ancient people of the original kingdom of Israel. Judaism celebrates specific guideposts by which the community is to perpetuate itself, and it embraces its traditions as both worthy in themselves and reflections of an all-pervasive daily spirituality within the members of the community as they interact with one another.

Today, of course, the role played by Jewish ritual and by predetermined forms of worship, will vary, depending on the nature of the emphasis on the Law accorded by contemporary traditions. At the foundation of all Jewish practice, however, is an all-encompassing approach, one that seeks to translate the incredible detail and diversity of God's creation to a holy form of human celebration (often, quite detailed itself). The basic aim of Jewish worship, then, is to see *all of life* as *liturgy.*

The overarching religious belief of Judaism is that all of life should be seen as a ritual in honor of the Creator. Orthodox, Conservative, and Reform are in agreement on this point, but their emphases and their definitions of the word "ritual" differ.

Worship in the Orthodox tradition places a heavy emphasis on word-for-word recitation of specific prayers in specific situations. There are specific prayers to be recited upon awakening, before eating; there is even a prayer of thanksgiving following a trip to the bathroom, in which the believer praises God for the wonder of the body and its functions.

**What's It Mean?**

**Liturgy** is public worship or ritual.

The Conservative approach to worship is less formalized but still keyed to tradition. The Conservative practitioner's approach to questions of formal religious worship embraces ritual as one expression of values like loving God and helping others, rather than a commitment to specific prayers for every conceivable situation. Conservative Jews could be said to follow the popular saying "There's a time and a place for everything."

Reform Jews, while embracing some specific forms of religious worship, are just as likely to find legitimacy in an unscripted response to day-to-day activities—a response rooted in the idea that action itself is a form of prayer. Members of the Reform movement are more prone to see prewritten, predetermined prayer designed for particular day-to-day situations as something that distances one from the actual experience of God's creation.

The Reform school is not anti-prayer—far from it. It's just that the multiplicity of instruction and repetition found in the other two traditions, and particularly in Orthodox Judaism, tends to be seen by Reform Jews as an obstacle to spiritual growth rather than an aid.

Every branch of the faith is sincere in its approaches. The question is how to realize the principles laid down in scripture and tradition.

## Dietary Laws

Just as prayer and common worship had a distinct social advantage to subjects of the ancient kingdom of Israel (social cohesion and a sense of purpose within the community), specific dietary rules served a purpose as well. The dietary rules set down in the Hebrew Bible may have seemed unusual to the Israelites' neighbors, but they ensured the health and well-being of the people, and served as yet another example of the fulfillment of God's promises to his people.

### Bet You Didn't Know

The word *kosher* refers to that which is in accordance with the established standards of Jewish ritual, typically food and its preparation. Meat that is kosher comes from animals that both chew a cud and have cloven hoofs (such as sheep and cows), and that are killed in accordance with special slaughtering procedures. Kosher meat must be prepared in such a way as to remove all traces of blood. Seafood is considered kosher if the animals caught have scales or fins. Poultry is kosher if it is slaughtered and prepared in the same manner as meat. Kosher dietary guidelines prohibit the consumption of dairy products at the same time, or immediately before or after, a meal including meat products. Separate cooking and serving utensils are required for dairy and non-dairy meals.

Ritual cleanliness and the avoidance of unclean animals remain all-important parts of the Jewish tradition, just as they were an important part of survival in Biblical times. Like the circumcision of males, specific dietary demands help to define and distinguish both the individual and the community he or she is a part of. To the practitioner, however, such considerations are secondary. These injunctions are, first and foremost, God's law.

## What Happens in the Service?

Group prayer is extremely important in the Jewish tradition. The number, complexity, and purpose of the prayers recited during a service at a synagogue will vary according to the hour of the day, the day of the month, and the branch of Judaism in question. Those wishing to pray alone may do so, but must eliminate certain prayers meant for group recitation.

Hebrew is the sacred language of Judaism. Orthodox services can be counted on to incorporate the most Hebrew in the ceremony; Reform tends to use the least. Similarly, Reform and Reconstruction services tend to be shorter than their Orthodox and Conservative counterparts. According to long-observed custom, a communal service requires a quorum, or *minyan*, of at least 10 adults (persons over the age of 13) to proceed. Orthodox Jews, as well as many Conservative practitioners, require 10 *men* for a minyan.

# The Basic Service Consists of ...

The *Amidah,* a group of grateful salutations and prayers of praise to God.

The *Sh'ma,* a pledge of faith, the centerpiece of which is the all-important declaration from Deuteronomy: "Hear O Israel, the Lord is our God, the Lord is One."

A public reading of a passage from the Torah. The *aliyah,* or "going up," refers to the act of being summoned to participate in this reading, a distinct honor.

### On the Path

The fundamental elements of the service in a synagogue/temple may be presented in brief or lengthy variations, depending on the demands of the situation and the particular branch of the Jewish faith. Morning, midday, and sunset prayer services typically run from 15 to 30 minutes; Friday evening or Saturday morning services are considerably longer.

A rabbi will lead the service. A cantor will sing and lead the congregation in song.

## Shabbat

The *Shabbat,* or "repose" that follows six days of work-day activity, parallels the account in the book of Genesis of God's rest after the Creation. The day begins on Friday at sunset and continues until nightfall on Saturday. Work is prohibited at this time, but the definition of "work" can very quickly become a matter of (intricate) discussion among practitioners. Buying, selling, and negotiating, however, are all acknowledged as prohibited activities for Jews during this period, which is also known as the Sabbath.

Regardless of the branch of Judaism under discussion, prayer services undertaken on the Sabbath are the longest and most intricate of them all. Friday evening services may last anywhere from half an hour to three times that length of time; the Saturday morning service may go as long as three full hours.

# Major Observances

Following are thumbnail sketches of some of the most important observances within the Jewish faith. For more detailed information on Jewish rituals and celebrations, see the fine books *How to Be a Perfect Stranger* (Arthur J. Magida, Editor, Jewish Lights Publishing, 1996) and *This Is My God: The Jewish Way of Life* (Herman Wouk, Pocket Books, 1974).

# Rosh Hashanah

This is the Jewish New Year, a holiday that takes place on the first and second days of the Hebrew month Tishrei, roughly the middle of September to the middle of

October. (The Hebrew religious calendar is based on the phases of the moon, not on the Gregorian calendar we go by in daily life.)

Rosh Hashanah celebrates both the religious New Year and the creation of the earth as described in the early chapters of the book of Genesis. Some branches celebrate both days of this holiday; others (i.e., the majority of Reform congregations) only the first day. Work is not performed.

## Yom Kippur

On this day, which takes place shortly after Rosh Hashanah on the tenth day of Tishrei, practicing Jews the world over observe the Day of Atonement. From the sundown that marks the beginning of Yom Kippur until the sundown of the following day, believers forego food and drink, do no work, and repent for misdeeds of the year just past.

## Sukkot

The harvest celebration known as the Feast of Booths lasts for eight days and generally takes place late in the month of October (using the secular Gregorian calendar). It is common to perform no work at the beginning and end of the celebration, but the number of days observed in this manner vary.

## Chanukah (Hanukkah)

The beneficiary, perhaps, of undue media attention because of its (coincidental) placement near the Christian observance of the birth of Christ, Chanukah is often presented as a "Jewish alternative" to Christmas. This is unfortunate, as the Festival of Lights deserves honor, attention, and recognition on its own terms and within its own tradition. The holiday known as the Festival of Lights celebrates the victory of the Maccabees over the Syrians in the second century B.C.E. It begins on the twenty-fifth day of the Hebrew month of Kislev (usually early- to mid-December). Work is permitted during Chanukah.

**On the Path**

Jewish congregations will require males (even males of another faith) to wear a small headpiece called a *yarmulke* (YAM-uh-kuh) during services. Orthodox congregations require that men and women sit in separate areas.

**Watch It!**

The habit many Gentiles have of referring to Chanukah as the "Jewish Christmas" can be a source of frustration among practicing Jews. The celebration of this (minor) holiday involves the commemoration of events that precede the birth of Jesus by over 150 years.

*The menorah is used during the festival of Chanukah.*

# Purim

A festival celebration commencing on the fourteenth day of the Hebrew month Adar (usually late February or early March), Purim commemorates the deliverance of Persian Jews from destruction, as recounted in the book of Esther. This joyous festival is preceded by a day of fasting, and soon gives way to general merrymaking. Work is permitted on Purim.

# Pesach (Passover)

This major holiday, which begins on the fifteenth day of the month of Nisan, honors the delivery of the Jewish people from slavery in Egypt. According to the book of Exodus, God issued a set of instructions for the Israelites: They were to prepare a special feast in great haste before the departure from Egypt. With no time for bread to rise, the bread at the meal would have to be unleavened. Exodus also reports that God arranged for the Angel of Death to destroy the first-born males of the Egyptians, and to "pass over" the marked houses of the Israelites, killing no one within. The Passover celebration, during which practicing Jews abstain from foods prepared with yeast or any other leavening agent, is observed (usually beginning in late March or early April) for seven days by Reform Jews and for eight by members of the other major branches. Many Jews (especially those who follow the Orthodox tradition) perform no work on the first and last two days of the period, but observances vary.

**On the Path**

Purim is marked by gift-giving and generosity toward those in need.

## *Shavout*

This holiday celebrates both the spring harvest season and God's gift of the Torah. It takes place on the sixth and seventh days of the month of Sivan, which corresponds to May or June in the secular Gregorian calendar. As a general rule, Orthodox Jews do no work on these days; a number of Conservative and Reconstructionist practitioners follow the same practice, but Reform Jews celebrate Shavout for a single day.

# Life Rituals

The baby boy is at the center of the *brit milah* (covenant of circumcision), the ritual removal of the foreskin enacted in accordance with Genesis 17:10. This ceremony takes place on the eighth day of the baby boy's life. A parallel naming ceremony for infant girls is known as the *brit hayyim* (covenant of life) or *brit bat* (covenant of the daughter). This, too, occurs on the eighth day of life.

At the age of 13, a Jewish male marks his entry into the community as an adult during his *bar mitzvah* (son of the commandment). The female counterpart is known as a *bat mitzvah* (daughter of the commandment), and can be held for females as young as 12. The bat mitzvah was first celebrated in the twentieth century.

The Jewish marriage ceremony is known as the *kiddushin* (sanctification). It takes place under a wedding canopy known as a *huppah*, and incorporates the ritual breaking of a glass underfoot, an act that commemorates a sad event in Jewish history, the destruction of the Temple in Jerusalem in 70 C.E.

Funeral observances in the Jewish tradition follow distinct guidelines that may vary depending on the branch of Judaism in question. (Reform Jews, for instance, permit cremation, while Jews of most other traditions observe injunctions against the practice.)

---

### The Least You Need to Know

➤ Jewish customs, rituals, and dietary guidelines provided both social cohesion and rules for law abiding life among ancient Israelites, just as they do for practicing Jews today.

➤ The moment-to-moment celebration of life itself, in all its diversity, underlies Jewish worship, observance, and ritual, although different branches of the faith take different approaches to the ideal forms of this celebration.

➤ Major Jewish holidays include Rosh Hashanah, Yom Kippur, and Passover.

---

# Part 3
# Christianity

*There is virtually no nation on earth that is without some community of Christian believers.*

*Although its adherents are to be found around the world, and acceptance of Jesus as the Messiah, the Son of God, is central to the faith, Christianity's "basic doctrines" defy simple explanation. In part, this is because of the many divergent traditions and structures that have emerged over the centuries as the result of disagreements over doctrine and practice; in part, it is because the role and teachings of Jesus himself remain, after two millennia, a fundamental mystery.*

# Chapter 7

# Christian Beginnings

**In This Chapter**

➤ Learn about the origins of Christianity

➤ Explore the historical development of the various branches of the Christian church

➤ Learn why broad generalizations about the Christian faith can be dangerous

Christianity grew from a tiny sect in first-century Palestine to become one of the world's great faiths. In this chapter, you learn about how it has developed, what forces have influenced it, and some of the diverse pathways it has traveled over the first two thousand years of its existence.

## The Man at the Center of the Faith

The simple and familiar name "Jesus Christ" offers a great deal of information about the influences that shaped Christianity.

"Jesus" is a Latinized form of the Greek "Iesous," a transliteration of a Hebrew name most contemporary Christians probably would not recognize: Y'shua. And "Christ" is not, properly speaking, a name at all, but a description. It is a variation on the Greek word "Christos," which means "the anointed one." This word is, in turn, a translation of the Hebrew "Messiah"—in Jewish tradition, a figure chosen and anointed by God who would bring salvation to Israel.

*The Holy Spirit, pictured as a dove. The New Testament describes a dove (the "Spirit of God") descending upon Jesus at his baptism.*

### Bet You Didn't Know

A few historians have suggested that all we can know for certain about Jesus of Galilee is that he was crucified in Jerusalem—probably on charges open-ended enough to sound like blasphemy to the Jewish religious leaders of his day and like sedition to the Roman authorities. However, most scholars now accept the basic Gospel picture of Jesus—that he conducted a popular ministry that embraced sinners and social outcasts; occasionally challenged the religious authorities of the day; and promoted love, tolerance, and faith. Jesus' claim to be the Messiah won him bitter enemies as well as followers, and was probably one reason for his execution.

Christians believe that Jesus was both God and Man, born on earth to redeem the human race. They accept and celebrate his ethical teachings, which emphasize unfailing mercy and forgiveness. They also believe that after he was betrayed by Judas Iscariot and condemned to death by Pontius Pilate, Jesus rose again from the dead, enabling humans to achieve true salvation. Christians anticipate the return, or Second Coming, of the risen Jesus.

### What's It Mean?

The four New Testament **Gospels,** Matthew, Mark, Luke, and John, are the received accounts of the life and ministry of Jesus. None were assembled, at least in their current form, during Jesus' ministry. The sources, dates of composition, and degrees of interrelationship of the various Gospels have given rise to centuries of scholarly work. The first three accounts share such strong similarities of material and viewpoint that they are regarded as "synoptic" (i.e., "same eye") Gospels. John presents a notably different, and probably later, tradition.

The name "Jesus Christ" captures a fateful (and, at the time, controversial) moment in the history of the church. These two words served to introduce Jesus, and the Jewish concept of a redeemer for the subjugated nation of Israel, to a distinctly non-Jewish audience. The various messages sent to that audience laid the foundations of modern Christianity.

In other words: The figure at the center of this faith is described at a distance, in translation, as the result of Greek cultural influences in the Mediterranean societies where the faith first gained wide acceptance among non-Jews. It was after this phase of its development that Christianity began the ascent that would lead to its status as one of the world's major religions.

Who was the "real" Jesus? A feeling of removal from Jesus the person sometimes arises among today's Christians, and understandably.

Today, we may expect written history to be an attempt at a neutral accounting of events, not realizing this is a modern value that cannot be applied to the sacred writings of antiquity. The compilers of the *Gospels* didn't set out to answer the modern questions, "What was Jesus really like?" and "What was the precise sequence of the events in his life, historically speaking?" Assembled from

### On the Path

Christians, by and large, accept the Bible as the inspired word of God. The Christian Bible includes 39 sacred Hebrew and Aramaic books, as well as 27 books from the years following the ministry of Jesus. Christians refer to the first group of books as the Old Testament, and the second group of books as the New Testament. A number of books and fragments frequently grouped with the Old Testament, known as the Apocrypha, are also held to be inspired by some Christians.

various sources a generation or two after Jesus' ministry, and written in Greek, rather than the Aramaic he spoke, the Gospels are part history, part faith testimony—not contemporary journalism or biography.

# Mystery

The "translation" problem goes beyond the question of how to refer to Jesus. Think of the many difficulties associated with integrating the religion of one culture into a separate (and very different) culture. In the case of the Gospels, faith in Jesus had to be translated from the Judaism of first-century Palestine to the Greek- and Latin-speaking (or "Hellenistic") culture of the late Roman Empire.

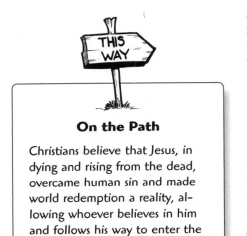

### On the Path

Christians believe that Jesus, in dying and rising from the dead, overcame human sin and made world redemption a reality, allowing whoever believes in him and follows his way to enter the kingdom of heaven.

An aura of mystery appears to have surrounded Jesus from the moment he emerged in Palestine as a teacher. For many believers, the same aura attaches itself to his teachings to this day. In first-century Palestine, many people apparently could not encounter Jesus without asking, "What kind of man is this?"

For two thousand years Christians have worked to lessen the distance between their own hearts and the demanding, puzzling figure at the center of their faith. Whether they lived in cultures that oppressed and persecuted followers of Christianity, cultures that claimed to follow Jesus' teachings as their social blueprint, or cultures that took no position one way or the other, Jesus' followers have had to make their own journeys to resolve fundamental questions about the man whose ancient ministry continues to exert a profoundly modern influence.

# Christianity in the World

Christianity is a rich, diverse faith that, like the other major religions, encompasses many schools and points of view. It is, today, a global religion. Some of the major events within the history of that faith are identified in this chapter.

## *Cultural and Historical Adaptability*

Jesus has sometimes been called the most influential person in Western civilization. This is probably because of the extraordinary reach and influence of the religion that sees him as its founder.

The word "Christianity" certainly applies to a staggeringly wide range of worship, and the religion the word describes has been a powerful social force for centuries in widely varying settings. (In his book *The 100: A Ranking of the Most Influential Persons in History,* Michael H. Hart observed that "(t)here is no question that Christianity, over the course of time, has had far more adherents than any other religion.") Because Christianity is an adaptable faith, however, it's extremely difficult to make across-the-board statements about it or, perhaps, logical assessments of its fundamental ideas.

## An Unfinished Faith

One reason to be wary of the use of logical tools to describe Christianity is that it is not (for most believers) a closed, concluded system. Christians, in living out their faith, do not look backward to a specific historical period but forward to redemption and resurrection through Jesus.

This orientation not only affirms the conviction that good will ultimately prevail over evil but also calls believers to be vigilant in living out the Gospel message in daily life. Christians are reminded that their faith is a direction, not a static set of principles. Some would even say Christianity is a "work in progress."

With these cautionary points in mind, you're ready to take a closer look at the history and development of this influential monotheistic faith.

# Peter and Paul—And Beyond

It is very important to recall that Christianity began as a form of Judaism and that not only Jesus but his earliest followers were observant Jews. This fact is often overlooked by Christians today who may not always realize the impact of early arguments concerning Jesus within Judaism.

The Apostle Peter, a disciple of Jesus (*Apostle* means "messenger" or "envoy"), is today regarded as the first bishop of Rome. The Christian congregation in Rome was to play a leading role in the survival and development of the faith. Another Apostle, Paul, was a contemporary of Peter, although he never met Jesus. A devout Jew, Paul gave up persecuting Christians after receiving a call from Christ to preach salvation to the Gentiles. Paul went on to become the foremost Christian theologian of the faith's early years and the main architect of the faith's expansion into the Gentile community.

Intermittent persecution by Roman authorities followed Christianity's emergence as a religion separate from Judaism, and both Peter and Paul are

### What's It Mean?

The **Pauline Epistles** are ancient letters attributed to Paul, offering guidance to particular congregations of the day and to the Christian church as a whole. The epistles are part of the New Testament and have had an immense impact on Christian doctrine and practice.

assumed to have died martyr's deaths in Rome. Although the extent of persecution has sometimes been exaggerated, Christians were seen by many Romans as disloyal and even immoral. Sporadic local persecutions and occasional imperial crackdowns brought suffering to Christian communities, including torture, loss of property, and very often violent death. Such measures proved ineffective, however, in halting Christianity's progress.

### On the Path

The life of St. Francis of Assisi, born in Italy in the late twelfth century, has inspired many Christians. As a young man, Francis relinquished a life of wealth, choosing instead a life of joyous poverty. Francis saw the suffering of Jesus in the poor and the sick, and the beauty of Jesus in nature. He eventually founded the Franciscan Order. Francis is one of the most beloved figures in Christianity.

### What's It Mean?

A **schism** is a division or state of disunion within a church. In Christianity, the schism between the Eastern and Western wings of the church (1054) led to separate groupings today known popularly as the Orthodox and Catholic churches.

# Development, Conflict, and Acceptance

The majority of members of the early church appear to have belonged to the lower classes and were looked down on as such. Their communities were small, poor, and scattered among the cities of the Empire. Inner spirituality formed a large part of Christian experience. Understanding and interpreting the mystery of Christ and of salvation often led to sharp conflicts and divisions.

Upper-class skeptics marveled at how members of a religion that emphasized love could put so much energy into attacking other Christians, especially while their faith was still under attack. Then in 312 C.E., something dramatic happened. A future emperor, named Constantine, converted to the Christian faith, following a vision which told him that he would gain a military victory.

After defeating his military rivals, Constantine assumed political power and issued decrees forbidding the persecution of Christians. His actions made Christianity respectable in the Empire and encouraged conversions to the faith among all classes of people.

With the weakening and failure of imperial power in Western Europe after 400 C.E. the popes, retaining religious leadership, also began to emerge as a powerful social and political force in their own right in the West. Over the next several centuries, Christianity expanded and developed under papal leadership.

At the same time, however, disputes between the Latin-speaking church of the West and the Greek-speaking church of the Byzantine Empire in the East were leading to separation. Pope Gregory VII, who was successful in undertaking ecclesiastical reforms in the West, was unable to prevent this division. Formal *schism* came in 1054. By that time, missionary efforts had brought Latin Christianity to most of Western Europe.

As city life revived in the thirteenth century after centuries of stagnation and decay, new religious orders of layfolk and clerics were formed to teach and preach the faith. This period also saw the building of great cathedrals and the founding of the major universities of Europe.

The century of St. Francis and St. Dominic saw the papacy assume a position of extraordinary prominence in both the culture and political life of Western Europe. This time was marked by stability, intellectual openness on certain topics, and unchallenged religious and social authority. But these same years also gave birth to the *Crusades* and the first of the Inquisitions, under which the church conducted secret trials to identify and eliminate heretics. This period of church history was also marred by various forms of institutional corruption.

The later Middle ages witnessed a papal schism and a series of bitter power struggles at Rome, resulting in competing claims for what had become the most powerful office in Europe. The papal office itself was claimed by two, and, for a while, three, claimants. Finally, an extraordinary Council was called (at Constance, 1414–1418) both to end the papal schism and to reform the church in head and members. The Council was able to secure unity in the papacy, but not to reform church abuses.

By the beginning of the sixteenth century, calls within the church for reform were becoming ever more insistent. Complaints about abuses, both at Rome and elsewhere, were loud. These complaints centered on a bloated and money-hungry bureaucracy, unblushing office seeking, the practice of concubinage by too many members of a clergy sworn to celibacy and a series of entangled religious and military alliances. Doctrinal misunderstandings concerning practices like indulgences (too often seen as a kind of payment to excuse sin), and about the grace won by Christ for all believers, were viewed with dismay by many.

European Christianity was ripe for reform, and when the changes came, they took the form of the Protestant Reformations.

### What's It Mean?

The **Crusades** were a series of military conflicts initiated by European powers during the eleventh to the thirteenth centuries. Their stated aim was to gain control of the holy places in the land where Jesus had lived—regions then under the control of Muslims. Although the Crusaders managed to take Jerusalem briefly in 1099 and establish a Latin Kingdom in Palestine that lasted 200 years, they were eventually repelled, leaving Muslim rulers in charge.

# The Protestant Reformations

The Reformations began, as their name implies, as an attempt to reform the excesses of the Roman Church *internally*. The result, instead, was the formation of a number of churches separate from papal authority. The roots of the movement actually extended far into the past. John Wyclif, for example, had headed a dissident movement in the fourteenth century. The catalyst of the Protestant Reformations, however, was Martin Luther's famous 95 theses, which may or may not have been posted on the door of the castle church at Wittenberg in 1517, but which certainly sparked a firestorm of controversy.

### On the Path

The Protestant Reformations extended to England in the sixteenth century when King Henry VIII, supported by his Parliament, defied the authority of the pope and named himself as head of England's church. This came about because the pope had refused to accede to Henry's request for a dissolution of his marriage to Catherine of Aragon.

Luther, a professor of theology, did not intend to separate from the Roman church when he wrote his 95 theses. His purpose was to address matters of salvation that concerned him deeply. Luther was a firebrand, however, and he refused to back down when his call for debate on doctrinal issues led him into direct conflict with church authorities. In 1519 he openly denied the authority of the church on religious matters; in 1520 he was excommunicated by the pope and condemned by the Holy Roman Emperor. (By then, however, Luther had many supporters.) In 1521 an attempt to heal the rift only led to greater support for the revolt against Rome.

Luther's doctrines (examined in the next chapter) gained wide support in Germany and elsewhere, and a number of political leaders embraced his cause, not least because they stood to gain economically by confiscating church property. A new class of capitalists, too, looked to benefit from a more open, less centralized social structure. But to read too much into these economic motives would be a mistake.

The criticisms Luther and his colleagues launched against corruption were shared by many laity and clergy. His revolutionary insistence on direct communication with God, unmediated by a priest, struck a chord with believers throughout Europe. Tragically, matters of conscience led to decades of bloody warfare between rival Christians.

Eventually, the rift did lead to significant reforms within the Roman Church. Doctrinal orthodoxy became an imperative, and clerical celibacy became more of a reality. But the religious divisions in Europe remained deep.

Profound war-weariness, commercial interest, and skepticism about competing religious claims eventually ended the religious wars. In Europe, territory was divided among the various factions. England became guardedly pluralistic, although the rise of Puritanism showed there was plenty of energy left in that country for religious debate. In the aftermath of the European Reformations, and in North America especially, varieties of Protestantism proved a rich source of new Christian thought and worship.

# Beyond the Divisions

In the long period following the Protestant Reformations, the leaders of the various Christian factions have attempted to transcend old conflicts, with varying degrees of success. To one degree or another, most of the divisions of Christianity have had to come to terms in recent years with the demands and opportunities of life lived in a time of rapid social and technological change.

Today, an increasingly vigorous *ecumenical movement* has helped to unite disparate factions of the church in ways that would once have been considered unthinkable. Representatives of prominent Protestant and Orthodox Eastern churches, for instance, were in attendance as observers during the Second Vatican Council, at Rome, which convened in 1962 and opened the way to significant new reforms within the Roman Catholic church.

In the modern era, scientific inquiry and heavy secular and commercial influence have discouraged the faith of some Christians while reinforcing and strengthening the faith of others. As the global church enters the new millennium, it finds itself gaining adherents in lands that once seemed far beyond its influence. "Christianity" may never again be the religious wing of a mighty political empire, but its essential principles endure. Empires crumble, but great religions go on. The Christian emphasis on mercy, forgiveness, reconciliation, and love has transcended even the (serious) limitations of the institutions that have propagated the faith over the centuries.

### What's It Mean?

The **ecumenical movement,** an ongoing effort to promote unity among the various Christian denominations, has been a potent force in twentieth- century Christianity.

## The Least You Need to Know

➤ The figure at the heart of Christianity, Jesus, has been the subject of mystery and veneration for centuries, and categorical pronouncements about him should be treated with skepticism.

➤ The Western, or Latin, Christian Church emerged as the dominant religious force in Western Europe and held that position for centuries.

➤ Disagreements with the Eastern Church in 1054 led to one major rift in Christianity; the Protestant Reformations of the fifteenth century created another.

➤ The excesses and limitations of the various Christian churches have not prevented the faith promulgated by those churches from becoming one of the world's most important religions.

# The Many Christian Denominations

Christianity can be divided into three main branches: the Roman Catholic Church, the Orthodox Eastern Churches, and the Protestant Churches. In this chapter, you'll find out about all three.

## Roman Catholicism

The word "catholic" originally referred to the global community of Christian believers and is still used this way in some contexts.

When Roman Catholics make use of the word Catholic, they are usually referring to the huge worldwide group of Christians who identify themselves as being in communion with the bishop of Rome, the pope. This group accounts for roughly half of all Christians on the planet. In this chapter, the terms "Catholic" and "Roman Catholic" will refer to this group of believers.

# What Catholics Believe

Roman Catholics, like all Christians, accept Jesus Christ as the Son of God.

Many aspects, however, of Catholic faith and observance stand in contrast to the practices of other Christians. Some of the most important distinguishing characteristics of the Roman Catholic faith are these:

➤ Acknowledgment of and participation in particular sacraments: baptism, confirmation, the Eucharist (that is, sharing in the 'transubstantiated' body and blood of Christ when Holy Communion is shared during Mass), penance (also referred to as confession), the anointing of the sick, marriage, and holy orders (for those entering the clergy).

➤ Acceptance of the Church as the repository of complete, divine revelation.

➤ Acknowledgment of the spiritual authority of the pope and the bishops of the Church as coming directly from Christ, who assigned earthly dominion over spiritual matters to the apostles (also known as *apostolic succession).* One of these apostles was Peter, regarded as the first bishop of Rome.

## What's It Mean?

The doctrine of **apostolic succession** holds that, in transmitting authority to the Apostles, Jesus initiated a chain of authority that has extended in an unbroken line to current Catholic bishops. The group of bishops, united with the pope, form a body called the Episcopal College. Roman Catholics believe that the members of this body have been given the commission to pass down the teachings of Christ and, at special times, to articulate matters of doctrine with the assistance of the Holy Spirit.

➤ Acceptance of the human soul's immortal status, with each person accountable for his or her actions and choices.

➤ Belief that God exists in an objective sense, and is understood as triune in nature.

➤ Celebration of the grace of God as poured forth in the hearts of believers, who are so changed as to become the children of God.

➤ Celebration of the message of Christ as both a belief and a way of life.

This list sets out the most obvious "external" or "institutional" features distinctive of the Roman church. It is worth noting, too, that Catholics accept that:

➤ The church is committed to a divine mission.

➤ God is concerned with human affairs and can be reached through prayer.

Roman Catholics accord special honor to the Virgin Mary. This veneration relates to her role as the mother of the savior of all humankind. Roman Catholics believe that, because of the redemption brought by Jesus, Mary, like her son, was preserved from the stain of original sin, which is seen as touching all other members of the human family. This view of Mary is known as the doctrine of the Immaculate Conception.

The Roman Catholic Church also teaches that, having finished the course of her earthly life, Mary was assumed, body and soul, into heaven. This teaching is known as the doctrine of the Assumption.

## The Trinity

The notion of the "triune" God, which is distinctively Christian, is both important and fundamentally mysterious. Catholics regard it as one of the profound truths of their faith.

The Profession of Faith that says that the Son, Jesus Christ, is truly God and truly human was debated in the third, fourth, and fifth centuries. Many councils were called during this period to defend the full mystery of the Incarnation of the Son, the Second Person of the Trinity, maintaining a full divine and human nature of Jesus Christ united in one divine person.

### On the Path

Roman Catholics, along with Orthodox believers and some worshipers in the Anglican and Lutheran traditions, venerate Jesus' mother Mary in a special way, regarding her as the Mother of God. This veneration arises from the faith understanding of the divine and human natures united in the person of Jesus.

### Bet You Didn't Know

The Trinity of Father, Son, and Holy Spirit should not be interpreted as meaning that Catholics (or believers within other Christian systems) view God as an essentially male deity. The divine essence is not considered as having a gender.

Similarly, the three dimensions should not be seen as somehow separate and incompatible with one another. The triune God is both one *and* three. If such a doctrine seems to defy rational explanation, this may be just as well. The dogma (teaching) of the Trinity is held by Catholics to transcend logical analysis or philosophical demonstration.

## Expansion—and a Rift

For the first centuries of its existence, the Church's history was essentially identical with that of organized Christianity, which evolved in an atmosphere of passionate debate. (See Chapter 7, "Christian Beginnings.")

From its earliest beginnings, Christianity can be seen as a religion on the move, spreading rapidly, if not always gently, into many nations. In part, this was because of the universality of the faith, but it was also, in part, because church authorities were willing to incorporate local traditions and imagery within the broader context of established Christian worship.

In 1054, the Western church formally split with the Eastern wing of the faith. Serious divisions between the two had, however, been in evidence long before.

## Challenge and Change

From the ninth century C.E. to the early sixteenth century, the Western Church was *the* religious component of Western European society. Since clear divisions did not yet exist between religious bodies and other social institutions, the Church was often a dominant social influence within the kingdoms of that era.

**On the Path**

Religious orders within the Roman Catholic Church have served to energize and reinvigorate the institution for hundreds of years. Members of these orders, which include (among many others) the Dominican, Benedictine, Franciscan, and Carmelite movements, seek to imitate the life of Jesus: They own no property, pursue a celibate lifestyle, and follow a discipline of strict obedience.

The Protestant Reformations, which led to a long and bloody military struggle, as well as a new pluralism within European Christianity, began as an internal attempt to reform the "Mother Church." The Reformations were neither the first nor the last campaigns mounted by believers to reform church practices.

A pattern of vigorous reform, growth, complacency, and renewed reform is not difficult to make out over the centuries of the Catholic Church's development. Catholics view the seemingly countless cycles of change and reform within their faith as part of an ongoing historical process of development, one fully in keeping with the church's divinely appointed role.

The most recent, and perhaps the most dramatic, of the reforms took place in the early to middle 1960s, with the Second Vatican Council (Vatican II). As a prelude to any review of Vatican II, it is worth remembering the work of the *First* Vatican Council, which began in 1869.

The First Vatican Council is remembered chiefly for its expression of the doctrine of papal infallibility, a much-discussed (and routinely oversimplified) statement that when the pope speaks officially ("ex cathedra") on matters related to faith or morals, he acts as pastor of the universal church and is given a special gift of the Holy Spirit to preserve the teaching from error.

Catholics believe that the pope teaches and believes as a member of the universal church. By definition, such teaching would not represent a contradiction of fundamental doctrines already revealed.

The idea that Catholics consider the pope to be correct in his every utterance is a common misconception. Only formal pronouncements concerning faith or morals fall under the doctrine of papal infallibility. A pope could not use this doctrine to enforce compliance with a decree that God is not three persons but two, or to dictate that Jesus be regarded as having been born in Dayton, Ohio. Such fundamental issues are beyond the reach of the pope's authority.

For critics, the doctrine of papal infallibility epitomizes what they see as a kind of rigid orthodoxy within the church. The Second Vatican Council, however, openly embraced some long-ignored initiatives for change—taking many observers, both within the church and outside it, by surprise.

Among the most important reforms were the acceptance of contemporary local language (rather than Latin) in the Mass, and a forthright embrace of broad ecumenical principles. The Council also issued a direct condemnation of Anti-Semitism.

# The Orthodox Church

The Orthodox Church (or, as it is also known, Orthodox Eastern Church) represents the dominant form of Christian worship in Greece and in a large region of eastern Europe. As a church it claims an unbroken history dating from Apostolic times when the Christian message was carried to such Greek-speaking communities as Ephesus, Antioch, and Corinth. The Orthodox system is also present in parts of the Middle East.

### What's It Mean?

Among the most prominent of the Catholic orders has been the Society of Jesus, whose members are commonly known as **Jesuits.** The intellectual accomplishment and energetic missionary work of the Jesuits have been one of the high points of modern Catholic history. The order was founded in response to the Protestant Reformations by Ignatius of Loyola.

### Watch It!

Although most people understand on an intuitive level what is meant by the words "Catholic" and "Orthodox," careless use of the terms without their initial capital letters can lead to confusion. Followers of the Eastern tradition emphasize the catholicism (universality) of their faith, just as believers within the Roman church realize the value of embracing and understanding orthodoxy (established and accepted belief) in addressing important faith challenges.

## Shared Origins, Different Rites

Because the eastern and western churches were united during their first thousand years of existence, they agree on many significant matters of doctrine. Their most important differences have to do with emphasis and practice.

Long before the formal split with the Western church in the eleventh century, for example, Eastern churches differed with Rome on the use of unleavened bread during religious ceremonies (Orthodox services today employ leavened bread), on the West's alteration of the Nicene creed to include explicit reference to the Holy Spirit's "proceed(ing) from the Father and the Son," and on the role of the pope.

*Western Cross (left),*
*Eastern cross (right).*

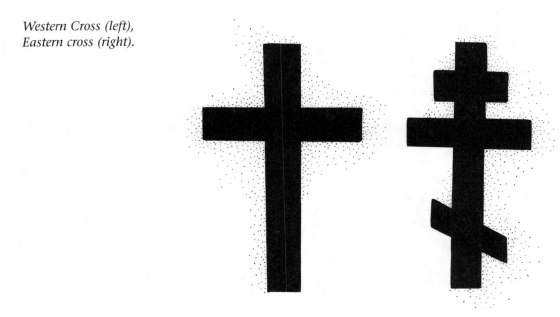

Another obvious difference is the eastern tradition's embrace of the liturgies of St. John Chrysostom and St. Basil. The Orthodox liturgy is sung, rather than spoken, and it is not generally a matter of daily observance.

Parish priests in the Orthodox tradition may marry before they are ordained. Infants may receive communion.

Orthodox places of worship are renowned for their beauty and elaborate ornamentation. Icons, gilding, carved ornamentation, incense, and screens veiling the high altar are some common elements of Orthodox liturgy and sacred space and serve to emphasize the transcendent nature of the divine.

## Organization

On an organizational level, the Orthodox tradition is less centralized than its Catholic counterpart. This is because it developed over the centuries through a number of *patriarchates,* a form of regional religious administration under the leadership of patriarchs.

In fact, within the Orthodox Eastern tradition, individual national churches operate with great independence from their counterparts, and national identity plays an important role in daily worship. The Russian Orthodox Church, which represents the largest community of Orthodox believers, was ruthlessly suppressed during much of the Soviet era. It reemerged, significantly, during World War II, and flourishes in the period following Communist rule.

## The Orthodox Church Today

A number of national Orthodox churches exist today, each representing the traditional patriotic traditions of its believers. Among these, the Greek and Russian branches are the most prominent.

Several autonomous Orthodox groups have established separate hierarchies in the United States, and although some of these churches are in communion with one another, no single confederation of Orthodox faiths has emerged. Given the nationalistic and cultural emphasis of most Orthodox traditions, it's likely that a variety of Orthodox voices will continue to add to the richness of America's religious life.

# Protestantism

From a single point of origin, the European religious revolutions of the 1500s, the religions designated as "Protestant" form the most diverse strand of the three great divisions within Christianity. The variety can be more than a little intimidating, because the collection of Protestant views presents a rich profusion of Bible-based traditions. The authors respect and honor the validity and devotion of the many Protestant traditions, not all of which can be identified here.

**On the Path**

Icons, paintings depicting Jesus and particular saints, are an important part of Orthodox practice. Objects of deep reverence by believers, they are considered windows through which the viewer can catch a glimpse of the divine during times of prayer and contemplation.

**Watch It!**

Does it really make sense to group Episcopalians with the Amish, Seventh-Day Adventists with Congregationalists, and Lutherans with Quakers? All these groups, of course, reject the authority of the pope, but generalizations about any faith system are dangerous, and broad statements about the Protestant traditions can be particularly tricky. In this family, denominations incorporate stark differences in doctrine and approach.

"Protestantism" is an umbrella term for a set of traditions that came into existence after the Reformations. If there is a single common thread among the traditions in this group, it is probably rooted in ideas of group autonomy and respect for individual experience. It has been said, for example, that Catholics come to Christ through the church, while Protestants come to the church through Christ.

This is not to say that most early Protestants believed in religious toleration and pluralism. (In the sixteenth and seventeenth centuries, such ideas were reserved for the radical fringe.) The guiding accents in the Protestant experience have been the formation of communities and the power of direct experience. Protestants claim "the priesthood of all believers," by which they assert that lay believers have the same access to God as clergy—that all have a religious vocation, whether farmers, factory workers, parents, or ministers.

Two other fundamental doctrinal points set Protestant Christians apart from believers in the Roman Catholic tradition. The Bible itself is regarded as the source of infallible, received truth, and the believer is justified by God's grace, obtained through his or her faith in Christ—not by good deeds or the mediation of any religious institution.

In practice, the vast majority of Protestant denominations have also rejected the notion of clerical celibacy. A few, including the Shakers, advocated celibacy among *all believers*, relying on the recruitment of outsiders to perpetuate the faith.

### On the Path

Lutherans appealed to the New Testament writings of the Apostle Paul in support of the notion of "justification by grace, through faith." The dispute over whether a human's good works could augment God's grace, or be accumulated in surplus by the church (like a bank account), was a matter of intense dispute between Luther's followers and the Catholic Church.

A word of warning: What follows is a beginner's summary. The outlines of major Protestant movements and doctrinal issues that appear below are meant as an introduction to the group in question, and not as the last word on any tradition or practice.

# Faith, Not Works

Martin Luther, the first and one of the foremost Protestant reformers, interpreted certain passages of the New Testament to mean that God's grace alone, and not the good works of individuals, served as source of salvation through faith. Luther's doctrine won an immediate following among academics, clergy, and laity.

John Calvin was another reformer of significant influence. An exiled French theologian of the generation after Luther, Calvin devoted his life to the ideal of building a truly Christian society based on charity, humility, and faith.

For Calvin, theology was important, but it was the starting place, not the goal. His vision of a church governed by elders (in Greek, *presbyteros*) led to the founding of, for example, the Presbyterian Church. "Reformed" churches in Holland, Germany, and France look back to Calvinist roots.

# Other Major Denominations

The Anglican Church, whose American branch is known as the Episcopal Church, rejects the authority of Rome but agrees with Roman Catholicism on many issues of doctrine. Followers of both the Anglican Communion (in England) and the Episcopal Church (in the United States) have embraced a commitment to positive social change.

For millions of Christians, worship and practice have been profoundly affected by the *Book of Common Prayer,* the service book of the Anglican Communion.

The Methodist church was founded by the English cleric John Wesley. This denomination emphasizes repentance, individual faith, and responsibility for the betterment of society at large. The tradition takes its name from the commitment of Wesley and his colleagues to lead lives governed by "rule and method" in religious study. Methodism is among the largest Protestant denominations in the United States.

Baptists, of which there are many varieties, represent the largest American Protestant denomination. Unlike most other branches of the Christian faith, Baptists insist that baptism, to be valid, must be a conscious adult choice that accompanies full acceptance of Jesus as one's personal savior.

Many Baptist traditions (as well as other denominations within the Protestant tradition) place heavy emphasis on New Testament passages that highlight the importance of being "born again." Baptists often see a direct, conscious acknowledgment of Jesus as Savior as the best means to this end.

Congregationalism, which traces its lineage from the Nonconformist movement in England, honors the Christian community as a covenant of faithful

**On the Path**

In 1536, John Calvin wrote the highly influential theological work *Institutes of the Christian Religion,* which explicitly rejected the authority of the pope and set out the doctrine of predestination for which Calvinism is well known.

**On the Path**

The Great Awakening, a period of religious revival and highly emotional preaching styles during the eighteenth century, led to rapid growth for a number of Protestant denominations. One of the greatest preachers of this period included the Congregationalist Jonathan Edwards and the Presbyterian William Tennent.

individuals. Each local church operates autonomously, acknowledging only Christ as its head, and respecting the relationships of the various congregations as interactions between members of the Christian family. Fellowship and cooperation are at the heart of Congregationalism.

In the twentieth century, two important movements within Protestantism have had profound influences on Christian worship in the United States. One is Fundamentalism, which holds that all statements in the Bible are literally true. Fundamentalist approaches to Christianity are broadly popular in the United States.

Pentecostalism is a global movement emphasizing an ecstatic experience of God, often resulting in *glossolalia* (speaking in tongues). Major Pentecostalist denominations include the Church of God in Christ and the Assemblies of God.

# Different Drummers: "Distinctive" Protestant Movements

The Quakers (or Friends) reject the necessity of ordained ministers and external sacraments, viewing all aspects of life itself as sacred. This pacifist tradition holds that every believer is gifted with "inner light." Friends gather in weekly meetings to pray silently together and to share revelation as the Spirit dictates.

**On the Path**

One person's comfortable orthodoxy may be the force that galvanizes another to launch a new religious movement. Protestantism contains countless examples of such movements; some have endured, some have not. The varieties of these movements, each with its distinctive approach to doctrine and practice, are seen by some as instances of Christian fragmentation, and by others as a source of tremendous richness and strength.

Extraordinary piety and a commitment to live as simply as possible mark the practices of active Mennonites, who refuse, on religious grounds, to hold public office or serve in any military capacity. The Mennonite tradition traces its roots to the radical fringe of the early Reformation, the Anabaptists. Another such group are the Amish, who reject many modern technological advances and severely limit contact with the outside world.

The Unitarian Universalist Association, which includes both Christian and non-Christian members, is among the most open and tolerant of Protestant religious traditions. Unitarian Universalists reject the doctrine of the Trinity, seeing Christ as a great teacher, not a divine incarnation. They tend to avoid dogma as restrictive and even presumptuous, choosing to emphasize inclusiveness and understanding rather than a specific religious creed.

The Christian Science movement, founded by Mary Baker Eddy, holds that the spiritual world is the true reality, compared to which the material world is an illusion. Christian Scientists believe that sin and illness can be overcome by spiritual powers. For this reason they tend to avoid medicines and medical procedures in favor of divine healing.

Seventh-Day Adventists celebrate the Sabbath on Saturday (rather than Sunday) and anticipate the imminent Second Coming of Christ.

Jehovah's Witnesses accept the Bible as factually true in every detail and anticipate the coming of God's kingdom after the battle of Armageddon, which is considered imminent and which is expected to be followed by a thousand-year reign of Christ on earth.

Followers of the Church of Jesus Christ of Latter-Day Saints (the Mormons) pursue a system of beliefs that accepts the divine revelation of the Bible but differs markedly from the doctrines accepted by most other Christians. Church tradition holds that an angel dictated a new and contemporary revelation, the *Book of Mormon,* to the American founder of the faith, Joseph Smith. Mormon practices and beliefs, which originally sanctioned polygamy, were extremely controversial during the nineteenth century. The sect endured hardship and persecution, and eventually relocated in a dramatic westward migration under the leadership of Brigham Young.

# The Quilt

Hundreds of movements, countermovements, splits, and alliances have occurred within the Protestant tradition over the centuries. Only the best-known can be touched on here. We close by reminding you that Protestantism can be thought of as a quilt of many squares, each square distinctive and important. To appreciate the quilt fully, any observer must first acknowledge its extraordinary complexity, and then the rich history of diversity to be read along the many seams.

**On the Path**

An influential movement (particularly during the 1960s and 1970s) was the Ecumenical mission, which sought to promote union and acknowledgement of common spiritual principles among Christians.

**The Least You Need to Know**

➤ Roman Catholicism draws its energy not only from its ancient practices and teachings, but also from a tradition of internal reform, which periodically reinvigorates the faith.

➤ The Orthodox Eastern Church of today is a grouping of autonomous churches, many with strong national identities.

➤ Protestantism's emphasis on revelation and the formation of community has led, over the centuries, to an astonishing variety of religious expression.

# Christian Celebration

No single chapter in a book such as this can say all there is to say about Christian ritual and celebration, or about every tradition's religious calendar. This chapter offers a brief look at the major Christian holidays, what they mean, and how observances can vary. So without further ado ...

## Advent

In Western churches, this season of preparation for Christmas begins on the Wednesday nearest November 30 (St. Andrew's Day) and lasts until Christmas itself. Catholics observe Advent with fasting and repentance but also with joy, in anticipation of the feast of the *Nativity,* or birth of Jesus. This event is described in the Gospels of Matthew and Luke. Most Christians view Jesus' birth as the fulfillment of certain prophecies enshrined in Hebrew Scripture. The New Testament relates Jesus' birth as miraculous, in that his mother, Mary, was a virgin when she conceived.

Orthodox believers observe Advent with a 40-day fast from meat and dairy products.

Since medieval times, Advent has also been acknowledged as a time for preparation for the Second Coming of Jesus and an opportunity to acknowledge his presence in the daily lives of believers.

# Christmas

Perhaps the most familiar of all Christian holidays to secular Western society, Christmas, the feast of the Nativity, is less important than Easter in the Christian religious calendar. The manner of its observance—austere or jubilant, serene or Bacchanalian—was a matter of intense dispute in England after the Protestant Reformations.

Catholics and Protestants celebrate Christmas on December 25, shortly before Epiphany. (In the Eastern Christian tradition, Epiphany originally incorporated the celebration of Christ's Nativity.) The familiar date is celebrated in the West as the date of the birth of Christ, and as an opportunity to exchange gifts, but it is worth remembering that the observance did not gain wide acceptance until the fourth century C.E.

### On the Path

Secular influences on the Christmas holiday began to emerge noticeably in the nineteenth century, and in the U.S. the approach of the "big day" has assumed heavy commercial and economic overtones. Many Christian churches have felt it necessary to undertake campaigns to remind believers of the spiritual nature of Christmas. Even in our advertising-driven era, however, the day is observed by means of certain distinctively Christian elements. One of these is the crèche, the scene of the infant Christ Child in a manger in Bethlehem. This presentation was originally made popular by Franciscan monks.

Christmas emerged in the Middle Ages as the preeminent popular festival of the year, and it has featured strong secular as well as religious influences from that time to the present day. Despite its contemporary commercial overtones, Christmas has a profound meaning that transcends materialism. It is the time when Christians, reflecting on the mysteries and paradoxes of Christ's Incarnation, respond with generosity, renewal, gratitude, and celebration.

## Epiphany

*Epiphany,* celebrated each year on January 6, commemorates the visit of the Wise Men to the newborn Jesus as recounted in the Gospel of Matthew. "Epiphany" means "manifestation" or "showing forth," usually of divine nature. The word has been used for centuries to describe gentiles' encounter with Jesus, symbolized by visitors from the east coming to humble themselves before the infant Messiah.

# Lent

Lent is a season of repentance and fasting that serves as a spiritual preparation for the joy of the Easter festival.

The observance of the first day of Lent on Ash Wednesday, the seventh Wednesday before Easter, is of ancient origin. In a number of Christian settings, it is marked by the imposition of ashes, a ritual in which worshipers come forward to receive a smudge of ashes on their foreheads. By this act the church echoes the words in Genesis regarding human mortality: "Dust thou art, and to dust shalt thou return."

### What's It Mean?

An **epiphany** may also describe a manifestation of the divine in one's own experience, through a vision, for example.

### Bet You Didn't Know

The time of Epiphany, in addition to celebrating Jesus' appearance as king to the gentiles, also commemorates Jesus' own baptism and his first miracle, the transformation of water to wine at Cana as described in the Gospel of John. All three events are aspects of Jesus' manifestation to the world.

The eve of Epiphany is often referred to as Twelfth Night, a name most know now only as the title of a play by Shakespeare. As a celebration, Epiphany is considerably older than Christmas. Although often relegated to footnote status in the aftermath of the (highly secularized) Western Christmas, Epiphany remains an important, if little publicized, Christian feast day.

### Bet You Didn't Know

If you haven't actually received ashes yourself on Ash Wednesday, you have probably encountered people who have. Sometimes the bearer of the ashes finds herself fending off the well-meaning handkerchief: "Yes, I know I have something on my forehead..."

But did you know where the ashes of Ash Wednesday come from? They are the ashes of the palms that were carried in the previous year's Palm Sunday celebration. In this way, believers acknowledge, with a touch of irony, Jesus' abandonment by even his closest followers during the final days and hours of his life—just one week after his royal welcome to Jerusalem.

# Palm Sunday

Palm Sunday is the final Sunday of Lent and the last Sunday before Easter. It is a day of acclaimation and rejoicing, but also of somber anticipation. Palm Sunday marks the first day of Holy Week, the week in which the betrayal and suffering of Jesus are remembered.

*The palm, traditional Western symbol of Christ's triumphal entry to Jerusalem. (Worshipers in eastern churches, for whom palms are scarce, use other plants.)*

The New Testament relates that as Jesus entered Jerusalem for Passover, crowds hailed him as a savior, scattering palm leaves in his path. In commemoration of the event, and as a prelude to the events of Holy Week, many Christians carry palm fronds on that day.

# Good Friday

The Friday before Easter recalls the death of Jesus on the cross. It has been marked since ancient times by fasting and other penitential rituals, as well as by meditation on the Stations of the Cross, a series of fourteen images depicting the passion, or suffering, of Christ.

Orthodox, Anglican, and Catholic churches do not celebrate the Eucharist on Good Friday. The gift of Holy Communion they receive on that day is consecrated the day before, in order to reserve Good Friday as a day of mourning.

# Easter

Easter is the single most important holiday of the Christian year. It celebrates the resurrection of Jesus after his crucifixion and proclaims the spiritual rebirth of believers through their union with the risen Christ.

Easter is a springtime holiday. The Sunday on which it is celebrated is a time for joy and praise from the faithful at the perpetuation and renewal of life through God's grace. It is a commemoration of the power of Christ to conquer death itself.

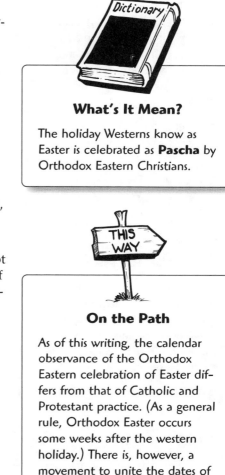

**What's It Mean?**

The holiday Westerns know as Easter is celebrated as **Pascha** by Orthodox Eastern Christians.

**On the Path**

As of this writing, the calendar observance of the Orthodox Eastern celebration of Easter differs from that of Catholic and Protestant practice. (As a general rule, Orthodox Easter occurs some weeks after the western holiday.) There is, however, a movement to unite the dates of celebration.

# Pentecost

Derived from the Jewish festival of Shavout celebrating the spring harvest, the Christian feast of Pentecost commemorates the gift of the Holy Spirit on the disciples following Jesus' resurrection and ascension. By this gift the church believes itself to be in union with the risen Christ, who, through the Holy Spirit, guides, upholds, comforts, and enlightens the faithful on earth. The holiday, which marks the birth of the Christian church, is held to be second in importance only to the Easter festival.

The New Testament, in the Acts of the Apostles, relates that on the day of Pentecost the Holy Spirit descended on Jesus' disciples in the form of tongues of flame, accompanied by a sound like rushing wind. Filled with the Holy Spirit, the disciples began proclaiming Jesus' resurrection in all the languages of the world, so that the crowds who listened to them marveled. The feast of Pentecost celebrates the church's call to bring the good news of Christ to all people.

Pentecost is observed on the Seventh Sunday after Easter. In some traditions it is accompanied by vigils of penitence. An English name for Pentecost is Whitsunday.

**On the Path**

For Jehovah's Witnesses, the memorial of Christ's death is the one day of the year set aside for religious observance. It takes place on the first evening of the Jewish Passover.

# The Feast of the Assumption

This feast, held on August 15, is the oldest feast in honor of Mary. It is celebrated both in the West and in the East; especially Roman Catholics commemorate Mary's assumption, body and soul, into heaven. Roman Catholics and Orthodox believers alike see Mary as the first human to receive the full fruits of life in Jesus' resurrection.

For Roman Catholics, the Feast of the Assumption (August 15), and the Feast of the Immaculate Conception (December 15), establish Mary as the image of the worldwide church. Believers within the Catholic faith see in her the realization of what the Church (the "bride of Christ") will be.

# New Year

The official beginning of the Orthodox church year is September 1. Believers within this branch of the faith celebrate this new beginning in a religious context. There is no equivalent New Year celebration in the Western church.

# Is That It?

Well, no. There are scores of other holidays within the various Christian traditions. The Catholic faith, in particular, is known for its profusion of holidays in honor of particular saints. The celebrations we have described represent the major dates of observance familiar to Christians, however, and are a good beginning point for those just encountering or rediscovering the faith.

## The Least You Need to Know

➤ Easter is the most important Christian holiday.

➤ As of this writing, Easter (or Pascha) is celebrated according to one calendar tradition among believers in the West, and another among Orthodox believers.

➤ Along with Easter, other important Christian observances include Christmas, Epiphany, Ash Wednesday, Good Friday, Pentecost, and the Feast of the Assumption.

➤ Despite strong influences from consumer society, Christmas retains its special spiritual character.

➤ In addition to the major holidays discussed in this chapter, Christianity is enriched by many variant traditions within the manifold expressions of the faith.

# Part 4

# Islam

*The battles Muhammad's Arabian warriors fought during his lifetime and afterward were important in historical terms, of course, but they do not reflect his most enduring influence on human affairs. For that we must look to the Islamic faith, which has retained its extraordinary appeal and power from Muhammad's day to ours. Today Islam boasts over 900 million adherents, of whom fewer than 20 percent are Arabs.*

*In this section of the book, you'll learn about the history and development of this major world religion.*

# Chapter 10

# The Early History of Islam

> ### In This Chapter
>
> ➤ Learn about the origins of the Islamic faith
>
> ➤ Encounter Muhammad, the preeminent figure of this religion
>
> ➤ Find out about the Five Pillars: the principles and obligations observed by every Muslim

The word "Islam" translates as "submission" (that is, submission to God).

Islam is the third great monotheistic faith. Its emergence can be traced to the mission of the Prophet Muhammad in the seventh century. It is the faith of a steadily growing number of Americans (six million at last count).

The religious system laid out by Muhammad draws on elements of Judaism and Christianity, as well as on Arab traditions in existence at the time of the faith's initial development. The fundamental revelation of Muhammad does not conflict with either Jewish or Christian religious principles: It states that there is one God, a God who requires of human beings both moral behavior (action, not simply belief) and devotion. Those who follow Islam are known as Muslims.

Muslim means "one who submits." The Islamic faith teaches social and personal codes of conduct affecting both men and women. This is done in keeping with the dictates of the Sharia'ah, or Law (rooted in the teachings of Muhammad, but formulated after his death), that embraces not merely certain aspects of human activity, but the entirety of human endeavor in all spheres.

### Bet You Didn't Know

Islam accepts both the Hebrew Scriptures and the New Testament as authentic divine revelations. The Qur'an, Islam's holy scripture, is acknowledged as the final word of God. Similarly, practitioners of the faith view Muhammad, a merchant born in Mecca around C.E. 570, as the final prophet of God, the last in a long series of prophets that includes both Moses and Jesus.

It is ironic that westerners should look on Muslims as followers of something strange and inaccessible. Islam is intimately related to Judaism and Christianity. Although major cultural differences certainly exist among the faithful of different lands, there is no good reason for a westerner to view Islam or Muslims as "foreign" or frightening. Media stereotypes notwithstanding, westerners have more in common with Muslims than they may realize.

### Watch It!

People often think of Muhammad, who lived in the seventh century of the C.E., as the founder of Islam. This is not what Muslims believe. Although Muhammad is known within the Islamic tradition as God's final prophet, he is not considered by Muslims to have "invented" Islamic faith.

# Who Was Muhammad?

Muhammad's historical impact has been immense. The man whose mission consolidated the Islamic faith has directly affected social and religious institutions through his teachings for over 14 centuries. Few, if any, historical figures have left such a clear and recognizable mark on human affairs.

Muhammad was born in Mecca; his family was part of the Hashim clan of the powerful Kuraish federation. His mother and father died shortly after his birth, and the future prophet was raised by his uncle. At 24 he married a wealthy widow and went back to Mecca and became a prosperous merchant in his community.

Although Muslims deny the divinity of Jesus, they honor him as a major prophet. They also recognize the angels Gabriel and Michael, familiar to both Jews and Christians. The Islamic conception of devils involves the evil jinn.

At the age of 40 Muhammad began to perceive a powerful force in his life. A series of mystical experiences led him to conclude that he was being summoned to proclaim the word of the supreme and single God, Allah. Muhammad's message—that there was only one God, and that idolatry was an abomination—was controversial, because existing ancestral faiths in Arabia worshipped a number of gods.

Muhammad was a gifted and persuasive preacher. He envisioned not only a single God but a single unified church embracing the faith. His devotion to this mission and his charismatic power must have been important contributing reasons for his success.

Muhammad's insistence on monotheism and his egalitarian ideas met with trial and opposition. His efforts to establish the faith in Mecca were met by setback after setback. Adherents of the faith proclaimed by Muhammad were persecuted and his family broke off relations with him.

## The Migration

In Yathrib, (later known as Medina, the "City of the Prophet") Muhammad was to find his first shelter from persecution. By C.E. 622, about 12 years after he is regarded as having first received his revelations from God, Muhammad developed a significant following at Medina. In the summer of 622, he organized an exodus (the word in Arabic is Hegira) of his followers at Mecca to go to Medina. The year of the Hegira (622) is celebrated by Muslims as the first year of the Muslim era.

Over the next few years, as Muhammad attracted more followers, a series of military conflicts between Medina and Mecca took place. After agreeing to a truce to aid pilgrims, Muhammad reversed himself in 630 when he felt that the treaty had been violated. He roused his forces, captured Mecca with little effort, and proclaimed the end of idolatry. He also extended a blanket amnesty that was, considering the wartime tensions of the past years,

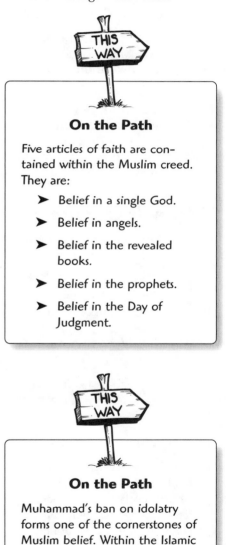

**On the Path**

Five articles of faith are contained within the Muslim creed. They are:

➤ Belief in a single God.

➤ Belief in angels.

➤ Belief in the revealed books.

➤ Belief in the prophets.

➤ Belief in the Day of Judgment.

**On the Path**

Muhammad's ban on idolatry forms one of the cornerstones of Muslim belief. Within the Islamic community, artistic representation of the image of Allah is forbidden.

remarkably lenient. Four men were executed, but pardons were extended to all others, including some bitter enemies.

The Arab Islamic state was a reality. Shortly after this consolidation, in 632, Muhammad died in Medina.

# The Qur'an

Muhammad's initial vision is said to have occurred around the year 610 in a cave near Mecca, where the angel Gabriel (Jibril) appeared to him and told him to "recite." The revelations received during this encounter were to become the opening lines of the Qur'an, or "recitation."

Muslims believe that Muhammad's many divine encounters during his years in Mecca and Medina inspired the remainder of the Qur'an, which was compiled by his secretary Zaid in Thabit. The final form of the Qur'an was determined by the caliph Uthman nearly twenty years after Muhammad's death. Uthman pronounced in favor of Zaid's collection and ordered that all other versions be destroyed.

## How It Originated

The Qur'an is a complex, majestic document. It is one of the most important books in human history. It is believed to have been dictated to scribes by Muhammad himself or reconstructed from memory based on his teaching.

The Qur'an is written in Arabic and considered authoritative only in that language. Translations of it are not regarded as inspired. It consists of 112 sutras, or chapters, the first of which (beginning "Praise be to Allah") is universally incorporated in the daily prayers of Muslims.

### What's It Mean?

The **Qur'an,** which is held by Muslims to consolidate and fulfill all past revelations from God, sets out a rigorous monotheism. For Muslims it is the Word of God, whose instrument was the Prophet Muhammad.

## What It Teaches

The Qur'an contains three kinds of teachings: direct doctrinal messages, historical accounts that also resonate with metaphorical meaning, and mystical expressions of sublime beauty—expressions that are hard to summarize in rigid formulaic terms but that nevertheless inform and support a broadly stated divine message.

The Qur'an also contains a number of stories that parallel events familiar from Jewish and Christian traditions. It also calls for faith in Allah, warns of the consequences of unbelief, and outlines specific moral duties. The Qur'an emphasizes Allah's unity ("There is no God but God"). It encourages the faithful to acknowledge both their dependence upon Allah ("I am not the Absolute") and their ultimate unity with Allah ("I am nothing separate from or other than the Absolute").

The Qur'an teaches that human life, which lasts only a short while, is a test. We will be rewarded or punished for our actions in a life after this one. Rewards and punishments will begin immediately after the funeral, but there will also be a Day of Judgment and a resurrection.

### Bet You Didn't Know

Did you know that Muslims, like Christians and Jews, consider themselves children of Abraham? However, only Muslims claim their lineage through Ishmael.

In the Hebrew book of Genesis, God made an everlasting covenant with Abraham. According to this book, Abraham's first child, Ishmael, whose mother was not Abraham's wife Sarah but Sarah's maid, Hagar, was ordered out of the tribe after Sarah gave birth to Isaac. Muslims say that Ishmael then came to Mecca and settled there, and that his descendants became Muslims. Muslims thus consider themselves to be direct descendants of Abraham, and to this day they honor both Abraham and Ishmael as prophets. The descendants of Abraham's son Isaac, according to both Islamic scripture and the Hebrew Bible, formed the tribes of Israel.

# The Five Pillars

The Qur'an outlines five obligations, or pillars, as essential to the lives of Muslims. They are as follows:

**The Five Pillars of Islam**

> ➤ *Confession of one's faith in God and in his prophet Muhammad.* "There is no God but God; Muhammad is the Prophet of God" is the basic confession of faith in Islam, and it infuses Islamic culture.

> ➤ *Ritual Worship.* Formal periods of worship are observed five times every day: before sunrise, after midday, at mid-afternoon, shortly after sunset, and in the

### On the Path

In addition to carrying out the commitments outlined in the Five Pillars, Muslims observe a general obligation to "commend good and reprimand evil." They also forswear gambling, usury, and the consumption of alcohol and pork.

### What's It Mean?

The **Hajj** is the pilgrimage to Mecca, required of Muslims at least once, although many exceptions are made for special cases. Those who fulfill the obligation are entitled to add "al-Hajj" (pilgrim) to their name.

fullness of night. Muslims direct their recitations and petitions toward the city of Mecca, where stands the ancient and supremely holy shrine known as the Kaaba.

➤ *Almsgiving*. The Zakat, or "purification" tax on property, is paid by all Muslims for the benefit of the poor, who include one's kin, the needy, and at times, the wayfarer. The amount of the Zakat is fixed. It is usually about $2^1/_2$ % of one's wealth, but in some circumstances it may be more.

➤ *Fasting*. Fasting is observed during the holy month of Ramadan (see Chapter 12, "Ramadan and Other Obsevances.")

➤ *Pilgrimage*. Every Muslim who is of sound body, sane, and able to afford the journey is expected to make a pilgrimage, or *Hajj*, to the holy city of Mecca at least once in his or her lifetime. Other pilgrimage traditions are associated with the ancient Kaaba as well.

## Expansion and Evolution

Today Islam claims between 600 and 900 million adherents in the Middle East, Africa, India, Central Asia, and many other regions of the world. Despite invariable differences in emphasis from region to region, Muslims have shown a remarkable sense of shared community and purpose.

In the next chapter you'll learn about the development of the Islamic faith after Muhammad's death and the complex relationship between the Sunni and Shiite sects. You'll also find out about the important role played by separate Muslim traditions like Sufism.

## The Least You Need to Know

➤ The fundamental monotheism of Muhammad is not out of keeping with Jewish or Christian religious principles because Islam was influenced by those faiths.

➤ Practitioners of Islam are known as Muslims: "Those who submit" to God's will.

➤ Muhammad's mission was a momentous event in human history.

➤ Muslims believe in a single God who requires of human beings both moral behavior and devotion.

➤ The Qur'an is held by Muslims to consolidate and fulfill all past revelations from God.

➤ The Five Pillars constitute the heart of Muslim observance and practice.

# Chapter 11

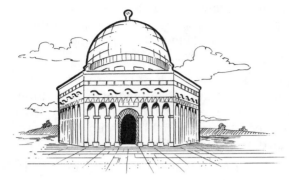

# The Later Development of Islam

## In This Chapter

➤ Find out how Islam changed after Muhammad's death

➤ Learn about the Sunni sect, the largest movement within Islam

➤ Find out about the origins and practices of the Shiite sect

➤ Examine the differences between the different groups

➤ Discover the guiding ideas behind the multifaceted, mystical, and ascetic Sufi movement

The philosophies within Islam today are not the only traditions that have shaped the faith. Over the centuries, schools, factions, and scholarly disciplines have enriched this faith almost unimaginably. Islam in turn has enriched other faiths, including Judaism and Christianity.

Like Judaism and Christianity before it, Islam encountered division and disagreement as part of its growth and development. In this chapter, you learn about the principal sects and schools of thought that have emerged and prospered over the centuries.

## Division and Discord

Although Muhammad's teachings clearly laid out a vision of a devout and united Islamic community, the years following his death were often tumultuous.

### What's It Mean?

**Caliph** was a title bestowed on the designated successor to Muhammad in leading the Islamic faith. The caliph emerged as a political leader and defender of the faith within the Islamic theocracy. Ottoman sultans assumed control of the office after their conquest of Egypt in 1517; the title was abolished in 1924.

Deep divisions within the assembly of Muslim believers led to a number of serious conflicts about the future of the faith. A group known as the Kharajis, restless at what they perceived as disarray and nepotism on the part of the third *caliph,* claimed the support of the Qur'an in waging holy war against him.

The militant Kharajis found a host of reasons to rebel against centralized authority. During the early centuries of Islam's development, they faced constant opposition from recognized Islamic leaders. The group was eventually eradicated, but other conflicts developed.

One was the result of an influential rational movement that arose in the eighth and ninth centuries C.E. Its leaders held that the rational faculty of man, without benefit of revelation, was capable of determining moral issues definitively. This group saw the Qur'an as having been developed in time and not eternal in nature, as many mystics believed. (As you will see in a moment, this "rational" approach to matters of faith was eventually discredited in Islam.)

### Bet You Didn't Know

The argument within early Islam about whether the Qur'an was created in time or was somehow eternal can be compared to early Christian debates about the temporality or eternity of Christ. In fact, as many Muslim scholars have pointed out, the Qur'an is to Islam very much as Christ is to Christians: It is "God among us," a kind of "self-portrait" of the divine.

## The Word

Muslims consider the Qur'an to be inspired only in its original Arabic, in the very words Muhammad received from heaven and passed along to his followers. That is why a translation into English or any other language is likely to be called "the meaning of the Qur'an," rather than simply "the Qur'an." For Muslims, what is "lost in translation" is the authenticity of a direct quotation from God.

The Qur'an, preserved in a formal Arabic that gradually became antiquated, was eventually supplemented by the *Sunna*. This assembly of traditions (collected in *hadith*, a word that refers, literally, to particular individual traditions) recounts the acts and sayings of the Prophet Muhammad.

These collections offer insight on correct behavior. Differing lineages and competing interpretations of the various accounts have persisted for centuries. Practical disputes have relied heavily for resolution on one of the most important sayings attributed to Muhammad: "My community will never agree in an error."

# The Sunni Sect

The views of the rationalist movement, which saw the Qur'an as other than eternal, were eventually accepted by the caliphs of the period, but a vigorous counterreaction arose in the tenth century. This movement eventually became known as the Sunni, or "orthodox" school of theology. The Sunnis overcame the rival teachings and emerged as the dominant force within Islam. Today, about 90 percent of Muslims worship within the Sunni tradition.

The Sunni ("orthodox") sect's emphasis on fundamentals—its opposition to schisms and its intolerance of dissent—did not lead to narrowly defined doctrine. Today, those known as Sunnis are culturally and religiously diverse. Instead of trying to achieve unanimity on questions of doctrine, Sunni Islam has opted for a broadly accepted set of theological principles.

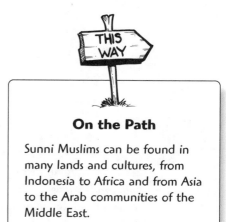

**On the Path**

Sunni Muslims can be found in many lands and cultures, from Indonesia to Africa and from Asia to the Arab communities of the Middle East.

Statements about the "doctrines" of Sunni Muslims must be made with great care. Bear in mind that the sect has extended into many parts of the world without requiring uniformity on every question of faith and practice. An emphasis on the individual's direct relationship with Allah, without any human mediator, distinguishes the Sunni sect, but this emphasis has not prevented individual Sunnis from exercising religious influence.

# The Shiite Sect

Only one major sect distinct from the Sunnis has survived in Islam. It is the Shiite sect, and it is of even more distant origin than the Sunni. This sect places a heavy emphasis on the role of individual leaders.

The Shiite sect originated not as a religious movement, but as a political faction in the bitter seventh-century disputes over succession to Islamic state leadership. Early Shiites emerged in opposition to the central government, supporting the claim of Ali, the cousin of Muhammad.

Eventually, the political orientation of the group incorporated a religious dimension. This broadening of the Shiite movement is generally traced to the death of Ali's younger son, Husayn, at Karbala in C.E. 680. The right of members of this family to succeed as leaders of the Islamic nation became a matter of Shiite faith.

The Shiite's vision of the early history of the Islamic faith differs sharply from that of the Sunni Muslim. Sunnis accept the first four caliphs as legitimate successors to Muhammad; Shiites do not.

Shiite Islam is the official religion of Iran, and the form of worship observed by communities of believers in India, Pakistan, Iraq, and other areas. It accounts for perhaps 10 percent of the world's Muslims.

Shiites reject the claims of the first three Islamic caliphs. The division is much more than an ancient historical dispute. For Shiite Muslims, *how* human leadership is carried out within the faith is crucial.

## The Imam

Shiites accept a doctrine focused upon a figure known as the imam, whose leadership allows a full understanding of the truths of the Qur'an.

### Bet You Didn't Know

Most Shiite Muslims belong to a group known as Imamites, or the Twelve Imam division. The *imam* is a religious leader, regarded as sinless, with a direct lineage to Ali, the cousin of Muhammad. Imamites hold that there were 12 imams, beginning with Ali and proceeding in a direct line to Muhammad al-Muntazar, who is considered to have disappeared from human view in C.E. 878. The twelfth imam is believed by Shiites to rule the world to this day, and is ultimately regarded as the only legitimate source of leadership.

The Twelve-Imam Shiites are not the only component of the Shiite sect. Another, considerably smaller branch is that of the Ismailites, who acknowledge seven imams.

Shiite clerics derive their considerable authority from their role as the deputies of the twelfth imam. They are considered to possess complete knowledge of the Qur'an and its implementation. Clerics may be referred to as mullahs or mujtahids. Individual members of the Shiite clergy benefit from a religious tax (khums) on Muslims; there is no formal hierarchy.

Shiites incorporate distinct approaches to ritual and practice. The Shiite sect permits individual believers to mislead others about their faith when failing to do so would result in personal danger. It also acknowledges temporary marriages, unions that may be established for a specific, predetermined period of time.

## Beyond Liberal and Conservative

Some scholars have called Shiite Muslims the "liberal" wing of Islam. The label does little besides highlight the shortcomings of terms like "liberal" and "conservative" when talking about faith.

It is true that the Shiites focus less than the Sunnis on rigorous logic and on the credentials of past authorities when they interpret the Qur'an. It is also true that the Shiites emphasize free will in a way that the Sunnis do not.

The Shiite tradition's emphasis on clerical authority, however, is just one reason that a "liberal" designation is problematic. It is probably better to say that Shiite practices focus on the imam as inspired conveyor of truth, and leave it at that.

### Bet You Didn't Know

The role of women in various Islamic societies is complex, more so than outsiders may think. Westerners tend to assume that Islam itself limits the rights of women. Actually, apart from certain stipulations about inheritance and laws concerning witnesses, Islamic rights and duties apply to both sexes. Ancient cultural traditions have done much more to shape the status of women than religion and doctrine. That is why Muslim societies can differ so dramatically in their approaches to this issue.

# The Sufis

The Sufis are the mystics of Islam. Every faith has its mystics—men and women who seek union with God through contemplation, *asceticism,* and prayer. Mystics

### What's It Mean?

**Asceticism** is a practice or set of practices such as fasting, going without sleep, and tolerating rough conditions, that disciplines the body so that the **ascetic** can concentrate on achieving spiritual perfection and union with God.

### On the Path

Sufism has made significant literary and theological contributions to Islam over the years. Conservative Muslims, however, have often viewed the movement with skepticism. Many Sufi practices, like the worship of saints; the incorporation of unfamiliar customs, and the repetition of the name Allah, sometimes with music; have been viewed as heretical by certain Muslims.

are usually both inside and outside their religious tradition: inside because they approach God through the forms of that tradition; outside because their personal revelations cannot be confirmed and are not always condoned by the rest of the community. Mystics both enrich and threaten their religious establishment. Revered by some and suspected by others, they often symbolize the prophetic voice of the faith.

Early Islamic figures revered by the Sufis include Ali (the cousin of Muhammad whose claim to the caliphate caused such controversy) and Hallaj, a tenth-century figure who shocked some of his contemporaries by claiming unity with God.

Two essential Sufi's ideas are complete reliance upon God (tawakkul), and perpetual remembrance of God (dhikr). Rabia al-Adawiyya, an influential early figure, condemned religious devotion that was motivated by a desire for heaven or a fear of punishment. For her, love for God was the sole valid expression of devotion to the Divine.

Historically, the Sufi's emphasis on dissolution into the Divine has sometimes resulted in conflicts with religious authorities. Hallaj's proclamation "I am the Truth" earned him crucifixion in C.E. 922.

Still, the Sufi movement mostly developed inside the lines of orthodox Islamic practice. By rejecting the worldliness of Muslim life, early Sufism did much to reinvigorate the faith, and to reinforce notions of an individual believer's progression toward the divine through continuous personal devotion.

Sufi orders have emerged in various parts of the world. Their flexibility and sensitivity to local tradition and custom have helped them to flourish and endure for centuries. These orders played an important role in extending Islam to new parts of the world, as well as in solidifying cultural and commercial ties.

## The Least You Need to Know

➤ There are two main divisions within Islam: the Shiite sect and the Sunni sect.

➤ The Sunni sect is by far the larger of the two groups. Its broad platform of essential doctrines has won adherents in many geographic and cultural settings.

➤ The main group within the Shiite sect, dominant in Iran and elsewhere, places a heavy emphasis on the lineage of the imams (regarded as the successors to Muhammad) and on the authority of clerical representatives acting as deputies of the unseen twelfth imam.

➤ The mystical and ascetic Sufi movements, which seek direct contact with God, have been highly influential over the centuries.

# Chapter 12

# Ramadan and Other Observances

---

**In This Chapter**

➤ Learn about daily Muslim observances

➤ Find out about important requirements and traditions that affect non-Muslims attending services

➤ Get the key facts about Ramadan

➤ Learn about other important Islamic holy days

---

In this chapter, you find out about daily worship rituals, the settings for Muslim worship, and Ramadan, the holy ninth month of the Muslim calendar. You also learn about a number of other important significant annual observances within Islam.

## Day by Day

Muslims pray five times a day; at dawn, noon, mid-afternoon, sunset, and in the evening. Although these prayers, which are typically not more than ten minutes in duration, may be undertaken in a mosque, they are considered just as valid when offered in other settings.

The Muslim believer's everyday activities stop at the five predetermined times of prayer to Allah. These prayers must be rendered faithfully and with full attention, regardless of one's physical location. Before beginning to pray, the worshiper removes his or her shoes and performs a cleansing ritual (*wadu*) for the hands, face, mouth, and feet. This literal physical cleansing reflects a symbolic spiritual purification.

*Intricate detail is a hallmark of Islamic religious art and design.*

At noon on Friday, the Islamic sabbath day, the Islamic community gathers in the mosque for a service of prayer lasting 30 minutes to an hour. Shoes are not worn in the mosque, and men and women pray separately so as not to distract each other (local arrangements for this differ from place to place). The Friday gathering is an important time of coming together for the local community, a time to renew relationships and share community concerns.

### Bet You Didn't Know

Within the mosque, representations of Allah, or of any human, plant, or animal, are strictly forbidden. Muslims consider such images idolatry and an unlawful imitation of the creative power of God.

Many mosques feature abstract decorative elements of extraordinary beauty and detail. The great mosques, such as that of Suleiman I in Istanbul, are among humanity's supreme architectural accomplishments. Repeated linear decorative forms called *arabesques* combine geometry and art in a symbol of divine unity and a sublime expression of faith.

Once the *wadu* (ritual washing) is complete, believers face Mecca and begin a series of rituals that involve bowing, prostration, and the recitation of established prayers. The number of prayers will depend on the point in the day at which the prayers take place.

If you are not a practicing Muslim, you should not attempt to join the prayer line. There will usually be a separate area in the *mosque* for non-Muslim guests who wish to observe prayer services.

# Important Islamic Life Rituals

Like most other major religions, Islam has special observances for major life events. Following is a brief summary of some of the most important customs.

## Welcoming Ritual

The birth ceremony is known as an *akikah*. This informal observance can take many forms, depending on the nation or culture in which the family lives. (Many Muslims do not celebrate any form of *akikah*.)

## Initiation

Initiation, or *shahada*, marks a young Muslim's formal entry into the faith. There is no set age for this rite; it commonly takes place during one's middle teens.

**On the Path**

Muslim prayer makes use of memorized recitations. Those who have recently joined the faith take part in group prayer and proceed under the guidance of a member of the clergy until the appropriate prayers are committed to memory.

**What's It Mean?**

A **mosque** is a building used by Muslims for worship and prayer. One wall, known as the **qibla** wall, always faces Mecca.

The ceremony must by witnessed by a prescribed number of adult Muslims. During the shahada, the individual making his or her formal proclamation of faith repeats, in Arabic, the sentence "There is no God but God; Muhammad is the prophet of God." The ceremony is held either in a private home or in a mosque. It may follow a regularly scheduled prayer service.

## The Marriage Ritual

This ceremony, seen as a sacred contract between the parties, takes place in the mosque's main sanctuary. By Western standards, the Islamic wedding rite may seem brisk and even lacking in formality. Witnesses simply observe the groom's formal offer

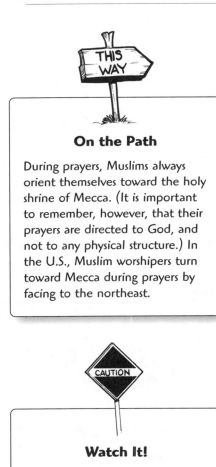

**On the Path**

During prayers, Muslims always orient themselves toward the holy shrine of Mecca. (It is important to remember, however, that their prayers are directed to God, and not to any physical structure.) In the U.S., Muslim worshipers turn toward Mecca during prayers by facing to the northeast.

**Watch It!**

Women attending Muslim religious services in American mosques should respect Islamic custom by wearing a head scarf. For reasons of modesty, Muslim girls and women cover their hair completely. And although there are no hard-and-fast rules on the subject, it is best to remember that less jewelry is definitely more in this setting. Be especially careful to avoid jewelry that incorporates people, animals, Jewish or Christian religious imagery, astrological symbols, or other potentially offensive depictions. (This goes for men as well as women.)

of marriage and the bride's formal acceptance of it. An officiant will offer a sermon on the subject of marriage. There is no elaborate ceremony associated with the event.

After the marriage comes the *waleemah,* or reception. This can take place virtually anywhere, including the mosque where the marriage occurred. There may be music and dancing, but needless to say, there will be no alcohol.

## Funerals and Mourning Periods

An Islamic funeral service, like the marriage ritual, is straightforward. It may incorporate a service at a funeral home, and it will include the recitation of *janazah,* prayers for the dead, at the gravesite. Islamic practice does not sanction cremation, and burial takes place within 24 hours.

Islam limits the official period of mourning of the death of a family member to 40 days. No other rules are laid down regarding how long the bereaved should mourn. In practice, Muslims can be expected to assume regular work duties a few days after the funeral. When in doubt, call the family directly.

Most female Muslims do not engage in social activities for 40 days following the death of an immediate family member. Males may follow less stringent guidelines.

## Ramadan

The holy festival of Ramadan occupies the whole of the ninth month of the Islamic calendar. (Since this calendar is lunar, the corresponding Ramadan dates in the solar Western calendar system change from year to year.) During Ramadan, which is the name of both a month of the year and a period of religious observance, adults embark on a rigidly observed period of abstention, reflection, and purification.

Between sunrise and sunset during Ramadan, adult Muslims do not smoke, eat, drink, or have sex. They are encouraged to read the Qur'an from beginning to end during the holy month, which celebrates the first revelation of the Islamic scriptures.

**Bet You Didn't Know**

The holy month of Ramadan, which falls in no fixed season because of the lunar Muslim calendar, is a time of daily repentance and fasting. Muslims are expected to forego all indulgences, to reflect on their past misdeeds, to reinforce basic personal discipline, and to express gratitude to Allah for his continued direction and daily presence in the life of the believer.

The very young, those who are physically ill, and members of certain specially designated groups (such as soldiers) are excused from Ramadan obligations.

# Other Important Islamic Holy Days

Ramadan is the most widely known observance in Islam, but other holy days are also celebrated. Each of the following is reckoned according to the lunar Islamic calendar, so Western calendar dates cannot be given.

## Lailat ul-Qadr

Lailat ul-Qadr represents the final ten days of Ramadan. During this period, Muslims celebrate Muhammad's first experience of divine revelation, which is regarded as having occurred on a single night sometime during the final ten days of the month. The actual date of the Prophet's first revelation is not known. Muslims may spend most of their time in a mosque during this final portion of Ramadan.

## Id al-Fitr

Id al-Fitr is the feast period that follows the conclusion of the month-long fast. It takes place at the end of Ramadan and lasts for three days. It is typically observed with banquets and the exchange of gifts. Id al-Fitr is also the time when alms are given, as mandated under Islamic law.

**On the Path**

The night of Muhammad's first revelation is known as the "Night of Power."

# Id ul-Adha

Id ul-Adha, in which animals are slaughtered to benefit the impoverished, takes place two to three months after Ramadan. It celebrates the faithfulness and obedience of the patriarch Abraham.

# Al-Isra Wal Miraj

Al-Isra Wal Miraj is celebrated on the 27th day of the seventh month of the Islamic calendar, Rajab. It marks Muhammad's divinely supported journey from Mecca to the discipline of five-times-daily prayer observed by Muslims ever since.

# Maulid al-Nabi

Maulid al-Nabi celebrates the birth of Muhammad the Prophet and is held on the 12th day of the third month (Rabi awwad). It is a very popular festival, with evening festivities beginning a week or two before and ending on the day of the feast.

---

### The Least You Need to Know

➤ The daily life of a Muslim incorporates regular prayer to Allah.

➤ A mosque is a building used by Muslims for worship and prayer.

➤ Prayer may take place in any setting, but the person praying must be physically oriented toward Mecca if possible.

➤ The holy month of Ramadan, which falls in no fixed season because of the lunar Muslim calendar, is a time of daily repentance and fasting.

➤ Between sunrise and sunset during Ramadan, adult Muslims do not smoke, eat, drink, or have sex.

➤ Other important Muslim observances include Lailat ul-Qadr (the final ten days of Ramadan, which celebrate the night of Muhammad's first experience of divine revelation), and Id ul-Adha (in which animals are killed for the benefit of the impoverished, in remembrance of the faithfulness and obedience of the patriarch Abraham).

➤ Lailat ul-Qadr is the final 10 days of Ramadan and is when Muslims spend most of their time in a mosque.

---

# Part 5

# Hinduism

*The beliefs and practices described by the word "Hinduism" form one of the oldest living religions on Earth. Not one single person in history can be credited with the development of this faith.*

*As you will learn in the chapters that follow, the absence of a single founder is only one of several fascinating "gaps" outsiders may encounter in examining this faith. (Another "gap:" formal doctrine!) These "missing pieces" result from our preconceptions, not from a deficiency within Hinduism. Someone who is unfamiliar with the traditional religious practices of India might expect them to look more like other great religions. But Hinduism, a label that incorporates countless sects and practices, is, as it has always been, unique and sufficient within itself.*

# Chapter 13.

# That Old-Time Religion

In this part of the book, you learn about the mysterious early centuries of Hinduism, its development over perhaps 4,000 years, and the close association of its many rituals, practices, and texts (such as the Bhagavad Gita) with the people of India.

As you are about to learn, Hinduism is missing something most of the other major world religions consider absolutely essential: a start.

## No Founder

Hinduism, which claims about 800 million practitioners worldwide (most originating in India or of Indian descent), is unique among humanity's major religions in that it cannot be traced to any specific individual or historical event. The faith, which is as diverse as India itself, is an extraordinary collection of variations and expansions—some ancient, some more recent.

This profoundly varied religion places a heavy emphasis on attaining freedom from the perceived world and on eliminating ties to the material plane of existence, eventually including one's personal identity. For all Hinduism's complexity, interconnection, and continuing development, this distinctive mystical core endures.

### Bet You Didn't Know

Scholars believe that Hinduism arose about 3,500 years ago out of interactions between conquering Aryans and traditions already present on the Indian subcontinent.

Hindu means "Indian." The diverse religious practices included under this name make up the dominant (though by no means the only) religious tradition in India, but practitioners themselves do not describe their faith in a limited or nationalistic way.

Because Hinduism arose from no single person or institution, it is seen as eternal and unchanging in its essence. Believers regard it as having existed forever.

### On the Path

A kind of inspired pragmatism supports the Hindu faith, unlike the history-based approach of many other world religions. Loosely connected beliefs and principles are combined with techniques like meditation and formal study to bring about personal spiritual development.

It's a mistake to try to extract one "belief system" from Hinduism's vast array of traditions and rituals. That's why some people prefer not to use the word Hinduism at all but to speak of the religions of India. Although it is possible to identify broad elements within the faith, Hinduism in its structure expresses the profound diversity of humanity's experience of the Divine. Free of absolute or formal doctrines, Hinduism has shown remarkable adaptability in its approach to the cultivation of mystic and transcendental experiences.

## The Biggest of Big Tents

"Those who see all beings in the Self, and the Self in all beings, will never shrink from it." So reads a passage in the *Upanishads,* a holy text that seeks to reconcile the (apparent) discord and profusion of physical existence into a single entrancing harmony. The lines are relevant both to the spiritual journey of the individual and to the countless tools Hinduism provides to help expedite that journey.

A westerner seeking to compare his or her faith's religious doctrines to those of Hinduism is likely to come away shaking his or her head. Precise doctrines are hard to come by in this faith.

Still, there are a few broadly accepted principles. The best way to get at these may be to take a quick look at the roots of the Hindu faith.

# The Indus Valley Civilization

The story of Hinduism begins about 1,500 years before the birth of Jesus. In the Indus Valley in modern-day Pakistan, a sophisticated urban people had lived for perhaps a millennium. This still-mysterious agricultural and mercantile culture is now known as the Indus Valley Civilization. It used a form of pictorial writing that contemporary scholars have not been able to decode completely.

The Indus Valley Civilization in its heyday exceeded, at least in geographical terms, the influence of two other ancient civilizations—Egypt and Mesopotamia.

It is possible that this ancient civilization, which may have been centrally governed, was in a period of decline around 1500 B.C.E., when a wave of Aryan invaders from the northwest conquered the region. The Aryans propagated their own language and practices in the Indus valley, but they did not wipe out the cultural heritage of the Indus people. Instead, through a complex set of interactions that scholars still do not fully understand, they assimilated many local practices and beliefs and combined them with existing Aryan rites.

### Bet You Didn't Know

Among the many images discovered by twentieth-century archaeologists in the remains of the Indus Valley Civilization are what seem to be depictions of Shiva, one of the greatest gods in today's Hindu pantheon. In contemporary Hinduism, Shiva has various aspects. His depiction in the symbolic form of a phallus (he appears to have been regarded as a fertility figure by the Indus people) is balanced by his role as the great cosmic destroyer.

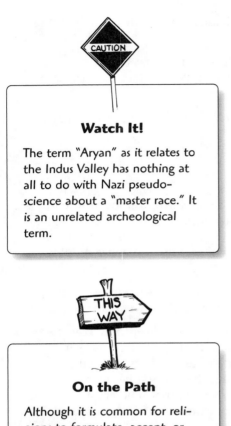

These rites involved the celebration of Brahman, a word now taken to describe an eternal, absolute reality beyond the multiplicity of forms. Other Aryan worship centered on fires, on the singing of hymns, and on the veneration of ancestors.

Modern science is not entirely sure that the Aryan warrior bands consciously incorporated existing Indus Valley rituals. Some scholars believe that the Aryans failed to secure total control of the Valley, and that small pockets of indigenous religious worship continued to thrive.

An ancient union of utterly different religious practices formed the first of many adaptations associated with Hinduism. What could better illustrate the richness and elasticity of the Hindu faith?

It is always dangerous to use modern language to describe an ancient process, but the very earliest Hinduism on record suggests what could cautiously be called an "inclusive" approach to competing cultural and religious claims. As Hinduism developed, it would continue to stress convergence rather than suppression in its encounter with other faiths.

Did Hinduism emerge as the gradual result of contact between the two traditions over the centuries? Or did it develop from an intentional set of decisions to combine forms? We don't know.

A hallmark of today's Hinduism, however, is the reconciliation of tensions and differences between religious structures. This character seems to have been essential to the development and growth of the faith.

# One and Many

Hinduism is an ongoing, pragmatic, and inspired synthesis, not the product of any strict ideology or doctrine. This is both its distinction and its greatness. Although it is not a religion that can be traced to a single revelation, neither is it a random "patchwork quilt" of fragmented ideas.

The earliest historical data shows Hinduism expanding and synthesizing the ancient practices of "competing" cultures. These practices became more meaningful and coherent because of their contact with one another, resulting in important new tools for self-discovery that extended the faith to its next phase of development.

The same features are in place to this very day! The most vigorous recent revivals of Hinduism, for instance, reflect its contacts with Christian morality, introduced by colonialism and missionaries in the nineteenth century, and with the twentieth-century movement for Indian independence from Britain.

But back to our story ...

# The Vedic Period

The Rig *Veda*, the earliest and among the most revered of the holy scriptures of Hinduism, was developed between 1500 and 1200 B.C.E. Legends associated with the Aryan warrior aristocracy and the adapted Indus Valley traditions influenced this collection of hymns.

There are 1,028 hymns in the Rig Veda. These make up the first portion of the Veda, and are one of the world's oldest religious scriptures.

Three other collections—the Samaveda, the Yajurveda, and the Atharaveda—were assembled during the first millennium before the beginning of the C.E. Together with the Rig Veda, these make up the Samhitas, or basic Vedas.

Between perhaps 800 and 300 B.C.E. (scholars are unclear about the dates), further writings were appended to the Vedas. These included the Brahmanas (including an explanation of ceremonies discussed in earlier Vedas), the Aranyakas, and the Upanishads. This last collection proved to be one of the most influential in the development of Hinduism.

The name of these texts means "sitting near," that is, near the feet of a sage or master. The Upanishads are direct accounts of advice from spiritually advanced mystics. They mark the final phase of development of the sacred Vedas and the beginning of elements of Hindu philosophy familiar to believers today.

The Upanishads set out the principle of reincarnation. In this sacred book emerged mystical

**What's It Mean?**

**Veda,** a Sanskrit word meaning "knowledge," refers to the great collection of early Hindu religious scriptures. The Vedas outline spiritual principles accepted by Hindus as fundamental to their religion. Vedic teachings emphasize the notion of a single supporting reality, manifested in Brahman, or eternal reality. All Hindus embrace the authority of the Vedas.

**On the Path**

Hinduism is rare among major religions in that it promotes the worship of animals. The homage paid to particular animals is best understood as part of the worship directed toward the particular deities regarded as riding on them.

Orthodox Hindus regard cattle and peacocks as sacred, and will not permit their slaughter under any circumstances.

disciplines designed to help the believer escape the cycle of death and rebirth. Believers are reminded that clinging to faith in one's own separate identity is like assuming an alias, making recognition of the true Self impossible.

The hymns of the Rig Veda appear to incorporate notions of heaven and hell, with the virtuous proceeding to heaven upon death. But around 600 B.C.E., a new trend of thought emerged, one that accepted the principle that a human spirit, in an ongoing quest for perfection, returns again and again in varying forms after the death of each physical body. Freedom from this cycle was seen as a preeminent spiritual goal. This doctrine is known as *reincarnation*.

# The Faith Develops: Circles of Life

The emergence of the doctrine of reincarnation had several striking effects on Hinduism. For one thing, it placed an emphasis on individual spiritual development, the better to attain release from the cycle of birth and death. For another, a reverence for all forms of life began to emerge, and sacrifices meant to impress or pacify the various gods became less and less common.

Teachings arising out of the notion of reincarnation allowed Hinduism, over time, to transfer primary focus from one set of gods (Brahma, Indra, Agni, and Varuna) to another (Vishnu, Shiva, and Shakti). For many faiths this kind of transition would have been traumatic, possibly leading to a major schism or bloody religious wars. Under the conception of divine incarnation (gods assuming flesh), however, Hinduism was able to establish a more or less seamless succession of teachings that allowed believers to accept one god as incarnate within another!

### Bet You Didn't Know

Hindus believe that there are four specific yogas (disciplines) that can serve as pathways to enlightenment: *janana yoga,* which summons the power of the mind and emphasizes meditation; *bhakti yoga,* which encourages the direction of one's love to God; *karma yoga,* which involves service to others; and *raja yoga,* which combines elements of all three of the above into a single practice and includes the popular discipline of *hatha yoga.* Hatha yoga is meant to help the practitioner develop complete control over the body.

The multitiered system that is so pronounced within Hinduism has given it certain unique advantages. The ancient, flexible structure of the faith and its tolerance for widely divergent elements has allowed it to extend across a huge social and geographic landscape. As it did so, it focused on distinctive and enduring spiritual ideas, and cultivated, over time, acceptance of such distinctive elements as the *mantra* and the principle of *karma*.

Karma is an impartial principle of cause and effect under which actions in a past life may have an effect on one's present situation. Similarly, deeds undertaken in the present life may have an effect on both short-term developments and on one's later incarnations. Only those who escape the cycle of birth and death may be said to go beyond the reach of karma.

*This is the symbol for AUM, the Hindu "syllable of supreme reality." This vitally important mantra (incantation or prayer) symbolizes, in its three sounds, the Hindu triad of Brahma, Vishnu, and Shiva. Buddhists and Sikhs also attach great significance to the utterance.*

# Hindu Philosophy

The influence of the Upanishads and the later emergence of Buddhism pointed Hinduism toward a formal enunciation of philosophical principles. Six ancient schools of Indian philosophy acknowledge the Vedas as a religious authority; all have played important roles in the development of the religion, but they should not be misconstrued as "dogma" that is universally accepted and promoted by Hindus.

Classical Schools of Indian Philosophy

* *Nyaya* was a logical school that emerged in the sixth century B.C.E., and sees clear thinking and analysis as essential means on the path to higher realities.

* *Vaisheshika* examined physical reality and offered a six-tiered system for categorizing it. This school emerged in the sixth century B.C.E..

* *Samkhya* emphasized the principles of matter and soul and is perhaps the oldest of these six methods. It stresses the evolution of the cosmos and of "the person."

* *Yoga* built on the Samkhya model, and developed patterns meant to help instill personal, physical, and spiritual discipline. It developed in the second century B.C.E.

* *Purva Mimamsa,* which emerged in the second century B.C.E., offers guidance in interpreting the Vedas.

* *Vedanta,* perhaps the best known of these schools, gave rise to a number of disciplines, each placing emphasis on the transcendent messages of the Upanishads, the final portion of the Veda. This school came into existence around the first century C.E.

In addition to forming the platform for the various schools of Indian philosophy, the Upanishads gave rise to one of the masterpieces of human religious thought, the *Bhagavad Gita.* This Sanskrit classic is usually elevated to the level of the Upanishads when authoritative Hindu scriptures are discussed. It is not, technically at least, a formal part of the Hindu canon, but its influence over the centuries has been so immense that it might as well be. In a nation with many "Bibles," it has emerged as the most popularly revered of them all.

The *Bhagavad Gita* is an epic poem relating the dialogue between the human Prince Arjuna and the beloved Lord Krishna (one of the most important Hindu deities) on the eve of a great battle. In it, Krishna imparts spiritual wisdom that reinvigorates the faltering Arjuna. The text emphasizes union with God by means of love, selflessness, and total devotion.

**What's It Mean?**

The **caste** system is a social hierarchy ordering marriage and social roles. Over the centuries, Hindu India has developed a complex and rigid social structure incorporating thousands of individual castes.

# Social Realities

The system of *castes* has been a distinctive part of Indian religious and social life for centuries. There are thousands of castes, each one differentiated from the others by its religious practices, among many other factors.

Operating simultaneously with a caste system has been a broader method of caste-related social ranking. The major classes in this system are: *Brahmins* (a scholarly elite long associated with the priesthood), *Kshatriyas* (the ruling and military class), *Vaisyas* (merchants and farmers), *Sudras* (the peasantry), and, beneath the other four designations, the so-called untouchables, assigned the most menial jobs. Although twentieth-century reforms began to address some of the most glaring inequities of the system, rendering untouchability illegal, entrenched distinctions among social castes have persisted.

The words "Brahma," "Brahman," and "Brahmin" can be intimidating for those encountering Hinduism for the first time.

*Brahma* is a specific creator god who, despite a decline in popularity since the sixth century of the C.E., is still regarded as one of the supreme deities in the Hindu pantheon. *Brahman* is a Hindu term for ultimate reality without change, or eternity, and may be conceived as the supreme being or single God. (Just to keep things confusing, this word is sometimes rendered as Brahma, but the two concepts are nevertheless distinguishable.) A *Brahmin* is a member of the prestigious priestly class (caste) in India; to this day, only members of this group are allowed to read from the Veda. (Just to *continue* to keep things confusing, the word Brahmin is sometimes rendered as Brahman.)

Contemporary Brahmins are likely to work in careers having nothing at all to do with religion, but they are still situated in positions of high status in India.

**Watch It!**

Use great care when employing the words Brahma, Brahman, and Brahmin. These frequently confused expressions can cause unintended offense.

## Hindu Beliefs

Hinduism is a massive religious system with a glorious profusion of entry points. Can any devotional practice on this large a scale support specific propositions of faith? The surprising answer is yes.

The following core beliefs are broad enough to support the activities of, for instance, both the devotees of the sun god Surya and the Vedantist celebration of an ultimate and impersonal Reality. Although they should not be mistaken for a religious creed or catechism, they do represent shared positions commonly accepted by Hindu believers.

Hindus believe that ...

➤ The Vedas present authoritative and divinely inspired teachings.

➤ Brahman (or the Absolute) is both essentially impersonal and, at the same time, personal; it is made manifest in a variety of forms, which are best understood as symbols of divine truth.

➤ Brahman may be reached through many different paths.

➤ What is commonly considered to be reality—the physical world—is actually temporal, illusory, and capable of concealing the divine truth from all but the wisest people.

**121**

➤ The doctrine of karma ensures full accountability for every thought, action, and word. Hardships and inequalities in this life may be explained by actions and decisions undertaken in previous lives.

➤ The doctrine of reincarnation holds that one is trapped by the cycle of life and death until one attains true realization.

➤ A devotee may embrace any number of revealed forms of the Absolute, and he or she may do so in any number of ways.

➤ Family life and social interaction are marked by four stages: the student, the householder, the seeker, and the ascetic. Believers in the last category improve the lot of the world at large through the process of their renunciation.

➤ Life has four goals: righteousness, earthly prosperity and success, pleasure, and spiritual liberation.

In the next chapter, you'll learn more about the complex, many-faceted approach that Hinduism takes to God (with a capital "G"), and to its many gods (with a lower-case "g").

---

### The Least You Need to Know

➤ Hinduism, which is as diverse as India itself (the nation with which it is strongly associated), is an extraordinary collection of variations and expansions—some ancient, some more recent.

➤ Hinduism is regarded as having existed forever; it has no founder.

➤ Specific, universally held doctrines do not play a major role in the Hindu faith.

➤ A series of loosely connected beliefs, such as a common acceptance of authoritative scripture, combine with a huge number of techniques for personal spiritual development within Hinduism.

➤ Hinduism's many forms of religious worship are meant to help believers move toward the direct experience of the Absolute.

# Chapter 14

# God's Many Faces

---

**In This Chapter**

➤ Find out about the single guiding idea behind the Hindu faith and its innumerable expressions

➤ Take a good long look at the one God/many gods question as it relates to Hinduism

➤ Learn about some of the principal Hindu deities

---

In this chapter, you learn about the principal deities of Hinduism, (which claims thousands of gods), and about the unique blend of diversity and unanimity that supports this faith's many sects and practitioners.

## One God, Many Gods

Hinduism can be as simple or as complex as any particular believer (or explorer) chooses to make it. Since this is a book for beginners, the best way to begin a chapter on the Hindu conception of God (and gods) may be to take the simple approach first.

Here it comes: don't blink!

There is something eternal and inherently divine within the human heart, and that "something" is not different from that which is eternal and inherently divine and permeates all of creation. The purpose of human existence is to discover a path that will lead to direct experience of this "something."

The principle you've just read lies at the heart of the Hindu faith, which accepts God as both a grounding, absolute Reality and as the exponent of innumerable changing processes. All the same, an important issue arises ...

## Does Hinduism Celebrate a Single God or a Profusion of Gods?

It's a fair question.

The answer such a query receives from the vast and ancient Hindu tradition can sound strangely ambivalent to a newcomer of the faith, and may even be mistaken for flippant. It is, however, an ancient and quite profound response, one that has been worked out with exquisite care over a period of centuries. The answer is: Yes.

Monotheists in the familiar sense—those who believe, as Christians, Muslims, and Jews do, in a single *personal* God—are quite likely to have the feeling of receiving mixed signals from the Hindu tradition, with its inspiring principle of ultimate reality, and its occasionally bewildering profusion of specific deities.

The complex question of whether Hinduism is or isn't a "polytheistic" religion can be illuminated briefly by an imaginary dialogue.

*A Short and Inconclusive Discussion on Topics Related to the Divine*

*Newcomer:* So, which is it? One God, Brahman, or a whole bunch of gods?

*Hindu:* Absolutely. Or, if you prefer, not so absolutely.

*Newcomer:* This is a pretty important issue. Doesn't Hinduism address it directly somewhere?

*Hindu:* Of course.

*Newcomer:* And how is it resolved?

*Hindu:* You know, it's funny. Someone came in here just a millennium or so ago asking basically the same question. "How many gods are there?" he asked.

*Newcomer:* What was the answer?

*Hindu:* "How many do you want?"

*Newcomer:* Suppose I were to tell you that still sounds like fence-straddling?

*Hindu:* Suppose I were to ask you where human beings get off trying to tell the Brahman, the Eternal, the Ultimate, what forms are off-limits?

*Newcomer:* But it has to be one way or the other, doesn't it?

*Hindu:* If everyone understands the process of labeling the Divine to be the thing that's *really* limited, what difference does it make what forms are acknowledged?

*Newcomer:* I'm getting confused. What do the Vedas have to say about this?

*Hindu*: "This Self, what can you say of it but 'no, no'?"

*Newcomer*: "No, no?"

*Hindu*: No real description of Brahman is possible; but direct experience, through whatever method, discipline, or form of devotion, *is*.

*Newcomer*: So there's one God.

*Hindu*: From a certain point of view.

*Newcomer*: And there are lots of gods.

*Hindu*: From a certain point of view.

*Newcomer*: I'm still feeling just the tiniest bit woozy ...

*Hindu*: Don't worry. That doesn't last long. Keep practicing.

**On the Path**

The members of the various Hindu sects worship a dizzying number of specific deities and follow innumerable rituals in honor of specific gods. Since this is Hinduism, however, its practitioners see the profusion of forms and practices as expressions of the same unchanging reality.

## Having It Both Ways

It is not at all accurate to say that Hinduism *rejects* the concept of monotheism as it is understood within Judaism, Christianity, and Islam. But neither does Hinduism's monotheism *exclude* specific concepts and incarnations of the divine—including personifications that some would call polytheistic.

The two ideas are simply not seen as incompatible with one another in Hindu thought the way they are in the faiths just named.

In the Brihadaranayaka Upanishad, Vigadha, son of Shakala, asks Yajnavalkya, "How many gods are there?" After an appropriate citation of scripture, the answer comes: "Three hundred and thirty three." Yajnavalyaka is praised for the perceptiveness of his answer, and is then asked again: "How many gods are there?" This time the answer is thirty-three, and the response is once again praised. The process continues until Yajnavalyaka answers that there is a single God, an answer for which he is praised; but each of the preceding answers is also acknowledged as inspired and correct!

**On the Path**

Once Hinduism came to embrace the concept of reincarnation, larger questions of purpose and destiny became easier to address—though not necessarily easier to resolve. The idea of each person's being reborn into suffering in order to attain purity and freedom from rebirth is one element of a massive drama, a drama that cannot be separated from the larger human task of acknowledging the divine presence in all forms.

125

**Bet You Didn't Know**

The panoply of deities found in Hinduism are understood by believers as symbols for a single transcendent reality.

The earliest Hindu holy texts, which focus on matters of ritual sacrifice and are clearly polytheistic, envision the various gods in an extraordinary way: as manifestations of an inborn, singular governing force or principle, regarded as ultimate in nature *and* capable of taking on particular forms.

Is Hinduism polytheistic or isn't it? The best way to approach the issue may be to avoid the temptation to resolve the matter definitively. Put the question aside and simply consider that this grouping of faiths accepts *both* infinite and single expressions of the Divine.

# The Big Picture

The implications of the vastly scaled theologies of Hinduism, which regard revealed forms as inherently limited, illusory, and, ultimately, exceeded by Brahman, can be quite far-reaching. Consider the subject of human history.

Western ideas of clear, divinely inspired historical progression, for instance, are in contrast to the Hindu conception of cyclic action, which acknowledges both creation and destruction as forces governing human history. This is a far cry from the Christian idea of the final deliverance of humanity via the Second Coming, to take just one example.

Instead of a single (and perhaps vengeful) God judging the entire human race, Hinduism emphasizes a divinely appointed drama that must be played out repeatedly over a vast timeframe.

# A Brief Introduction

A book like this cannot begin to describe the vast grouping of Hindu deities in a responsible way. Following are short descriptions of a few of the most important deities in Hinduism as they have emerged over the centuries.

As you read on, please keep two things in mind: 1. Hinduism is an evolving religion, one that has constantly incorporated new practices and outlooks as spiritual needs have demanded. As a result ...2. Its panoply of gods is a shifting phenomenon, one that is constantly being transformed. The most important deities may engage in rivalries before being reconciled, or even combine with one another. Tracing the lineage, incarnations, and convoluted histories of a particular deity can be a daunting task indeed!

## The Big Three

*Brahma* is a personification of the Absolute, the creator of the world, which is perpetually destined to last for 2,160,000,000 years before it falls to ruin, at which time Brahma recreates it. The passage of one such cycle represents a single day in Brahma's life. One of the three supreme gods in the *Hindu triad,* Brahma is revered as the Creator within that grouping.

*Vishnu* has many incarnations, of which two are worthy of note here: as *Krishna* and as *Rama.* In the Hindu triad, he is the Preserver. Vishnu is seen as a force of transcendent love.

*Shiva* symbolizes the various potent forms of the energy of the Ultimate. Usually depicted with four arms and surrounded by fire, Shiva is the third supreme god in the Hindu triad. Shiva embodies both the creative force (he is closely associated with a symbolic phallus) and the idea of destruction. This is his role within the Hindu triad, but Shiva represents an ancient and complex figure whose most important attributes are not easily summarized.

## Some Other Important Deities

*Krishna,* an enormously popular Hindu deity, is an incarnation of Vishnu. He is seen variously as lover, trickster, cowherd, and military hero. First and foremost, however, he is the object (and source!) of extraordinarily devoted and unfailing love. Krishna's sexuality is often startling to westerners; he is frequently depicted as a seducer of wives and daughters—metaphorical expressions of the human soul's union with the Divine.

*Rama* is another incarnation of Vishnu; his story is told in the epic known as the *Ramayana.* Rama's tale celebrates the commitments of family life and the supreme value of virtue and right living; it also

### On the Path

Vishnu and Shiva, two preeminent Hindu gods, were initially depicted as rivals. True to form, the Hindu faith reconciled them and eventually merged them, as elements of the triad that also includes Brahma.

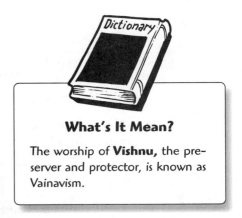

### What's It Mean?

The worship of **Vishnu,** the preserver and protector, is known as Vainavism.

127

illustrates the shortcomings of worldly possessions and authority. Rama has been described as "God incarnate as morality."

*Shakti, consort to Shiva,* goes by many other names as well, including Parvati, Kali, Uma, and Durga. She represents the creative force but may take the terrifying form of the destroyer-goddess. This seemingly paradoxical figure is sometimes worshipped in Shiva's place. This happens at times when Shiva is regarded as having entered a trance that makes him unable to heed the requirements of humanity. As you can see, Hindu forms of worship are remarkably fluid and adaptable.

There is a great deal more that could be said of Hinduism, and perhaps a great deal more that should be said about some of the cultural and gender roles associated with it—issues we have not tried to raise here.

The purpose of a book like this is not to make judgments, but to offer responsible introductions to the faiths of the world. Furthermore, in the end no judgment may be necessary. After all, there has never been a religion as well suited for constructive change as the Hindu faith.

**On the Path**

Worship of Shakti gave rise to Tantric devotion, a practice that employs supremely disciplined and focused sexuality as a pathway to unity with the Absolute.

Mahatma Gandhi, who spoke so powerfully and so eloquently on behalf of those injured by the caste system, may well have captured the true essence of this faith when he frankly refused to follow certain scriptural dictates. "My belief in the Hindu Scriptures," Ghandi said, "does not require me to accept every word and every verse as divinely inspired ... I decline to be bound by any interpretation, however learned it may be, if it is repugnant to reason and common sense."

Gandhi could expand "abstract" spiritual values into the real world. By adapting what could be used and transcending what could not, he modeled the most exciting and vigorous elements of Hinduism.

---

### The Least You Need to Know

➤ Hinduism features lots and lots of individual deities.

➤ Although some religions regard monotheism (worship of one god) and polytheism (worship of many gods) as incompatible, Hinduism is not one of them.

➤ Each of the many Hindu deities is regarded as a particular, and useful, form of the Ultimate.

➤ The Hindu triad includes the gods Brahma, Vishnu, and Shiva. Other important deities include Krishna, Rama, and Shakti.

# Chapter 15

# Respect for Life and Personal Growth

---

### In This Chapter

➤ Reincarnation ... the straight scoop

➤ The sanctity of life within the Hindu tradition

➤ Important patterns of Hindu worship

---

In this chapter, you find out more about the principle of reincarnation and about Hinduism's emphasis on personal spiritual purification, rather than regular worship within a congregation.

## Life and Death

The Hindu view of life and death is essential to the day-to-day observances of this faith.

Hindus believe that humanity is cast into a long cycle of repetitive incarnation, known as *samsara*. Hindus also accept as a transcendent goal one's ultimate escape from that cycle. Everyday life—our day-to-day experience of existence—is seen as a burden, very often a very painful one, thanks to the working-out of karma from our current lives and past incarnations. This process is seen as an intrinsic part of the human condition.

Spiritual progress, according to Hinduism, is all about avoiding rebirth. This notion can be a misleading one, however, especially for outsiders.

## "Watch Out for Rebirth"

It would be easy to assume that these principles would automatically lead to severe asceticism (practices that discipline the body) or even nihilism, a distaste for life itself. Nihilists, however, deny that human existence has any meaning or purpose. This is not the case in Hinduism.

Instead of dismissing existence as meaningless, committed Hindu practitioners seek, in countless ways, to cultivate a profound joy and celebration of the process of working out past karma. Their joy exists side by side with their pious desire to transcend the physical world.

To be sure, some extraordinary ascetic disciplines can be found in Hinduism. Familiar images of the lean-boned penitent; the holy person meditating alone on a remote hilltop; the guru who demands full rigor, attention, and devotion from his followers—these familiar roles do reflect a strand running through this complex faith, but they are not all there is to it.

### What's It Mean?

**Samsara** is the process of accumulated, karma-driven birth, in which the thoughts and deeds of past lives are addressed and resolved in subsequent lives. No aspect of existence is seen as separate from the dance of karmic resolution, and true freedom is regarded as impossible while the cycle of karma-driven birth continues.

Such ascetic disciplines must not be misinterpreted. And they are certainly not the only paths for spiritual development within Hinduism!

### Bet You Didn't Know

Recent Hindu leaders such as Swami Vivekenanda and Mahatma Ghandi have upheld spiritual movements within Hinduism that stress social awareness and compassion toward others, de-emphasizing the ascetic disciplines of the individual. Nevertheless, asceticism is likely to continue to represent an important current of belief and practice within Hinduism.

Within Hindu practice there are some schools that teach an intense, solitary self-mortification. Others promote the pursuit of one's spiritual destiny through home celebrations, sexual discipline, everyday life with one's family, service to others, and countless other methods. Hinduism makes room for an exhilarating array of disciplines, each of which reveres life as a profound gift and many of which are incorporated into "everyday" life.

# Religion, Religion Everywhere

For Hindus, each new incarnation offers the opportunity for growth. Believers pursue four life aspirations, each one recognized as spiritually valid: pleasure, development of wealth, righteousness, and liberation from the cycle of birth, death, and rebirth.

Life is seen as a sacred opportunity for a particular believer to embrace a particular, appropriate discipline at a particular time and hasten his or her journey toward union with Brahman.

For this reason, the line separating "religion" and "everyday life" in Hindu life can be difficult to make out.

# Where's the Sabbath?

Many non-Hindus are familiar with a conception allowing religious faith to act in support of, or perhaps as a supplement to, one's "habitual" existence. Many more expect religious life to take the form of regular weekly observance of established rituals, with congregations of fellow believers.

A Hindu practitioner, however, is perfectly at home in a situation in which such expressions of group devotion are comparatively rare. Other forms of religious discipline, however, are developed and pursued with full attention. The short message: Hinduism has no formal, universally acknowledged sabbath. It would also, of course, be accurate to say that Hinduism sees every day as the sabbath.

In a similar way, the absolute reverence for life, or *ahimsa,* is fundamental to the everyday experience of Hinduism.

**Watch It!**

The law of karma should not be mistaken as a system of divine reward or punishment. Karma is an impartial force, almost like the physical law of cause and effect. It takes no sides and is not filtered through a supreme entity. It affects even the minutest aspects of the human experience.

**What's It Mean?**

**Ahimsa** is the Hindu principle of reverence for life. The idea arose around 600 B.C.E. and led to the rapid growth of vegetarianism.

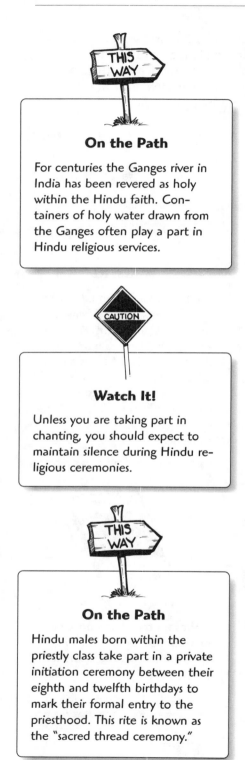

## On the Path

For centuries the Ganges river in India has been revered as holy within the Hindu faith. Containers of holy water drawn from the Ganges often play a part in Hindu religious services.

## Watch It!

Unless you are taking part in chanting, you should expect to maintain silence during Hindu religious ceremonies.

## On the Path

Hindu males born within the priestly class take part in a private initiation ceremony between their eighth and twelfth birthdays to mark their formal entry to the priesthood. This rite is known as the "sacred thread ceremony."

In recent years, some American Hindu believers have formed groups that practice Western-style traditions of worship—like weekly congregational gatherings on Sundays. Most, however, still practice the traditional forms.

"Purify us from all sides," reads the Atharva Veda in a hymn to the Earth. Later, it reads, "May Earth, clad in her fiery mantle, dark-kneed, make me aflame; may she sharpen me bright ... " An ancient emphasis on purification within Hinduism presupposes a unity with all created forms. This is the unity the dance of life is meant to express and uncover.

# Temples and Homes

Celebration of life in all its kaleidoscopic glory is an essential element of Hinduism. For this reason, temple worship and private worship rituals in the home are important Hindu disciplines. Of course, some believers practice no external worship whatsoever, choosing to cultivate awareness of the divine presence in other ways. Hinduism has many paths.

Hindu worship and religious observances may take place either in a temple dedicated to a particular deity, or in the worshiper's home, at small shrines that incorporate images of a god or goddess. Prayers are directed to the god or goddess, who is regarded as an honored guest. During worship, or *puja*, the consumption of sacramental food known as *prasad* may take place. It is blessed before it is eaten.

For those attending Hindu worship services for the first time, a gentle reminder may be in order. Chanting before an image or statue of a particular god, or offering that figure flowers, incense, or special oils, should not be looked down on as "idolatry." Outsiders have a difficult time understanding such forms of worship, but it may help to remember that in the Hindu tradition, devotion to *a particular form* of the nameless, formless, and ultimate reality is a way of honoring the one essential divine principle.

Hinduism acknowledges *any and every* depiction of the Absolute as both valid and inherently limited. It holds the eventual transcendence of such forms to be an important spiritual goal.

## What to Expect

Individual devotees may conduct particular worship rituals at whatever speed is comfortable to them. When more than one person is engaged in worship, group chanting may take place.

Outsiders will never be expected to take part in rituals that make them uncomfortable. Neither will they be excluded from any part of the service in which they wish to participate.

When in doubt about what will happen, ask *before* the services begin. The order of rituals can usually be confirmed ahead of time by talking directly with the celebrant.

**On the Path**

Although Hindus regard one's physical body as transitory, the soul, or *atman*, is seen as neither beginning nor ending.

# Celebrations

Following is a brief review of some of the most holy days within the Hindu faith. Needless to say, this is not a comprehensive list!

*Duhsehra/Durga Puja,* which is generally observed in the early autumn, is an observance of the triumph of good over evil.

*Rama Navami*, generally observed in springtime, is an important holiday centered on the god Rama.

*Krishna Janmashtami* marks the birthday of Krishna. It is generally celebrated in late summer.

*Shiva Ratri* is an all-night celebration of the Divine as manifested in the god Shiva. Shiva Ratri usually occurs in the latter part of the winter season.

# Life Rituals

Here's a brief summary of some of the most important life rituals within the Hindu faith.

*Infant welcoming ritual.* Hindus place great importance on the point at which a child first consumes solid food. This is an occasion for group celebration and a formal "rice-eating ceremony." It takes place about six to eight months after birth and is accompanied by religious rituals. It is often preceded and followed by a reception.

*Marriages.* In the Hindu tradition marriages are usually arranged, a contract between two families. Each incorporates five ceremonies: a verbal contract between the male parents or guardians of the bride and groom, the giving-away of the bride by her father or guardian, a welcoming ceremony for the new couple, a hand-holding ritual, and a walking rite. Hindu marriages generally take place after sunset.

*Funerals.* Funerals center on the cremation ritual known as *nukhagni.* After a predetermined period of days, depending on the caste of the deceased, a ceremony known as *shradda* marks the end of the family's mourning period and the journey of the soul of the departed.

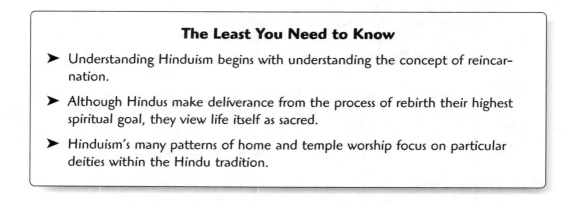

### The Least You Need to Know

➤ Understanding Hinduism begins with understanding the concept of reincarnation.

➤ Although Hindus make deliverance from the process of rebirth their highest spiritual goal, they view life itself as sacred.

➤ Hinduism's many patterns of home and temple worship focus on particular deities within the Hindu tradition.

# Part 6

# Buddhism

*We live in a world with a long and bloody history of conflict over religious ideas. Islam spread through large-scale military conquest. Violent conflicts between Protestant and Catholic parties tore Europe apart during the Wars of Reformation; in Northern Ireland the battle is still being waged. Acts of hatred and bloodshed between Hindus and Muslims have troubled India for centuries. Only somehow, Buddhism has translated the teaching of divine love and transcendent purpose into a pacifism capable of shaping human actions on a large scale. Indeed, pacifism and nonviolence have significantly shaped the destinies of countries where Buddhism has predominated.*

*To find out more about this enduring and influential world religion, take a look at the next three chapters of this book.*

# Chapter 16

# The Prince Who Left the Palace: Buddhist Origins and Doctrine

---

**In This Chapter**

➤ Learn the story of the Buddha

➤ Read about The Four Noble Truths

➤ Discover some of the most important ideas within Buddhism

---

Buddhism developed in India as a noncomforming system outside of Hinduism. Buddhists explicitly rejected the usefulness of the elaborate Vedic rites and refused to accept the caste system as authoritative. Despite these differences, however, Buddhism shares many fundamental beliefs with Hinduism, including the concepts of reincarnation, karma, and entering Nirvana, or absolute liberation.

Discover the origins of Buddhism in the momentous decision of Prince Gautama to disobey his royal father's orders and explore the real world on his own.

## The Legend of the Buddha

In the sixth century B.C.E. (we think), Siddhartha Gautama was born, the son of the wealthy and powerful ruler of a small kingdom. At his birth, the legend holds, an old sage foretold that the prince would become either an ascetic or a supreme monarch.

The boy's father, eager to ensure that his son would become the leader of his kingdom and a great warrior, sought to protect Prince Gautama from fulfilling the prophecy as an ascetic. He kept his son isolated in the kingdom, allowing him to live a life of

### On the Path

Buddhism holds that the sheltered prince Gautama had never encountered old age, illness, or death until he ventured outside the royal estate. That journey brought shattering revelations about human suffering. Eventually he encountered a man whose knowing smile reflected contentment and peace. Gautama asked his chariot-driver how the man could be happy in such a world, and was informed that he had just seen a holy man, one who had obtained complete liberation.

### What's It Mean?

A **Buddha** is a fully enlightened being. Siddhartha Gautama, the founder of Buddhism, became known as Buddha Tathagata ("he who has gone through completely"). Other names for this revered figure include Bhagavat (Lord) and, simply, the Buddha.

supreme luxury. He was determined that the prince should never want for anything—and never desire any other life than that of a monarch.

As a young man, Gautama married and became a father. It is said that, during his twenty-ninth year, he finally made his way out of the palace, where he was confronted by old age, illness, and death—realities that had previously been kept secret from him. The journey shocked him and forever changed his life.

## On to Asceticism

After this experience, Gautama reacted radically against the luxurious lifestyle that had brought him what he now recognized as an empty and useless existence. Vowing to become a holy man himself, he pursued a life of deprivation and asceticism. He forsook the palace and his family in search of liberation and a solution to the problem of human suffering. Years of intense spiritual searching followed.

During this period, Gautama became an itinerant ascetic, subjecting himself to intense physical disciplines. Yet spiritual progress remained elusive.

After one rigorous fast, he accepted a meal of rice cooked in milk from a local woman. This was a breach of established religious practice within the discipline Gautama was pursuing.

Having thus compromised the ascetic "war" against his own body, he sat on a straw mat beneath a Bodhi tree and made a vow not to move until he had attained true liberation.

On the morning of the seventh day, he opened his eyes and looked out to the morning star. At that moment, he became enlightened.

## The Awakening

Tradition holds that, upon attaining this awakening, Gautama/*Buddha* exclaimed that all beings possess enlightenment, but that some are blinded to this fact.

Buddhism, the faith that developed as a result of this realization, places a heavy emphasis on liberation from delusion—and by extension, from three habits that give rise to distorted human perceptions. Those habits are desire, anger, and ignorance.

# The Buddha's Path

By charting a path between extreme self-indulgence and rigorous self-denial, Siddhartha Gautama had attained true knowledge. His embrace of this path was a defining moment that led to his designation as the Buddha, or Enlightened One.

The Buddha was tempted to remain in seclusion for the rest of his life, but before long he encountered some of his earlier companions, fellow seekers who had pursued the ascetic path with him. They ostracized him at first because of his decision to violate the ascetic lifestyle. Eventually, however, they acknowledged the depth of his realization and decided to follow him. The Buddha's ministry had begun.

Having directly experienced ultimate awakening, he spent the rest of his life traveling the countryside, preaching, and organizing a monastic community, the *sangha*.

# Nirvana (Before It Was a Rock Band)

The Buddha's very first discourse, which he gave in a place called Deer Park, was known as "the setting into motion the wheel of the dharma." It revealed the basic doctrines of Buddhism.

*Dharma* in Buddhism refers to sublime religious truth. It also serves to describe, on a technical level, any particular facet of experience or existence.

Hindus also use the word *dharma*, but for them it has to do with a religious obligation, social convention, or individual virtue.

**What's It Mean?**

In Buddhism, a **sangha** is a community of monks, much like a Western monastery.

**On the Path**

Nirvana, the state of final liberation from the cycle of birth and death (recognized in both Hinduism and Buddhism) is held to be beyond definition. In the *Surangama*, Buddha describes Nirvana as the place *"where it is recognized that there is nothing but what is seen of the mind itself; where, recognizing the nature of the self-mind, one no longer cherishes the dualisms of discrimination; where there is no more thirst nor grasping; where there is no more attachment to external things."*

The Buddha accepted the principle of reincarnation. He believed that living beings are trapped within the physical cycle of birth and death under the law of karma until complete release is attained. His teaching mission was to enable disciples to attain a clear, deep, direct understanding of the obstacles they faced in their own spiritual lives.

**On the Path**

Even many non-Buddhists have acknowledged the purity of the Buddha's revelation and the profundity of his religion's basic principles. The simplicity and clarity of the core ideas of Buddhism have moved ancient Chinese philosophers, twentieth-century Beat poets, and contemplative Catholic monks, to name just a few.

The Deer Park sermon laid out the basic "roadmap" by which believers could avoid the obstacles that prevent people from understanding their true nature. It explained the steps one must take to gain direct experience of ultimate reality—Nirvana—just as the Buddha had.

In this talk, the Buddha laid out the Four Noble Truths that are still the bedrock of the faith two and a half millennia later. Although Buddhism has evolved in many ways over the centuries, expressed itself in a great many sects, and developed an extremely broad system of philosophical thought, these fundamental beliefs of Buddhism have remained unchanged since the Buddha's time.

The Four Noble Truths are a rarity among the world's major religions: a set of founding ideas that has never been used as justification for the acts of a warrior class or culture, or for any military exploit. There has never been a military crusade launched in the name of the Buddha, and considering the nature of the Four Noble Truths, it is doubtful that there ever will be.

*The Four Noble Truths*

The Buddha taught that:

1. *Life is suffering.* The very nature of human existence is inherently painful. Because of the cyclical nature of death and rebirth, death does not bring an end to suffering.

2. *Suffering has a cause: craving and attachment.* Suffering is the result of our selfish craving and clinging. This in turn reflects our ignorance of reality.

3. *Craving and attachment can be overcome.* When one completely transcends selfish craving, one enters the state of Nirvana, and suffering ceases.

4. *The path toward the cessation of craving and attachment is an Eightfold Path:*

    Right understanding

    Right purpose

Right speech

Right conduct

Right livelihood

Right effort

Right alertness

Right concentration

The Buddha also taught that the abiding self is illusory. Physical form, sensations, perceptions, psychic exertions, even consciousness itself—none yield an unchanging, independent self. And the human tendency to view the self as an independent, controlling entity is not merely a benign delusion, but a significant barrier to spiritual progress.

## Beyond Substance

The notion of "non-self," emphasized in the teachings of the Buddha, has frequently been misinterpreted. In fact, many westerners have dismissed Buddhism as "atheistic" or "nihilistic" because of it. Such labels may build barriers to understanding the faith. The limitation probably lies with familiar conceptions of what is and is not "God," and not with Buddhism.

The Buddha taught that any conception dividing one phenomenon from another—a blade of grass from a meditating woman, for instance, or a meditating woman from her own Buddha-nature—is illusory. Nothing exists independently or eternally.

According to Buddhist philosophy, a blade of grass, examined closely enough, is simply a transitory collection of processes. Indeed, the very label "a blade of grass" is misleading. Why? Because the lines dividing the smallest possible components of the blade of grass from the rest of creation are imposed by our own perceptions. They do not actually separate that (transitory) blade of grass from anything.

Nothing is permanent. No form endures forever; no single perceived manifestation fully expresses the supreme reality. The line between "a blade of grass" and "not a blade of grass" is an illusory one, in the end. Although it may be convenient in certain situations for the woman to use the term "blade of grass" to describe what is next to her as she meditates, or the term "enlightenment" or "Buddha-nature" to describe the eventual result of her sustained, disciplined practice, Buddhism reminds us not to

**On the Path**

Buddhism sees all manifested forms as subject to decay and division. Fixating on particular forms (even spiritual ones) is regarded as a form of delusion.

take such labels too seriously—even (especially) when that meditation appears to be promising, or incorporates the experience of *samadhi*.

For the Buddhist, developing the right kind of self-discipline offers a pathway out of delusion and toward true awareness. Holding on to what does not actually exist will only lead to suffering.

### What's It Mean?

**Samadhi,** in Buddhism, is understood as a state of single-minded concentration. Along with morality and wisdom, samadhi is seen as an essential tool for pursuing a path of self-awakening. (In Hinduism, this word describes the point at which an individual's consciousness merges with the Godhead.)

### On the Path

In Buddhism, the realization that the self has no true reality is more important than devotion to ascetic practices. Indeed, if such practices lead to pride, they do more harm than good. In the Buddhist tradition, the deities named in Hinduism are spirits who have not yet attained the final liberation.

The same principle of continuity between the meditating woman and the blade of grass is also applied to the God or distinct Supreme Being a non-Buddhist might suppose to be guiding the woman's meditation. All imagined separateness between perceived entities is, as it were, a hallucination.

It is as a result of this philosophy, and not out of cynicism or any lack of piety, that Buddhists reject the notion of a separate God that is somehow set apart from everyday experience.

## Gods

With such a doctrine, it is no surprise that Buddha taught that one should not seek divine intervention in this life. The familiar Hindu gods do indeed exist, he taught, but they do not hold dominion over daily human life. Instead they are subject to the same universal laws that human beings must observe.

Buddha's path focuses on the single-minded pursuit of an individual's spiritual goals, not on the establishment of new conceptions of the Deity.

The emphasis of the religion he founded is on meditation and the observance of important moral precepts, seen as expressions of one's own actual nature rather than as standards derived from external divine authority.

Both lay and monastic Buddhists commit to the following precepts:

➤ Not to kill.

➤ Not to steal.

➤ Not to act in an unchaste manner.

➤ Not to speak falsely.

➤ Not to take intoxicants.

In addition, monks vow:

➤ Not to eat at times not appointed.

➤ Not to view entertainments deemed as "secular."

➤ Not to wear perfumes or bodily ornaments.

➤ Not to sleep in beds that are too high or too wide.

➤ Not to accept money.

In addition, many other vows may accompany the pursuit of a monastic lifestyle.

# Teaching, Living, Dying

The Buddha is said to have spent 45 years teaching, ordaining monks and nuns, and promoting a solitary, secluded style of spiritual discipline. This method of self-discovery would profoundly affect the religious lives of millions of followers throughout Asia and around the world in the centuries to come.

The Buddha appears to have shown no interest in assembling a written record of his own teachings. His disciples transmitted the most important sermons orally; hundreds of years after his death, they were finally committed to paper. (Even these early scriptures, initially written in Sanskrit, are not extant; the earliest surviving accounts of the Buddha's teachings are in Pali, an ancient northwestern Indian dialect.)

Tradition tells us that the Buddha died at the age of 80 without naming a successor. His final words, passed along for centuries, form the perfect encapsulation of the faith he founded.

"All composite things decay. Diligently work out your salvation."

---

### The Least You Need to Know

➤ The Buddha's enlightenment beneath a Bodhi tree in India marked the beginning of Buddhism, a new religious tradition outside of Hinduism.

➤ The Four Noble Truths form the most important principles of the Buddhist faith.

➤ Buddhism sees all manifested forms as subject to decay and division, and acknowledges liberation only by overcoming selfish desire and craving.

# Chapter 17

---

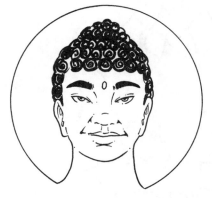
# Mahayana and All That

## In This Chapter

➤ Find out about Buddhism after the Buddha

➤ Learn about the history and development of the Theravada school

➤ Learn about the history and development of the Mahayana school

In this part of the book you learn about the two great divisions of the Buddhist faith, their differing approaches to spiritual life, and the many movements and trends within each. You will also get an idea of the most unusual and influential scriptures within the various Buddhist traditions.

## After the Buddha

The Buddha chose not to appoint a formal successor before he died, preferring to allow each of his followers to choose a path and to search within themselves for enlightenment. Soon after his death, however, a council convened to settle the growing differences among Buddhist followers.

This council, led by the monk Mahakasyapa, was the first of many such attempts to resolve differing views on the direction of the faith. Doctrinal disputes within the new religion were common in the centuries following the Buddha's death, and these disputes were not easily resolved. Many sects of Buddhism emerged, in part because of disputes over the details of monastic disciplines.

Eventually, 18 schools or disciplines were acknowledged. Of these, only one, the Theravada ("doctrine of the elders") school, still exists today.

*The lotus is a sacred symbol in both Buddhism and Hinduism.*

## What's It Mean?

In Mahayana Buddhism, a **bodhisattva** is one who deserves Nirvana but postpones entry to it until all sentient beings are rescued from rebirth and suffering.

## On the Path

Although Buddhism arose and developed in India in its early phase, it is now almost completely absent from that country. Of the few living in India who practice Buddhism today, many are from other countries.

# The Two Schools of Buddhism

There are no written records on the early development of Buddhism. The earliest Buddhist scriptures were written about four hundred years after the Buddha's ministry. Thus it is hard to be certain just what the Buddha said or taught.

The Theravada school, which views its most sacred teachings as those of the Buddha himself, emphasizes a solitary life of personal religious discipline. Around C.E. 100, however, a very different conception of Buddhism began to emerge as a powerful movement within the faith.

This view of Buddhism chose to focus less on the supreme virtues of a life of seclusion and more on the importance of compassion and service to others. The ideal of this wing of the faith was not the *arhat,* or perfected sage, but the *bodhisattva*—the advanced soul who deserves Nirvana but vows to postpone entry to it until all sentient beings are rescued from the wheel of rebirth and suffering. This became known as Mahayana, or "Great Vehicle" school of Buddhism.

The founder of Mahayana Buddhism was the revered philosopher Nagarjuna. His movement has exceeded the influence of the earlier Theravada path, with its emphasis on individual discipline and solitary practice. For this reason the Theravada school has been labeled the Hinayana ("Lesser Vehicle") school.

Theravada/Hinayana Buddhism survives today in Sri Lanka and Southeast Asia, while Mahayana Buddhism is likely to be found in Japan, Korea, Mongolia, and China.

## Theravada Buddhism

The Theravada school, with its emphasis on detachment and seclusion, reveres the way of renunciation—the pursuit of a rigorous, purifying lifestyle for the sake of spiritual goals. Of course, lay believers are apt to pursue a less ambitious spiritual regimen following a generally ethical way of life and perhaps helping to support the monastic orders.

## Theravada Scriptures

Theravada scriptures are in three parts, known as the Tipitaka, or Three Baskets. The three parts are the *Vinaya Pitaka* (monastic regulations), the *Sutta Pitaka* (discourses and discussions attributed to the Buddha), and the Abhidamma Pitaka (discussions and classifications relating to philosophy, psychology, and doctrine). Within the *Sutta Pitaka* is the *Dhammapada,* a summary of the Buddha's teachings on a variety of mental disciplines and moral issues.

**What's It Mean?**

An **arhat** is a holy person who attains enlightenment through solitude and ascetic practices.

---

Five More Things You Should Know About the Theravada School

➤ As one of the 18 major early schools of Buddhism, the practices and beliefs of the Theravada School are believed to reflect the essential early doctrines of Buddhism.

➤ The *arhat,* or worthy one, is sometimes known as the "solitary saint" within the Theravada tradition.

➤ Besides those already discussed, important texts within Theravada Buddhism include the Milindapanha (Questions of King Milinda), a dialogue about common problems in Buddhist thought, and ...

➤ The somewhat later Visuddhimagga (Path of Purification), which is a brilliant summary of Buddhist thought and meditative practices.

➤ A third-century B.C.E. council resulted in the expulsion of members of the sangha (monastic community) who were considered to have joined monastic orders for political rather than spiritual reasons.

# The Mahayana School

Around the first century B.C.E., the movement that would become known as the Mahayana school of Buddhism first emerged with the circulation of a new body of scriptures, the Mahayana sutras. In addition to promoting a new spiritual ideal, we find the idea of the bodhisattva, an Enlightened being who postpones union with the Ultimate for the benefit of all beings. Mahayana Buddhism also formulated an important spiritual principle: *sunyata*. This Sanskrit word for "emptiness" states that all ultimate entities, including the Buddha and the state of Nirvana, are empty, that is, completely undivided from the rest of the Supreme Reality.

The idea of Sunyata arose in the first century B.C.E. as a radical reassertion and expansion of the doctrine of non-self. Mahayana Buddhists argued that all ultimate entities—including the Buddha and the state of Nirvana—are empty. This view undercuts the common perception that the Ultimate is somehow separate or independent from direct experience. Does "emptiness" mean the same thing as "nihilism"? Not at all. Rather, it has to do with interconnection. When a Mahayana Buddhist holds that "all dharmas are empty," what is really being rejected is duality, division.

*Dualistic thinking*—the common assumption that the world is made up of separate entities—is seen by many groups within Buddhism as fundamentally delusional. Language, including this paragraph, reflects this dualistic way of thinking. Thus language is considered by Mahayana Buddhists to be of limited use in illuminating spiritual truths. Nagarjuna was of the opinion that nothing conclusive could be said in words concerning ultimate reality.

The doctrine of emptiness rejects as inadequate any conception of separate, independent existence, whether of individuals, objects, spiritual states, or anything else. Empty things are seen as transcending existence and non-existence; such things simply merge.

The Heart Sutra advises that "form is emptiness, emptiness is form." Interpreting these words could take a lifetime, and we will not presume to begin a

### What's It Mean?

**Dualism** is the attempt to explain phenomena by means of opposite poles: good and evil, black and white, old and new, "I" and "other," God and creation, and so on.

*Duality* is any example of this way of seeing.

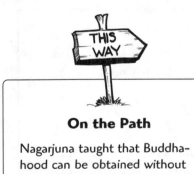

### On the Path

Nagarjuna taught that Buddhahood can be obtained without necessarily renouncing the world. According to this view, Nirvana is a reality that can be brought into existence in the present moment.

meaningful interpretation here. Consider, however, that emptiness is *not* different from the universe in which we live. All forms and processes, including true realization, are relative and interconnected. This fact for the Mahayana Buddhist, does not describe emptiness; it *is* emptiness.

## Mahayana in Black and White

The Mahayana division of Buddhism is divided into a large number of sects, each with a particular scriptural tradition. The many variations reflect centuries of teaching traditions and evolved points of emphasis. The variety can be daunting to the outsider, but in fact there is a great deal of overlap among the various holy texts. Even the Pali writings of Theravada Buddhism are accepted by most Mahayanists as inspired.

**On the Path**

Among the most widely studied of the (many) Mahayana scriptures are the Lotus Sutra, which emphasizes the grace of the eternal Buddha and counsels enduring faith; the Diamond Sutra, which arrests normal logical processes and focuses on the nature of emptiness; and the Heart Sutra, regarded by many Buddhists as the essence of true wisdom.

---

Five More Things You Should Know About Mahayana Buddhism

➤ The diverse Mahayana division of Buddhism differs from the Theravada school in placing a greater emphasis on the idea of grace—the assistance of the bohdisattvas.

➤ Many Mahayanists also accept the notion of Tathata, or Suchness, a governing principle of the universe that manifests itself as the pure Mind, or absolute and enduring Buddha-nature.

➤ Mahayana Buddhism places a special emphasis on the study of the *prajnaparamita* (perfection of wisdom) sutras.

➤ Among the many movements and sects of Mahayan Buddhism still active today include the nonacademic movements of Zen and the Pure Land sects, each of which is discussed in detail in the next chapter.

➤ One influential belief within Mahayana Buddhism is that the Buddha is eternal and absolute. This view regards the historical Buddha as a temporal form of the eternal Buddha-nature.

**Vajrayana** is a strand of Buddhism with ties to Hindu Tantric practice. It uses yogic discipline to transcend and redirect desire, the better to attain union with the Ultimate Reality.

# Tibetan Buddhism

Tibetan Buddhists revere the most important Mahayana teachers as bodhisattvas. They also incorporate an important tradition independent of both the Mahayana and Theravada traditions, *Vajrayana*.

Among the best-known Tibetan Buddhist scriptures is the *Bardo Thodol*, popularly known as the *Tibetan Book of the Dead*, an extraordinary book of instruction for the dying and for their spiritual guides. This complex work is neither easy to read, nor easy to forget once it has been read.

For many believers the *Bardo Thodol* is an essential companion to the principle expounded by the Buddha in the opening lines of the Dhammapada: "All that we are is the result of what we have thought; it is founded on our thoughts, it is made up of our thoughts."

## The Least You Need to Know

➤ After the Buddha's death, 18 formal schools or disciplines were acknowledged within Buddhism.

➤ Theravada Buddhism is the oldest surviving school of Buddhism, and the only one of the ancient grouping of 18 to endure.

➤ Mahayana Buddhism, which emphasizes compassion, service, and the notion of emptiness, has been an important trend in Buddhism since the first century B.C.E.

➤ Tibetan Buddhism incorporates both Mahayana traditions and Vajrayana, an esoteric strand of Buddhism associated with Hindu Tantric practice.

# Chapter 18

# Zen and Other Buddhist Schools Popular in the West

### In This Chapter

➤ A brief account of Zen's early history and development

➤ Various Zen approaches

➤ Other Buddhist schools

In this part of the book you learn about the history and development of Zen, one of the most notable and widely studied Buddhist schools in America. You also learn about other modern Buddhist schools.

## What Is the Sound of Zen Beginning?

The word "Zen" derives from the Sanskrit word *dhyana,* meaning meditation.

It's a little strange that the name of this much-analyzed sect of Buddhism has become a kind of catch-word for all that is elusive, vague, and baffling in Oriental thought. In fact, the derivation of the word "Zen" describes this school, and its outlook, perfectly. Zen's central tenet is not a particular rule, idea, or stated philosophy, but rather the personal practice of various forms of meditation.

In other words (a Zen student might ask), why bother with words?

Three Cool Things About Zen

> ➤ Explanations, scriptures, and dogma are viewed with deep suspicion in the Zen tradition.

> ➤ The direct personal experience of meditation—and *all* aspects of everyday life—is of paramount importance.

> ➤ Only through this personal commitment to actual, engaged *presence*, Zen students believe, can human delusion arising from greed, anger, and ignorance be overcome. Reciting dogma, instructions, or other people's conclusions just won't cut it.

**Bet You Didn't Know**

Zen is the Japanese name for this school. In China where it was founded, it's called "Chan." It is said that Zen was brought from India by a figure known as Bodhidharma ("Enlightened Tradition"). Because the Japanese term is most widely used in the west, we will use it in this chapter.

An American once asked Zen Master Suzuki Roshi to define the term "zazen" (sitting meditation). Rather than engage in a long-winded discussion of technique or terminology, the teacher answered by assuming the cross-legged meditation position on a nearby table and sitting quietly for half an hour!

Suzuki Roshi had given a perfect object lesson in "beginner's mind"—the state of openness and innocence that renders second-hand words and concepts obsolete.

# Bodhidharma Gets Things Started

Zen traces its origin to the legendary figure Bodhidharma of the Mahayana school of Buddhism. Bodhidharma is said to have arrived in China from India near the end of the fifth century C.E.

The earliest development of Bodhidharma's school is hard to trace. We know that he is said to have meditated for nine straight years in search of direct insight into the ways of enlightenment.

Eventually Bodhidharma took on the role of teacher to a group of disciples and passed his teachings on to a successor, Hui-k'o, known as the Second Patriarch. Under the Third Patriarch, Seng-ts'an, Zen came under the influence of Taoism, which emphasizes an open, noninterfering approach to the processes of nature.

Seng-ts'an observed:

> "*The Way is perfect like vast space, Where nothing is missing and nothing is in oversupply. Indeed, it is because of our choosing to accept or reject That we do not see the true nature of things.*"

## "Original Mind"

Bodhidharma's teaching lineage eventually extended to Hui-Neng, the Sixth Patriarch, who emphasized the importance of discovering one's own "original mind" and "true nature." These teachings have remained staples of Zen practice to this day.

In the eighth and ninth centuries C.E., Zen strengthened and developed its traditions of one-on-one instruction and direct experience of the enlightened way. While other schools of Buddhism were enduring a period of intense persecution in China, Zen continued to flourish—in part because of its lack of dependence on written texts, which could be (and often were) destroyed by those seeking to eradicate Buddhism.

Zen Buddhism survived because of its willingness to transcend standard forms, rituals, and written instructions. Today, it continues to teach practitioners to move beyond dependence on such trappings, even beyond dependence on standard forms of thought, into the direct experience of enlightened consciousness. This detached approach has allowed Zen to adapt well to social and cultural challenges over the centuries.

**On the Path**

Although Zen Buddhism is not the most popular Buddhist denomination in the West, it is among the most influential. Americans eager to explore new social and religious perspectives have been especially interested in Zen in the second half of the twentieth century.

**On the Path**

Bodhidharma is said to have described Zen as "*a special transmission outside of the scriptures. There was no need for dependence on words and letters; direct pointing to the real person; seeing into one's nature, which was identical with all reality, justified Buddha–life and led to attainment of Buddhahood.*"

## Two Schools

Two distinct approaches to Zen practice occurred in China. One focused on "sudden enlightenment" through such tools as *koans,* or anti-rational teaching riddles. The other school preferred to encourage its students to pursue zazen practice (cross-legged meditation) with no expectation of enlightenment, sudden or otherwise. This second school also rejected the method of the sudden enlightenment school, in which masters engaged in constant questioning—and occasionally even physical violence!

When Zen made its way to Japan, the "hard" and "soft" schools became known as the Rinzai and Soto schools, respectively. These two schools have profoundly influenced the development of Zen teaching, and are active to this day.

### What's It Mean?

A **koan** is a riddle that invites the student to evidence his or her ability to overcome barriers to enlightenment. "What is the sound of one hand clapping?" is a classic beginner's koan. One's ability to respond appropriately to a koan is a measure of spiritual progress.

# Next Stop: Japan

Although Zen eventually declined in China, it assumed a vigorous new life in Japan, especially among the medieval military class. As a result, it profoundly influenced the art, literature, and aesthetics of the country. The influences went both ways: The style of Zen with which most Westerners are familiar has a distinctly Japanese flavor.

### Bet You Didn't Know

Don't expect to find a lot of explanation in Zen training or practice. In this tradition, even the words of a revered teacher are suspect. Master Rinzai said, *"Rather than attaching yourselves to my words, it is better to calm down and seek nothing further. Do not cling to the past or long for the future. This is better than a pilgrimage of 10 years' duration."* Having broken Rinzai's own rule by quoting him, we now venture a second violation of Zen spirit by passing along an old and well-worn story.

Master Tung-shan was weighing some flax one day when a monk walked up and asked him, "What is Buddha-nature?" (Or in other words, "What is the nature of enlightenment?") Without hesitation, Tung-shan answered, "Three pounds of flax."

The moral: Committed Zen students strive to stay completely involved in the present moment, because that's the only place true enlightenment can ever be found!

Whatever culture it has occupied, Zen's first objective has always been to encourage direct personal experience on a moment-to-moment basis. Typically, this is accomplished (or at least attempted) by means of hours of solitary meditation under the guidance of a teacher. But periods outside of formal meditation, in the Zen model, are just as important as opportunities for direct experience and honest perception.

# Other Buddhist Sects

There are, of course, many other sects within Buddhism. These include the following:

## *The Pure Land School*

Pure Land Buddhists appeal to the grace of Buddha Amitabha (Amida), who, according to tradition, vowed, in the second century C.E. to save all sentient beings. This redemption, believers hold, is brought about by invoking Amitabha's name, and results in rebirth into the Western Paradise, a transcendent domain in which miraculous surroundings abound. From the Western Paradise, it is believed, entry to Nirvana is assured.

Pure Land Buddhism is an extremely influential devotional expression of Mahayana Buddhism, particularly in Japan.

Absolute reliance on the Buddha of Infinite Light is a central tenet of this expression of Buddhism, which enjoins believers to cultivate supreme and unwavering faith in the Buddha Amitabha.

From its earliest days, Pure Land Buddhism was notable for its occasional evangelical fervor, and for contrasting the bliss that awaited true believers with the torments of hell that were reserved for others. This doctrine, combined with the Pure Land Buddhists' rejection of human works as a means of spiritual salvation, has led this sect to be compared to Protestant Calvinism.

There are a number of branches within Pure Land Buddhism. Among the most notable is the Jodo Shinshu, the largest Buddhist denomination in Japan.

**Watch It!**

The point of Zen practice is not to become withdrawn or self-absorbed, but to discover the authentic self capable of participating in the world fully. Zen emphasizes not elite remoteness, but 100 percent involvement, with no distraction, in whatever one is doing. One American Zen school has adopted the slogan of a sneaker manufacturer: "Just do it."

**On the Path**

Believers within the various Pure Land schools pursue a spiritual path whose means of union with the Ultimate is an absolute reliance on the Buddha's grace. Individual exertion along paths of internal spiritual development are rejected as self-centered, or even insulting, to the Buddha Amitabha insofar as they reflect a lack of faith in his grace.

## Nichiren Buddhism

Nichiren Buddism (named after the Japanese Buddhist Nichiren, C.E.1222–1282) covers a number of different schools within Japanese Buddhism. Nichiren Buddhism's most notable expression in recent years has probably been the lay Buddhist movement known as Soka Gakkai, which claimed over a million Japanese adherents in 1993. Today, the various forms of Nichiren Buddhism play an important role in American Buddhist life, both in and out of the Japanese-American community.

# Celebrations

There are so many denominations and varying traditions within Buddhism that we can only touch on the most common here.

### On the Path

The Buddhist Churches of America, whose followers numbered 500,000 in 1993, is the most numerous American Buddhist denomination. It is an outgrowth of the Japanese Jodo Shinshu school.

## Nirvana Day

This is observed on February 15, the date on which the Buddha's passing is observed.

## Buddha Day

April 8 is the date on which the Buddha's birth is celebrated.

## Bodhi Day

Buddhists celebrate December 8 as the day on which Prince Gatauma took his place under the Bodhi Tree, vowing to remain there until he attained the supreme enlightenment.

---

### The Least You Need to Know

➤ Zen is one of the best known Buddhist schools in America.

➤ Zen Buddhism is rooted in direct experience and rejects scholarly abstractions.

➤ Other important contemporary Buddhist movements include the Pure Land and Nichiren sects.

➤ The three most important holidays in Buddhist tradition are Nirvana Day, Buddha Day, and Bodhi Day.

# Part 7

# Nature, Man, and Society in Asia

*In this section, you learn about three categories of Asian observance—Confucianism, Taoism, and Shinto—each of which has influenced millions.*

*All three schools challenge western assumptions about what is (and is not) "religious observance." Many westerners consider Confucianism, for example, to be a pragmatic philosophy, not a religion. Yet the sage Confucius has had a shaping spiritual and ethical influence on the Chinese people. Taoism is both a philosophy and a religious system, and also claims an impressive history of medical, literary, theatrical, and artistic influence. Shinto, the former state religion of Japan, shows how an adaptive religion can be both traditional in its faith to its ancient roots, and profoundly "secular" in any number of modern expressions!*

# Chapter 19

# Confucianism: Human Relations 101

Religion? Philosophy? Ethical system? Social tradition? Scholarly discipline?

Confucianism has been all of these things over the two and a half millennia of its existence. It endures today as a collection of diverse schools of thought closely associated with, and affected by, centuries of Chinese historical development. The school has seen its share of heady ascents and steep declines, but it has never faded completely from the scene.

Over its two and a half thousand years, Confucianism has periodically reinvented itself, introducing new strands of thought and reassessing and revising its practices. Yet, it continues to emphasize the harmonious way of life first expounded by the sage Confucius.

# Who Was He?

The name by which the supreme philosopher of ancient China is known in the West is a Latinized form of the Chinese phrase K'ung Fu-tse, which means "Master K'ung." For the purposes of this book, we'll use the name most familiar to English-speaking Westerners.

Confucius was largely self-taught. Interestingly, although his influence has been monumental and his teachings eventually resulted in a formal and imperial Confucian orthodoxy, no Chinese ruler ever wholeheartedly embraced Confucius's doctrines during his lifetime.

### Bet You Didn't Know

Confucius was born in 551 B.C.E. As an official in the state of Lu (today known as Shantung), he endeared himself to the public by advocating important reforms based on humane principles of administration. Deeply concerned about the dominant militarism of China, Confucius offered instruction for potential Chinese leaders to refine and stabilize the government according to principles of peace and equity.

Confucius was more interested in ethical and political matters than religious principles as such. The ideals of decorum and harmonious social interaction that he preached relied heavily on personal moral development and obedience to proper forms. He rejected any identification of himself as a sage, but this did not prevent a cult of honor and ritual sacrifice from arising around his name and image some centuries after his death.

Confucius has been called one of the most influential thinkers in human history.

# Five Interactions

Confucius's identification of five ethical relationships transformed Chinese thought and profoundly influenced social systems in China and other Asian nations for centuries.

Particular importance is usually attached to the relationship between parents and children.

These binding relationships are, within Confucian thought, founded upon and made possible by a compassionate, humane approach that incorporates a profound love. This broad principle requires only a single word for expression in Chinese: *jen*. Also essential to Confucianism is *li,* or seamlessly proper conduct between parties.

Jen expresses itself in *chung*, "faithfulness to oneself." But such faithfulness is not to be misunderstood as self-absorption. Confucianism depends upon attention to moral duties befitting a son or daughter (*hsiao*).

### What's It Mean?

**Jen** is the compassion and humanity arising from genuine love. **Li** is correct ritualistic and etiquette-based behavior between individuals.

---

*Six Relationships*

Parent and child

Ruler and minister

Government officials

Husband and wife

Older sibling and younger sibling

Friend and friend

---

# Opposition, Departure, Return

Confucius's reformist ideas won him the enmity of some powerful people in his home state. Eventually, he left Lu and pursued a mission he believed to be willed by Heaven. Although his disciples included some highly positioned people, Confucius himself never received the prestigious royal appointment he sought. It seems his outspoken approach with high-ranking members of the hierarchy may have doomed his dream of implementing his reforms.

Nevertheless, the accomplishments of Confucius were extraordinary. According to tradition, before his death in Lu in 479 B.C.E. he edited and compiled, with his followers, a number of vitally important texts. At the same time, he developed a body of teaching that is revered to this day in Asia and elsewhere in the world. His doctrines are considered to be reflected most authoritatively in the *Analects*.

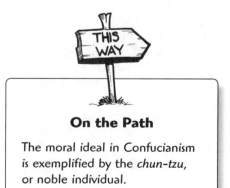

### On the Path

The moral ideal in Confucianism is exemplified by the *chun-tzu,* or noble individual.

## On the Path

Confucius's conduct-focused teachings often mirror important spiritual principles within other traditions. Where Christianity teaches, "Judge not, so that you will not be judged," Confucius observes, "The gentleman calls attention to the good points in others; he does not call attention to their defects. The small man does just the reverse of this." (*Analects* 12.16)

## What's It Mean?

*The Five Classics* are all believed to have originated well before Confucius's time. They are: the *Book of Changes (I Ching)*, the *Book of History (Shuh Ching)*, the *Book of Poetry (Shih Ching)*, the *Book of Rites (Li Chi)*, and the *Spring and Autumn Annals (Ch'un Chi)*, which chronicle major historical events.

# The *Analects*

The *Analects of Confucius (Lun Yu)* was not acknowledged as a classic until the second century C.E. The work records the deeds and sayings of "Master K'ung"—although this work was compiled not by Confucius himself, but by his later followers.

The bulk of the work consists of sayings and remembrances assembled not long after the death of the sage. The teachings of Confucius reflected in the *Analects* are straightforward and direct: If people pursue courtesy, correct form and etiquette, reverence, and humane benevolence within each of the five basic human relationships, harmony will exist at every level of society.

Although every individual within the social hierarchy must act righteously, in Confucian thought special emphasis is always laid on the virtuous conduct of the ruler of a state, whose deeds serve as moral patterns that affect the entire nation.

Confucius saw the family structure as the environment in which the virtues of a lifetime could be developed, virtues that would eventually benefit society as a whole. The teachings set out in the *Analects* view social hierarchy and correct action within it as necessities, a kind of extension of the family structure.

This emphasis on the family structure is not, however, an endorsement of rigid social roles. Rather, it sees the family as a series of constantly shifting relationships; one must be a child, for example, before one becomes a parent. Each of life's roles must be accompanied by appropriate discipline, regard for form, and ethical commitment.

# Other Literary Stuff

Confucius lived during a time of tremendous philosophical activity in China. During this time he and his followers oversaw the development and formalization of a number of important writings. These books are traditionally divided into two groups: the Five Classics and the Four Books.

Confucius seemed to have felt particular respect for the ancient *Book of Changes*, or *I Ching*. As an old man he is said to have remarked that if he were to be granted 50 more years of life, he would devote them to the study of this book and thereby escape significant error.

## Ch-Ch-Ch-Changes

In the East, the *I Ching* is regarded as the first of the Five Classics. It is also the most popular of all the Confucian classics in the West.

People sometimes forget that this remarkable book was not "written" by Confucius. It was timeless when he first encountered it; its earliest layer of text is now at least three thousand years old. Commentaries and appendices attributed to Confucius and members of his school would eventually be incorporated into the work.

The *I Ching* is a manual of divination for those seeking guidance. Whatever unfolding event or circumstance the reader wishes to explore, the *I Ching* has an answer. Advice is offered by means of 64 numbered six-line figures, known as hexagrams. The lines may be broken or solid; broken lines symbolize the universal yin (female or yielding) force, while solid ones reflect the universal yang (male or active) force.

### What's It Mean?

The **Four Books** incorporate the works of Confucius and Mencius (372–289 B.C.E.), as well as the commentaries of their followers. They are considered by many to be the fundamental teachings of early Confucianism.

They include the *Analects* (*Lun Yu*), the *Great Learning* (*Ta Hsueh*), *The Doctrine of the Mean* (*Chung Yung*), and the *Book of Mencius* (*Meng-tzu*). Together with the Five Classics, the Four Books make up the basic texts of Confucianism.

### On the Path

Within Chinese cosmology, *yin* and *yang* are the polar aspects of the primal energy. Interaction between these female and male, dark and light, passive and active principles is seen as a basic and observable element of cosmic development and evolution. Hexagrams within the *I Ching*, six-line figures developed by means of (seemingly) random patterns initiated by the reader, are thought to be symbolic of interactions between the yin and yang principles in the situation under examination.

To the sincere seeker, the *I Ching* is held to offer insights into the workings of any event or phenomenon. Come to the book with a question, and you will develop a hexagram that answers it. Talk about bang for your scriptural buck!

Hexagram 30 (Fire) is a good example of how this *I Ching* process works. With this hexagram the *I Ching* advises that "It will be advantageous to be firm and correct, and thus there will be free course and success. Let the subject nurture a docility like that of a cow, and there will be good fortune." A modern questioner might toss coins to develop the hexagram, perhaps in search of an answer to the question, "Should I ask my boss for a raise?"

*Hexagram 30 (Fire), named after the trigram, or three-line pattern, that appears in both the upper and lower positions. (Notice that the top three lines are, in this hexagram, identical to the bottom three.)*

## "Does It, You Know ... Work?"

Whether the book "really predicts the future" or not, the *I Ching* has passionate adherents in both the East and the West. (The psychiatrist Carl Jung was a notable devotee.) Many supremely skeptical Westerners, in fact, find in the *I Ching* a pragmatic and accessible (if occasionally vague) source of wisdom. Its profound Confucian study and analysis can be an excellent starting place for reflecting on the elemental forces affecting human relationships.

Perhaps that is why the *Book of Changes* has been applied longer, more consistently, and more thoroughly than almost any other collection of religious scriptures.

# After the Master

After the death of Confucius, his philosophy branched into two schools. One, led by Mencius, held that human intuition is inherently good and should serve as a guide to action and choice.

Mencius believed in working toward a world that would enable the good of the majority to be realized. In fact, he has often been recognized as an early advocate of democracy.

Another school within Confucianism was that of Hsun-tzu (312–230 B.C.E.), who argued that people are born with innately evil natures and require ritual (*li*) in order to cultivate true virtue. Hsun-tzu regarded ritual as worthy in and of itself, teaching that established codes of behavior were to be observed for their own sake.

Hsun-tzu placed a heavy emphasis on the observance of ceremonial rites and the practice of civilized arts such as music. It is one's birthright, he taught, to cultivate good in oneself, and to maintain this goodness, one must be ever vigilant and work against one's own (destructive) nature. He opposed what he viewed as the rarefied idealism of Mencius.

## Confucianism Tops the Charts

Before the Han Dynasty (206 B.C.E.–220 C.E.), Confucianist thought experienced a brief but precipitous decline. During the Han period, however, it experienced a powerful revival.

The works associated with Confucius were canonized and once again taught by scholars in the national academies. Candidates for government positions would be appointed based on their knowledge of the classic literature. Confucianism emerged as the dominant intellectual force in China.

After the Han dynasty, however, China fell into chaos. During this period of uncertainty, Buddhism and Taoism (see the next chapter) emerged as counterparts to Confucian thought. When stability was restored during the Tang dynasty (C.E. 618–906), high-level bureaucrats nurtured the teachings of Confucianism once again and secured its position as the official orthodoxy of the state.

**On the Path**

Mencius is considered to be the author of the *Meng-tzu*, one of the Four Books of orthodox Confucianism. In it he argued that human nature is intrinsically good, and that preexisting elements within the human character could, with practice and attentive nurturing, blossom into the mature virtues of benevolence, rightness, propriety, and wisdom.

**On the Path**

Confucianism's vigorous emphasis on the formation of the proper society and the establishment of ethical standards stands in stark contrast to the open, formless, impersonal, and effortless Taoist path (see the next chapter). Interestingly, however, the two schools are seen as complementary. Rather than serving as rival philosophies, the two systems are generally regarded as balancing and amplifying one another.

Over the centuries, Confucianism served as a platform for new debates and embraced new schools of thought. In the twelfth century C.E., the renowned thinker Chu Hsi advanced the notion that one's moral development, when carried out in harmony with transitions in the exterior world, permits one to "form one body with all things." Chu was the most notable of several important figures in the Confucianist renaissance that has become known as Neo-Confucianism—a period that is considered to have extended to the end of the Ch'ing dynasty in 1911, some 800 years later!

Neo-Confucianists incorporated ideas from Buddhism (especially Zen Buddhism) and Taoism to formulate a system of metaphysics—explanations for ultimate questions of existence. Previously, Confucianism had not addressed such issues.

# New Confucianism

With the collapse of the Chinese monarchy in the early decades of the twentieth century, Confucianism was increasingly regarded as decadent and reactionary. It was reinvigorated in the modern era by the efforts of Hsiung Shih-li (1885–1968), regarded as the inspiration for the New Confucianism. This movement sought to make the Confucianist tradition a model for the development of a harmonious and tolerant world civilization.

# The Changing, Changeless Way of Confucius

Twenty-five hundred years later, what is the way of Confucius?

It's still hard to describe the school founded by "Master K'ung" concretely. Is it a religion or not? Although late nineteenth-century attempts to have the philosophy acknowledged as the official state religion of China were unsuccessful, there is an important and enduring religious dimension to this tradition.

Confucianism, in all its many manifestations and through all its varying accents, has contributed in an important and distinctive way to the moral and spiritual traditions of untold millions of people. Its emphasis on humaneness, tolerance, harmony, and duty are in keeping with the world's great spiritual teachings.

The continuous evolution and development of this body of teachings has never altered its central and abiding concern: the encouragement of proper relations between human beings. Relationships are seen as most perfect when they are motivated by love and an understanding of reciprocity very similar in nature to the familiar principle, "Do unto others as you would have them do unto you."

Despite its many formulations and variations over the centuries, the fundamental ideas of Confucianism remain unshakable guiding forces.

Among the most important of these is that correct conduct arises, not through external force, but as a result of virtues developed internally through the observation of laudable models of behavior.

After Confucius's death, the master's emphasis on *jen*, or humane love, was eloquently taken up by Mencius, who continued the Master's work when he wrote:

> "All things are within me, and on self-examination, I find no greater joy than to be true to myself. We should do our best to treat others as we wish to be treated. Nothing is more appropriate than to seek after goodness." (*Meng-tzu*, 7a:4)

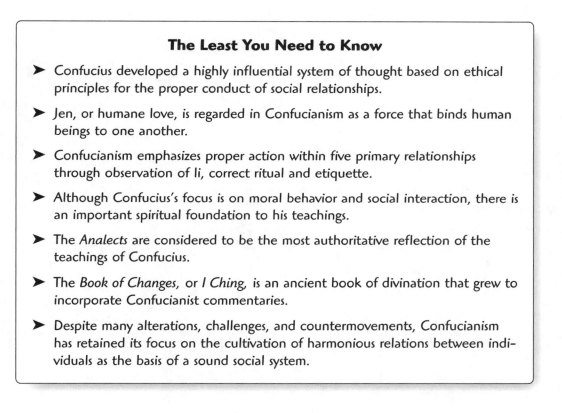

### The Least You Need to Know

➤ Confucius developed a highly influential system of thought based on ethical principles for the proper conduct of social relationships.

➤ Jen, or humane love, is regarded in Confucianism as a force that binds human beings to one another.

➤ Confucianism emphasizes proper action within five primary relationships through observation of li, correct ritual and etiquette.

➤ Although Confucius's focus is on moral behavior and social interaction, there is an important spiritual foundation to his teachings.

➤ The *Analects* are considered to be the most authoritative reflection of the teachings of Confucius.

➤ The *Book of Changes*, or *I Ching*, is an ancient book of divination that grew to incorporate Confucianist commentaries.

➤ Despite many alterations, challenges, and countermovements, Confucianism has retained its focus on the cultivation of harmonious relations between individuals as the basis of a sound social system.

# Chapter 20

# Taoism: The Effortless Path

## In This Chapter

➤ Learn about Taoism's complementary relationship with Confucianism

➤ Learn about the fundamental ideas of Taoism

➤ Try (like the rest of us) to establish a working definition of "the Tao"

➤ Find out why it caught on

In this part of the book, you learn about the influential religious and philosophical system known as Taoism, a tradition whose name, like its guiding force, defies complete explanation. Its practitioners would maintain that this inexpressibility is completely appropriate.

In recent years, Taoism, like Buddhism (another hard-to-put-into-words belief system), has given rise to a wave of articles, books, manuals, and essays in the West. To find out what all the fascination and fuss is about, read on!

## "Not to Be Impolite, But ..."

Taoism has a long and rich history that criss-crosses that of Confucianism. With Confucianism, it has served as a fundamental component of Asian spiritual and philosophical life for centuries. The fundamental doctrines of Taoism may be said to reflect a principle of action based on the natural world.

Unlike Confucianism, which advocates conformity and proper behavior within an ideal social system, Taoism illuminates a receptive approach to life.

The Taoist viewpoint sounds something like this: The individual should seek the truth by means of a patient, accepting focus on natural patterns and influences worthy of emulation.

Not surprisingly, the Confucian emphasis on social hierarchy and scrupulously correct etiquette within that framework is largely rejected by Taoism. It would be a mistake, however, to view Taoism simply as a critique of Confucian thought. The teachings of this school reflect spiritual principles of great antiquity, and their expression in Taoism is part of an ongoing process of growth, development, and interaction with a wide variety of beliefs.

### Watch It!

Although rigid Confucians may sometimes regard it as such, Taoism is not a subversive or anti-social system of thought. It does not hold social forms to be meaningless or without merit. It simply believes that conscious efforts to control people and events are counterproductive.

### Watch It!

The differences between Taoism and Confucianism have often been exaggerated. There are similarities; for example, both Confucianism and Taoism accept a cosmology embodied in the concept of yin and yang.

## Nature: Close to the Ground

The ideal Taoist lifestyle is that of the farmer, seeking complete harmony with the patterns of nature. If the seeker can live openly and without artifice, in touch with nature's rhythms, his or her day-to-day experience will lead directly to the power of the Tao.

Taoism elevates the principles of non-control and non-interference. To pursue the Tao means to abandon all restless struggling, no matter what form it may take.

Under Taoism, the ideal personal situation, attainable only through prolonged observation and meditation, is one of utter simplicity, profound faith in natural processes, and true transcendence of short-sighted craving and grasping.

## Words: The Tao Te Ching

The ancient Chinese religious and philosophical system known as Taoism derives from the *Tao Te Ching*, ascribed to the sage Lao-Tzu (d. 520? B.C.E.). The book is one of the most moving and sublime achievements of Chinese culture.

The writings of another brilliant philosopher, Chuang-Tzu (c. 369–c. 286 B.C.E.), have also become very important in Taoist practice. This challenging (and occasionally nonsensical) collection of satirical parables and allegories shines a light on the relative nature of all "rational" processes and assumptions. Today it is second in influence only to the *Tao Te Ching* in Taoist practice.

But the central text of Taoism has always been the *Tao Te Ching*. It has been translated into English in countless editions, and with the *I Ching*, is one of the most influential sacred Asian texts read in the West.

> *Taoism on the Neglected Art of Keeping It Simple*
>
> As to dwelling, live near the ground.
>
> As to thinking, hold to that which is simple.
>
> As to conflict, pursue fairness and generosity.
>
> As to governance, do not attempt to control.
>
> As to work, do that which you like doing.
>
> As to family life, be fully present.
>
> —*Tao Te Ching*

**On the Path**

Taoism's emphasis on spontaneity and self-reliance finds important parallels in Buddhism and in many other religious traditions, as well. Jesus' saying that only those who become as little children may enter the kingdom of heaven catches much of the guiding spirit of Taoism.

Brevity is the soul of wit—and of the *Tao Te Ching!* The book is one of the world's shortest primary religious texts. The entire work is less than five thousand words long. In its spare way, it describes a view of the world in which man, heaven, and earth function as interdependent entities.

The *Tao Te Ching* addresses matters of culture, emotion, nature, right action, language, and mysticism through reflections on the Tao. The term "Tao" has led scholars and translators to develop many wandering, scholarly explanations. An adequate one-word rendering of "Tao" into English remains out of reach.

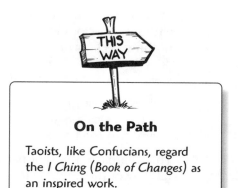

**On the Path**

Taoists, like Confucians, regard the *I Ching (Book of Changes)* as an inspired work.

# Wow: The Tao!

So, what *is* the Tao? We might as well ask: What is God?

Literally, *Tao* means "path" or "way." All the same, the scriptures of this faith advise that the "eternal Tao" cannot actually be named. We'll take a calculated risk, though, and follow the lead of other commentators by describing the Tao as a sublime

"Natural Order"—one marked by the effortless alternation of cycles (i.e., night and day, growth and decline) and an unconstrained, pervasive creativity that transcends impermanent expression. The Tao may best be described as "the way the universe works."

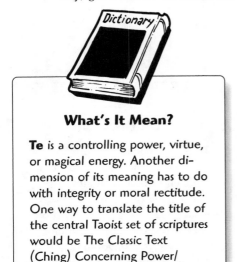

**What's It Mean?**

**Te** is a controlling power, virtue, or magical energy. Another dimension of its meaning has to do with integrity or moral rectitude. One way to translate the title of the central Taoist set of scriptures would be The Classic Text (Ching) Concerning Power/Integrity (Te) and the Way (Tao).

One thing is certain: The Tao is "sought" only through the most yielding approach. To reach unity with it, one must put aside all that is artificial, strained, and unnatural. Instead, one must seek to develop a personal code from the naturally arising and spontaneous impulses of one's own true nature. Such a code, Taoists believe, transcends narrow, externally imposed teachings and doctrines.

Emptiness is essential to Taoist thought. The enlightened person is thought to be like a hollow reed or bamboo shoot: empty within, upright and resolute without.

Taoists teach inaction, but this idea must not be misunderstood. True inaction, in the Taoist sense, is the most efficient possible action, the most spontaneous possible action, and the most creative possible action.

Maintaining contact with the Tao means allowing activity to spring spontaneously, without conscious effort, from a well of nothingness accessible to all. This "doing nothing" is known as *wu-wei*. A Taoist who acts in accordance with this principle does not pursue a life of sloth or laziness, but one in which the least possible effort yields the most effective and productive outcome.

A classic Taoist illustration of effortless action involves water, which naturally occupies the lowest possible position, but nevertheless exerts sufficient force over time to wear down the hardest stone.

This approach, the Taoists maintain, enables the believer to connect with the elemental flow of the universe itself.

Such unity with the mystical is known as *te,* a force that makes possible true liberation. It is taught that this power can allow the believer to overcome even death itself.

# Who Founded Taoism?

Lao-Tzu, author of the *Tao Te Ching*, may have been a committee, rather than a single individual.

Traditionally, he has been described as a sage living in the same period as Confucius—slightly older, we are told—who passed his teachings along to a border guard. The guard is said to have faithfully transcribed the teachings into the book with which centuries of spiritual seekers have become familiar.

There's a problem with this account, however. Confucius is known to have lived in the sixth century B.C.E., and internal evidence within the text of the *Tao Te Ching* points to a later compilation—possibly formalized around the fourth century B.C.E.

### Bet You Didn't Know

The *Tao Te Ching*, the central text of Taoism, is a brief and immensely influential book that uses poetic (or, if you prefer, cryptic and elusive) language to point out the futility of struggling against universal processes. It advocates instead a course of submission, flexibility, and profound self-awareness.

To believe one can somehow overcome or outwit the waxing, waning, creative natural order is held to be a great error. It is far more advisable, a Taoist would argue, to find a way to act in accordance with the unknowable, unnamable force that underlies all creation and is visible in every manifestation of it.

Western observers have tended to emphasize Taoism's serene and inscrutable side. The truth is, over the centuries, the system has expressed itself directly and pragmatically in political, military, mythological, artistic, medical, and scientific areas. Even certain doctrinal conflicts with Confucianism have yielded when the time was regarded as appropriate. The hallmarks of Taoism are flexibility and a vision of an inspired, continually reinvigorating, self-revealing path by the person of integrity.

## Old Voices

Today, scholars believe that the school we call Taoism arose from ancient beliefs and practices having to do with nature worship and predicting the future. Although scholarly debate continues, most regard Taoism's central scriptures as a collection of wisdom from Chinese sages over the centuries.

The person or persons who edited the *Tao Te Ching* and consolidated the various ancient teachings was probably responsible for giving Taoism the form we know today.

## New Voices

The Taoist tradition can be seen as a counterpart to Confucianism, but it also embraces features of Mahayana Buddhism. Today, Taoism is an independent system that incorporates the following:

➤ The rejection of calculated, restless, goal-oriented effort.

➤ Trust in the benefits of effortless, spontaneous action in accordance with the requirements of the time.

➤ Belief that the Tao manifests itself everywhere and in all situations.

➤ An understanding of the Tao as eternally new, fundamentally creative, and beyond literal expression.

➤ Emphasis on the importance of balance, especially on that which is communicated between the human realm, heaven, and earth.

Whether or not a single individual named Lao-Tzu articulated the principles of Taoism, these timeless teachings inspired one of the world's great spiritual traditions. If Lao-Tzu didn't actually exist, he may as well have.

### On the Path

Taoism, widely known for its simplicity and conciseness, has its complex face as well. Popular influences have created an elaborate pantheon of hellish and heavenly spirits, but Taoist priests have always understood these as expressions of the singular Tao.

## Back and Forth with Buddhism

Influenced as it was by Mahayana Buddhism, Taoism in turn played an important role in the development of the well-known school of Buddhism that Westerners know as Zen.

Taoists believe that the spontaneous, creative Tao can be seen everywhere. It renews itself continually and can never be exhausted. Practitioners who remain still and silent are held to be capable of discerning its directions, and thus to act in accordance with those promptings without preconception and in full possession of their true selves.

Some formulation of all of these beliefs came to be reflected within Zen Buddhism.

# How Has Taoism Expressed Itself?

Let us not try to count the ways—because it's pretty complicated.

Detailing the "expressions" of Taoism can be elusive, because it's served as an acceptable channel for innumerable principles and movements. It has existed on many levels, too, often with rituals that "mean" one thing to its lay believers and perhaps something broader to its priests and devotees. In keeping with its own teachings, Taoism has been quite flexible in adapting to times and circumstances.

## The Believers

Instead of asking what Taoism looks like in practice, we might ask whom it appeals to. Throughout history, those who have turned from worldly exploits as shallow and unrewarding, those who have become disillusioned with social agitation or military conquest, and those who have tired of the daily struggles over rank and position—have turned to Taoist teachings. In the faith, they have often discovered meaning within the unfolding dance of nature—and perhaps come closer to learning how best to perform their own roles within that dance.

## The Outside World

By its very nature, Taoism generally refrains from trying to influence political or social institutions. In this way it stands as a polar opposite to Confucianism. In fact, many of the ethical and social concerns of Confucian thought were dismissed by early Taoists as excessive, restless strivings out of step with the naturally unfolding harmonies of the universe.

This is not to say that there has never been any attempt to implement a Taoist political philosophy; there has been. The political side of Taoism holds that the best model for government is the undisturbed harmony of nature. From this it is argued that the duty of the ruler is to rule according to as few restrictions and directions as possible. It is sufficient simply to guide the populace away from want and turmoil.

# It Caught On!

Taoist thought and practice eventually met with widespread acceptance in Chinese society as a whole, in large measure because of interest in its relevance to medicine. One of its basic principles was the promise of eternal physical life.

## What Was That About Immortality?

For many Chinese, Taoism's nature-based teaching gave rise to a profound reverence for natural processes and a desire to retreat to the natural world. At the same time, Taoism encouraged a powerful embrace of life itself, expressed in health, long life, and even immortality. Thus, knowledge concerning the Tao was held to be a pathway to superior physical health and even the transcendence of death.

For centuries, Taoism has been associated with noninvasive herbal remedies, regular breathing techniques, and deep concentration as methods of promoting longevity and reducing stress. The great advances the Taoists brought to the medical arts in China have had much to do with the enduring popularity of the faith.

### On the Path

Interest in alchemy as a means of attaining the Taoist goal of long (or even eternal) physical life led to the development of many curatives and elixirs. A great many of these are still widely employed in Chinese medicine today.

## What Was That About Release?

Another reason for the enduring popularity of Taoism is its historical role as an ancient and reliable form of release (and, often, escape) from the cycle of historical processes and bitter political conflicts.

Taoism has served for centuries as a platform for individual spiritual growth—and as a respite from important, but perhaps ultimately unresolveable, questions about social structures. Taoism's emphasis on integrity, authenticity, and relaxed, attentive engagement with the world may be the best expression of "traditionalism" within this faith.

---

### The Least You Need to Know

➤ Taoism and Confucianism form complementary systems of thought.

➤ Taoism derives from the book *Tao Te Ching,* ascribed to the sage Lao-Tzu, but believed by scholars to be a compilation of many ancient sources.

➤ The fundamental doctrines of Taoism reflect a principle of action modeled on the natural world.

➤ Taoism elevates principles of noncontrol and noninterference to high importance.

➤ The Tao may best be described as "the way the universe works."

➤ True inaction, in the Taoist sense, is the most efficient possible action, the most spontaneous possible action, and the most creative possible action.

# Chapter 21

# Shinto: Harmony and Clarity

---

### In This Chapter

➤ Learn about the history and development of Shinto

➤ Find out about the many forms taken by kami (spirits)

➤ Discover how this adaptable faith has become a vital part of the Japanese cultural heritage

---

In this chapter, you find out about the history, development, and practices of Shinto, a native Japanese religious tradition that can also be found in the many countries in which sizable Japanese communities exist.

## Shinto: The Basics

Shinto is the indigenous nature-focused religion of Japan. It incorporates a number of ancient Japanese mythological rites and has undergone many formulations and structural revisions over the centuries. It is related to the religions of Manchuria, Korea, and the region today known as Siberia.

In its earliest known form, Shinto was without name, text, or dogma. Today, Shinto places a greater emphasis on tradition and ceremonial custom than on formal religious or metaphysical doctrines. In place of rigid intellectual structures, Shinto emphasizes the harmony of natural beauty and a clear, often distinctly poetic, appreciation of perceived reality.

## Bet You Didn't Know

Shinto is one of the world's oldest religions; its origins extend into the far reaches of pre-history. Formal institutionalization of many of its forms did not occur until the middle of the first millennium B.C.E., when it was considered necessary to distinguish native Japanese forms from Chinese religious influences.

Eventually, diverse mythological and ritualistic elements were combined into a single accepted creation account. Although there is no deity regarded as supreme over all kami, the sun goddess Amaterasu is accorded a high rank. Within Shinto, the emperor of Japan (whose temporal power has undergone many fluctuations over the centuries) is regarded as a direct descendant of Amaterasu.

First and foremost, Shinto is a form of nature worship; it took shape around the reverence of kami, or divine spirits—manifested and recognized in natural forces, objects, powerful individuals, and other entities. Today, Shinto continues to elevate established tradition and reverence over formal theological questions.

## What's It Mean?

The word **Shinto** is a Chinese transliteration of a phrase created in the late sixth century C.E. to distinguish native religion from others that had become widely accepted in Japan. The corresponding Japanese term, *kami-no-michi,* is commonly translated as "The Way of the Gods," or "The Way of Those Above."

Shinto's many rituals celebrate purity, clarity, and contact with the diverse forces of nature.

Essential to the Shinto faith is the word *kami,* which describes something possessing a power that an individual believer does not.

The word may be used to identify something that is physical, animate, and familiar (an animal or a person), spiritual (a ghost or spirit), or inanimate (rock formation or a personal computer). Believe it or not, the term kami, as applied to your Macintosh, does in fact carry a certain religious significance.

Contemporary Shinto observance reflects historical interactions with Buddhism and Confucianism. However, early forms of Shinto preceded the introduction of these faiths to Japan, perhaps by many centuries.

Shinto has historically promoted rituals that were closely linked to the seasons: to planting and harvest patterns—for instance, to the observance of the new year, and to times of ceremonial purification. For all the influence exerted upon it by other faiths, Shinto has retained its unique focus on personified natural forces.

# Two Big Dates

In modern times, Shinto has undergone two major periods of abrupt change. Social forces shaped the religion at two key points, one in the nineteenth century and one in the twentieth.

## 1868: Drawing the Line

The intertwining of Shinto with other forms (particularly Buddhism) eventually gave rise to a counter-reaction that tried to reestablish Shinto as a separate and distinctly Japanese religious form. (Catholicism, introduced by Jesuit missionaries in the sixteenth and seventeenth centuries, also experienced this "counter-reaction.")

Beginning in the 1700s, Shinto devotees undertook an energetic campaign to identify, distinguish, and reawaken old practices within their faith. This effort reached its full expression after the Meiji Restoration of 1868, when Shinto rites were formally separated from Buddhist practices.

Shinto's emergence as an important and truly independent religious form is often traced to political events of 1868 and the years that followed. During the second half of the nineteenth century and the first 45 years of the twentieth, the Shinto religion served as a vehicle for Japanese nationalism. Elements within the society strongly encouraged the use of the ancient mythological elements to venerate the emperor, the state, and, eventually, an aggressive military policy.

**Watch It!**

The common English translation of the word *kami* is "god," but don't let it mislead you. Kami has certainly been used in Shinto practice to describe supernatural beings, but not in the Western sense of an omnipotent God. A better translation may be "spirit" or "one residing above."

**On the Path**

Although Shinto priests continued to observe ancient customs of ritual purification and abstinence, the indigenous Japanese faith was practiced in (literally) close quarters with Buddhism for much of the nation's history. It was common, for instance, for Buddhist practices to extend into Shinto shrines, many of which were built adjacent to Buddhist temples and vice versa.

## 1945: A New Direction

After World War II, Shinto formally disclaimed its direct ties to the state. Under the direction of the occupying Allies, a number of dramatic reforms were enacted. The provision of public funds to maintain shrines was forbidden, and in 1946 Emperor Hirohito explicitly renounced his claim to divinity.

These changes in structure and emphasis were certainly not the first to be associated with Shinto. Although the faith now operates as one of a number of coequal religious forms in Japan, its vibrancy and ritualistic tradition are as important as ever to the cultural and religious heritage of the nation. The post-1945 period has been a productive and important one for Shinto, which continues to thrive in Japan and in other countries where Japanese have formed large communities.

### On the Path

Following the overthrow of military rule under the shogun, the Meiji Restoration of 1868 transferred political power to the Emperor. This movement also led to the promotion of Shinto, with its emphasis on the divine nature of the Emperor, as the official, state-sponsored religion of Japan.

## Day by Day

Shinto has become completely assimilated into day-to-day Japanese custom and tradition. Its rituals are accepted on so many levels as to be nearly indistinguishable from "everyday life." A new construction project, for instance, is unlikely to begin without a formal offering and ritual prayer ceremony overseen by a Shinto officiant at the site.

## In the Shrine

Shinto ritual embraces much more than religious practice conducted in shrines, but many of the most important events of the faith take place within these buildings. Shinto shrines are made entirely of wood and are generally situated near sacred trees and flowing water.

When a visitor enters a Shinto shrine through the *tori*, he or she is regarded as having left the world of finite things and entered the realm of the infinite and immeasurable, where the powerful kami may be invoked for the purpose of the ceremony at hand. Although many kami may be honored after one passes through the tori, in each shrine, one kami in particular is specially venerated.

### On the Path

In the second half of the twentieth century, new Shinto sects that explicitly emphasize the importance of brotherhood, world peace, and harmonious relations among nations have arisen.

# The Heart of Shinto

Shinto practice nourishes local traditions and promotes an awareness of kami and the natural world. It has more to do with traditions and beliefs than dogma or morality. As one of Japan's grounding institutions, Shinto has contributed to the extraordinary fusion of ancient tradition and cutting-edge, technologically influenced life in contemporary Japan.

## *Anything Missing?*

To an outsider, Shinto is perhaps most fascinating for what it doesn't have. Some things noticeably absent within the Shinto faith are:

➤ A founder. (Like Hinduism, Shinto claims no individual originator.)

➤ Written scriptures. The closest Shinto comes to these is the mythological history known as *kojiki*, or "documents of ancient matters," completed in C.E. 712 These writings deal with the ancient "age of the spirits," as well as court proceedings, but they are not revered in the way that inspired writings are in other faiths.

➤ Exclusionary patterns of worship. Believers may practice Shinto in combination with other faiths. Most Japanese follow both Buddhism and Shinto.

➤ Rigid dogma about the nature or form of that which is worshiped. No requirement is laid on any Shinto practitioner regarding his or her belief in specific kami.

➤ Strict formal doctrines or bodies of religious law. Beyond a few important "affirmations," the beliefs of this system are basically open-ended, not seen as conflicting with other faiths.

**What's It Mean?**

A **kami-dana** is a Shelf of the Spirits in the home of a Shinto believer, a miniature depiction of the holy central section of a shrine. In its center is a mirror that allows kami a means of entry and exit.

**On the Path**

Festivals honoring kami are central to Shinto practice. Important festivals include February 11 (National Founding Day in Japan), those honoring locally recognized kami, and the first days of each season. (Spring and fall festivals are particularly important.)

## On the Path

The doctrine of *yorozu-yomi*, or flexibility, allows Shinto to be adapted easily to the lives of many people. Under this principle, it is accepted that there are many kami—kami for every purpose, taking any number of forms. Kami may also be worshipped in any physical location, according to one's taste and inclination.

# Divine Power

Natural events are considered to be manifestations of heavenly energy within Shinto. Reasoning and dogma are regarded as unnecessary in the face of such forces; only the blessings of the kami are to be sought when one wishes to influence the course of natural forces and events.

Accordingly, Shinto places heavy emphasis on reverence toward nature; tradition, family, and ritual; and tranquility, individual ritual purity, and cleanliness.

This last point deserves a closer look. In the West we have the saying that "cleanliness is next to godliness," but the Japanese conception may be closer to "cleanliness is not distinct from godliness." Since the spirits are regarded as holding disorder and slovenliness in high disdain, a deep concern with bathing, personal cleanliness, and order takes on great importance in Shinto.

---

Core Beliefs

Shinto employs the word "affirmations" in talking about fundamental beliefs. The Japanese term carries the connotation of "things we agree are good." There are four affirmations in Shinto:

1. *The affirmation of family and tradition.* Shinto reveres the major life events, especially rites of birth and marriage. Since traditions are passed on generation by generation, Shinto places extraordinary importance on the central family unit.

2. *The affirmation of reverence toward nature.* The Japanese have a history of respect for physical beauty, perhaps because they live in one of the most beautiful parts of the world. Closeness to nature is a sacred component of Shinto devotion.

3. *The affirmation of physical cleanliness.* Shinto requires not merely symbolic or ritual cleanliness, but the real thing. One must be absolutely clean when one encounters the spirits, and so must one's surroundings!

4. *The affirmation of matsuri, or festivals held in honor of one or more kami.* Matsuri represents a chance for people to congregate, socialize, and honor the particular spirit or spirits associated with the festival.

# A Binding Force

Since its earliest days as a nation, Japan has employed the adaptable forms and practices of Shinto to promote a deep respect for nature and for life-affirming custom, continuity, and tradition. For centuries, in addition to reinforcing notions of sincerity, purity, and cleanliness, Shinto has celebrated divine forces and influence in a distinctively Japanese way.

Today Shinto continues to exert a powerful influence on the Japanese people, often in concert with other traditions. Its supreme adaptability and its avoidance of dogma allow it to flourish in a modern setting, where it can continue to stress the enduring harmony of nature and its relationship to daily life.

---

### The Least You Need to Know

➤ Shinto is the indigenous religion of Japan; its roots are prehistoric.

➤ Shinto is a form of nature worship.

➤ Preeminent among the innumerable Shinto kami, or spirits, is Amaterasu, the sun goddess, regarded as the source of the dynastic line of Japanese emperors.

➤ Shinto does not promote a system of dogma or a moral code.

➤ Ritual and tradition are essential to Shinto, as they are to all of Japanese culture.

➤ The four "affirmations"—tradition and family, love for nature, physical cleanliness, and matsuri (festivals honoring the spirits)—guide Shinto practice.

➤ Over the centuries, Shinto rites have become assimilated at a deep level in Japanese life.

---

# Part 8

# Old Paths, New Paths

*So far you've read about religions with quite large followings. A religion doesn't have to attract tens of millions of followers to exert a powerful influence on the lives of those who subscribe to it.*

*In this section, you learn about ancient patterns of worship that have evolved in indigenous settings; about other ancient patterns that have been revived or adapted in modern contexts; and about some of the new religious forms that have left their mark on the American scene over the past century.*

*You'll also find out how the religious traditions you've been studying answer some of the most important human questions. Don't be surprised if you discover some common ground in the process!*

# Ancient Creeds

Five religions—Judaism, Christianity, Hinduism, Islam, and Buddhism—are the primary focus of religious observance for the majority of the occupants of this planet. But it was not always so. As impossible to ignore as this grouping of five faiths is, another five traditions are worthy of attention as precursor religions.

In this chapter, we examine five important ancient faiths: those of the ancient Egyptians, Greeks, Maya, Druids, and Aztecs. Each is fascinating not only for the light its practices and founding myths shed on current systems of belief, but also for the social, cultural, and historical insights it offers on the civilization in which it operated.

## Ancient Egyptian Worship

The sheer diversity and scale of ancient Egyptian forms of religious observance are awe-inspiring. A full discussion of the subject is, unfortunately, beyond the scope of this short chapter. What follows is a summary of key points.

# Ancient Egyptian Worship: The Cultural/Historical Setting

The native dynasties of ancient Egypt extended from the founding of the First Dynasty circa 3110 B.C.E. to the conquest of the final native rulers of the New Kingdom by Alexander the Great twenty-seven centuries later. Periods of foreign domination intervened at various points during that period; after Alexander, a line of monarchs descended from, and named after, Ptolemy I (previously Alexander's general) ruled the empire.

Cleopatra, queen of the Nile (and daughter of Ptolemy XI), attempted to restore Egyptian power and influence—not least by means of her complex political and personal relationships with Julius Caesar and Mark Antony. Eventually Octavian (later the emperor Augustus Caesar) secured a period of unquestioned Roman control and ended the days of the Egyptian empire. Refer to the 31 B.C.E. portion of the timeline that follows.

The age, duration, and vitality of the ancient Egyptian civilization, which spanned a period exceeding three millennia, simply boggles the mind. Religious worship was a constant identifying and energizing force throughout this remarkable, and exceptionally long-lived, civilization. The condensed Ancient Egyptian Dynasties timeline that follows can serve as an adequate starting point for those interested in familiarizing themselves with some of the principal events.

Old Kingdom (circa 3200–2258 B.C.E.)

➤ Circa 3200 B.C.E.: Tradition holds that Menes, king of Upper Egypt, subdued the forces of the Lower Delta, forming a united kingdom of Egypt.

➤ 2884–2780 B.C.E.: Egypt emerges as a major trading nation.

➤ 2780–2680 B.C.E.: Earliest practice of sun-worship is believed to have occurred during this period. Mummification is initiated.

➤ 2680–2565 B.C.E: Construction of the great pyramids, monuments to the monarchs whose mummified bodies they house (and to the centrally organized Egyptian nation as a whole).

**On the Path**

A unifying theme of the period of ancient Egyptian empire was the divine or semi-divine nature of the pharaoh, or king. This tradition may well have had social and political origins relating to questions of national unity and identity.

**On the Path**

Mummification played an important role in ancient Egyptian religious practice. Ever-more elaborate embalming practices evolved over a period of centuries, always with the goal of faithfully preserving the deceased's likeness for eternity. Royal tombs were supplied with treasures meant for enjoyment in the afterlife.

➤ 2420–2258 B.C.E.: Period of rising commercial and military influence but steadily weaker and less effective political institutions, culminating in the collapse of the Old Kingdom.

Middle Kingdom (circa 2000—1786 B.C.E.)

➤ 2000–1786 B.C.E.: After an intermediate period not entirely documented, but during which centralized authority was restored, the Twelfth Dynasty presides over another flourishing Egyptian civilization. Writing standards are formalized and religious life is vibrant.

New Kingdom (circa 1570—31 B.C.E.)

➤ 1570–circa 1342 B.C.E.: Following a century of rule by the Hyksos, Amasis I ejects this group (which may have been Syrian) and launches the Eighteenth Dynasty, under which the Egyptian civilization ascends to its peak. The boy king Tutankhamen rules during this period.

➤ Circa 1342–945 B.C.E.: A series of weak rulers ensues; priests rise in influence and maintain a sort of worship-centered de facto government; period of general decline.

➤ 945–332 B.C.E.: Period notable for domination by outside powers, culminating in conquest under Alexander the Great.

➤ 323 B.C.E.: Death of Alexander the Great. His general Ptolemy eventually assumes control of Egypt and rules as Ptolemy I, founding a line of Ptolemaic kings, as well as the great library at Alexandria.

➤ 31 B.C.E.: Cleopatra—daughter of Ptolemy XI, and regarded as divine queen by her people, is defeated with her lover Mark Antony near Actium by the forces of Octavian (afterward the Emperor Augustus Caesar). Later, they return to Egypt, but eventually fall to the Romans and commit suicide. Octavian has Cleopatra's son and (titular) joint ruler Ptolemy XIV—almost certainly the issue of Cleopatra's earlier union with Julius Caesar—put to death. The final line of divine Egyptian monarchs comes to an end.

So much for the history. Let's look next at the view of creation taken by the Egyptians.

## Two Ancient Egyptian Creation Myths

One version of how the world came into existence: At the beginning, all that existed was Nu, the abyss of chaotic waters. Then the sun god arose from the waters by means of the power of thought.

Having no place to stand, the sun god fashioned a hill, and it is on that hill that the city of Heliopolis (literally, "City of the Sun") was erected. He joined with his own shadow to create a race of gods. Later, Shu and Tefnut got lost in the watery abyss of Nu. The sun god sent his own eye out to find them—and when the eye returned with his offspring, he wept tears of joy. Those tears became the first humans.

Another version of how the world came into existence: At the beginning, the sun god took on the identity of Khepri, the great scarab god. Khepri created everything—including the watery abyss from which he himself arose. He chose to breathe out air (the god Shu), and then moisture and rain (the goddess Tefnut).

Shu and Tefnut mated, and produced earth (the god Geb) and sky (the goddess Nut). At this point, with air, rain, earth, and sky created, the physical universe was in place. Later, Khepri wept when his children brought him his own eye, the sun, which had been hidden from him. His joyful tears were the first humans.

**On the Path**

The fact that there is more than one popularly circulated "creation" in Egyptian practice gives some sense of the scale and diversity of this faith.

**On the Path**

Despite variations in Egyptian creation myths, Geb and Nut were always regarded as parents of Osiris (god of the underworld), Isis (goddess associated with nature and renewal), Seth (sun god who eventually murdered Osiris and who came to represent evil), and Nephthys (faithful comforter of Isis).

## Key Concepts from Ancient Egyptian Observance

Among the most important points to remember about the religious practices of the ancient Egyptians are the following:

➤ Members of specific clans worshipped animal totems that were regarded as their ancestors. Many of these totems later emerged as gods.

➤ Major deities included Ra, the sun god; the inexhaustibly popular brother/sister/husband/wife pair, Isis and Osiris (central figures of the enduring *cult of Isis and Osiris*); Horus, their son; and Thoth, the god of learning. A large number of other gods, many of them combinations of humans and animals, were part of this system of worship.

➤ There was no single, specific set of ancient Egyptian religious beliefs, but rather a broad collection of practices and group-specific worship systems. As the empire expanded and solidified, however, many of these rituals took on national significance.

➤ Originally, the Egyptians regarded an afterlife as a privilege obtainable only by mummified kings. Later, during the New Kingdom, elite wealthy Egyptians also began to be accorded preparation for the journey to the next world.

One final note: In the fourteenth century B.C.E., pharaoh Ikhnaton launched an effort to acknowledge Aton as the official national god. It didn't catch on.

# Ancient Greek Worship

Roughly four thousand years ago, scholars believe, an invasion by Aryan warriors combined Aryan civilization with that of the Aegeans and Minoans. The likely result: a synthesis that would eventually become Greek culture.

The ancient Greek city-states had an incalculable influence on Western culture, and elements of their mythology and religious practice have pervaded both ancient and modern life.

## *Ancient Greek Worship: The Cultural/Historical Setting*

The vast Greek *pantheon* of gods suggests a combination of the religious practices and images of the Aryan victors with those of the conquered Aegean and Minoan peoples. Zeus, for instance, was the Aryan sky-god; his sister and wife Hera was a fertility goddess of the Aegeans. (These two gods fought a great deal, a situation that may be a reflection of real-life postwar social strife between the former combatants.)

Speaking very broadly, the great flowering period of Greek civilization occurred between the eighth century B.C.E., when colonies that later emerged as city-states were formed, and 146 B.C.E., when Rome took full control of the often-unstable network of Greek polities. During the glorious interim, Greek religion was a vital shared reference point. Without a common set of religious ideas and rituals, the forever squabbling city-states would probably have had far less of a sense of shared identity and purpose.

**What's It Mean?**

The **cult of Isis and Osiris** was one of the most influential and widespread religious practices of the ancient world. Worship of Isis and celebration of the mysteries related to the resurrection of her husband/brother Osiris spread to Greece, eventually becoming one of the dominant religious traditions of the Roman world. Isis remained an object of pious devotion for a remarkably long period of time; the cult associated with her was active for several centuries *after* Constantine I's conversion to Christianity.

**What's It Mean?**

A **pantheon** is the entire collection of gods featured in a particular culture's mythology.

The ancient Greek religion, which emphasized action and the cultivation of one's own personal virtue, helped to bind together a diverse and frequently divided nation—a nation that made stunning advances in politics, literature, the arts, philosophy, and architecture that echo today through virtually all major cultures.

In no small measure because of their religious values, the Greeks managed, at the right moments, to celebrate intellect, logic, open inquiry, thoughtful living, and creativity in a way that has served for centuries as a model to all humanity.

### On the Path

Minor variations on the Greek creation myth are common. This may have something to do with the confluence of cultures and traditions that occurred in a murky period (1100–800 B.C.E.) about which historians still have many questions.

### On the Path

Rhea's sister Titan Themis, symbolizing the principles of order and legality, eventually gave birth to Prometheus—who gave stolen fire to the human race and was punished for this crime by Zeus.

## The Ancient Greek Creation Myth

In the early times, shapeless Chaos reigned over a universe without light, a place where endless night and the vast region of death were the only realities. Then Eros (Love) sprang forth for reasons humans can never understand or explain, and with Eros, arrived light and order. With the arrival of light came Gaea, the earth, daughter of Chaos.

Gaea bore Uranus, heaven-god and first king of the universe. Uranus took his mother Gaea as his wife. Their children included the three Cyclopes (huge one-eyed beings) and the three Hecatoncheires (hundred-handed ones). Later, the twelve Titans were born. The original Titans were the huge children of Uranus and Gaea. Among their number were Cronos, Rhea, Themis, and Oceanus.

Uranus proved a poor father and husband, mistreating his own progeny, and Gaea fashioned a sickle out of flint and tried to incite her children to attack him. All were terrified at the thought—except Cronos, the youngest of the Titans. Cronos attacked and castrated Uranus, usurping his power. Where drops of Uranus's blood fell on the ground, the Furies sprang to life, ferocious pursuers of those who commit murder. Where Uranus's blood fell in the sea emerged Aphrodite, the exquisite goddess of love and fertility.

Cronos wed his sister Rhea and ruled as King of the Titans. Convinced that one of his own would rise up against him, Cronos ate his first five newborn children alive. To save the life of her sixth child, Rhea tricked Cronos into eating a stone wrapped in swaddling clothes. She hid her child among the nature goddesses known as nymphs, who raised the infant—named Zeus—secretly.

Grown to adulthood, Zeus disguised himself, returned to Cronos's domain, and tricked him with a drink. As he choked on Zeus's potion, Cronos coughed up the five children he had consumed. Zeus had thus reclaimed the lives of Hestia, Demeter, and Hera (his sisters), and Pluto and Poseidon (his brothers).

There followed a fierce battle against Cronos and the Titans loyal to him; Zeus prevailed and overthrew his father. He cast lots with his brothers, and it was determined that Pluto would rule the underworld and Poseidon would rule the sea, with Zeus exercising dominion over heaven and earth. Zeus, an amorous monarch, reigned at Mount Olympus as king of all gods.

## *Key Concepts from Ancient Greek Observance*

Among the most important points to remember about ancient Greek worship are the following:

➤ The Greek pantheon included: Zeus, the god of heaven; Hera, his sister/wife; Demeter, the earth mother; Apollo, who was connected with divination, the arts, medicine, and certain higher intellectual pursuits, and who watched over flocks; Hermes the war god; and many, many others.

➤ Greek practice emphasized mystery cults—secret groups led by a priest or other *officiant* that typically incorporated initiation rituals, some kind of purification ceremony, display of holy relics, dramatic recital elements, and dispersal of unique wisdom.

➤ The Eleusinian Mysteries were perhaps the most prominent mysteries of the period. The secrecy surrounding a number of their specific practices appears to have endured, but scholars do know that the rites involved the goddess Demeter and her daughter Persephone's return from the underworld. The Eleusinian Mysteries emphasized the immortality of the soul and the permanence of divine renewal.

**What's It Mean?**

An **officiant** is one who presides over a ritual or ceremony.

**What's It Mean?**

An **oracle** is the pronouncement of an officiant, offered at a shrine or in some other holy setting, as the divine answer to a believer's question. An oracle can also be the agency regarded as the source of that response.

➤ The Dionysian and Orphic Mysteries were also important to the Ancient Greeks. Dionysius was the god of wine and of sensual revelry; Orphic observance incorporated hymns and aimed at a final triumph over death.

➤ *Oracles*, such as the one at Delphi, were vital locations of Greek worship; so were the specific temples of gods associated with particular city-states and the healing centers dedicated to Aesculapius, the god of medicine.

➤ The philosopher Plato (427–347 B.C.E.) strongly influenced Greek religious practice. In the centuries following his teaching, Greek worship moved away from the idea (frequently expressed in Homer's writings) that the trials of humans served as amusements for the often-capricious gods of Olympus—and toward a devotional conception of ultimate underlying reality and the perfection of form.

One more point before we leave Greek religious observance: the region remained a cultural and religious center, and thus an influence on various ancient forms of worship, for some centuries after its annexation by Rome.

### On the Path

Why did the Maya desert their cities? Was there an environmental collapse? An incursion from another tribe that forced the exodus, but did not subdue the people as a whole? Some other catastrophe? In recent years, some have argued that the available evidence indicates that large numbers of Maya commoners left population centers to avoid being selected as victims of human sacrifice rituals. It's an interesting notion; the debate continues.

# Ancient Mayan Worship

Renowned for their pyramidal structures, their arts, and their mathematical system, the Maya of ancient times operated under a complex theocracy that, like that of the Aztecs, emphasized calendar-making. Their descendants occupy roughly the same regions of what is now southern Mexico and Central America. Modest rural settlements have characterized the region for centuries.

## *Ancient Mayan Worship: The Cultural/Historical Setting*

The zenith of the agriculturally centered Mayan civilization, one of the most important pre-Columbian peoples, occurred between C.E. 300 and 900. The reason for the gradual depopulation of their great cities between C.E. 900 and 1100 has been a subject of continuing debate.

At its height, the Mayan civilization appears to have operated not under a single ruler, but as a loosely organized gathering of semi-autonomous cities and villages. These units seem to have emphasized kinship and genealogy as important social and religious factors. Ties to the earth were always vitally important. Advances in agricultural techniques supported population growth in the ancient Mayan culture—and, by extension, the accompanying breakthroughs in mathematics, calendar-making, architecture, and the arts for which the old civilization is best known today.

## The Ancient Mayan Creation Myth

In the ancient times, before there were people, the gods Tepeu and Gucumatz reigned. If they thought something, it came into existence.

When they thought about the earth, it was born. When they thought about trees, or mountains, or any other feature of the landscape, it came forth. The moment they thought about animals, the animals were there.

Tepeu and Gucumatz soon realized, though, that something important was missing. Nothing that they had created was capable of praising them. And so they decided to create people.

The first people were made of clay—but the gods found that these dissolved when they got wet. The next people were fashioned from wood, but they were troublemakers, and so the gods sent a flood to rectify their mistake and start anew. Finally the gods appealed to the mountain lion, the coyote, the parrot, and the crow to help them find the right material from which to build superior beings. The animals found corn, and it was from corn that the gods created the Four Fathers from which all humanity traces its lineage.

## Key Concepts from Ancient Mayan Observance

Among the most important points to remember about the ancient religious practices of the Maya are the following:

➤ The Maya placed a high degree of faith in the ability of the gods to control and order events and human undertakings within specific time periods.

➤ Nature, time, and agriculture were preoccupations of religious life—and, indeed, of life as a whole—in Mayan society.

➤ Like the religion of the Aztec peoples of central Mexico, Mayan religion incorporated elements of human sacrifice to appease key gods.

➤ Among the many other important deities were Kinich Ahau, the sun god; Chaac the rain god; and the Maize god, strongly associated with the central obsession of the culture as a whole—ripened and healthy corn.

➤ Mayan mythology postulated four brother-gods who held up the sky. Each presided over a four-year span of time and represented one of the four directions. Colors associated with each of these deities were essential to Mayan religious and calendar-making practices.

## Watch It!

A common misconception associates the Druids with the creation of the huge primeval stone monuments of France and Britain. Although these mysterious edifices were once credited by scholars to the Druids and assumed to have been built as an expression of their religious practice, archaeologists have since concluded that the structures are actually older than even Celtic culture. The history and purpose of sites such as Stonehenge remains obscure. They may have been intended as observatories, or as centers of religious worship, or both.

## What's It Mean?

The word **pagan** derives from the Latin word *paganus*, meaning "someone from the countryside." Forbidden religious practices were often simply relocated to less-populated regions.

➤ Current scholarship suggests that ancestor worship was an important part of life in ancient Mayan civilizations.

Descendants of the ancient Mayans are alive and well in the region. Roman Catholicism has been the dominant religion since the Spanish conquest of the 1500s; however, many original traditions (including native religious practices) have been intertwined with their European counterparts.

# Ancient Druidic Worship

Druids were ancient priests who led nature-based religious ceremonies in Celtic Britain and other European regions. The Druids are known to have been active in the third century B.C.E. Archeological discoveries led to intense popular interest in Druidic practices during the eighteenth and nineteenth centuries.

## The Druids: The Cultural/ Historical Setting

What we know about the Druids' history arises primarily from what the Romans wrote about them. We learn from Julius Caesar that Druids in Gaul formed a federation that crossed over tribal boundaries, and it seems likely that a similar system operated in Britain. The Romans also noted that Druids met annually and exercised great influence over political and social matters.

In Gaul, Druids were fierce but ill-fated adversaries to Rome. Not even the Roman seizure of southern Britain in the first century C.E. and illegalization of native rituals, however, could completely eliminate Druidic practice, which moved to outlying areas and were branded as *pagan*, a term that endured for centuries.

Under attack from Rome, Druidic practice lost much of its political potency; it eventually yielded to the advance of Christianity in Britain circa C.E. 600, although suppressed rituals and oral teachings appear to have persisted in some quarters for many years after that. Modern practices based on Druidic concepts have become increasingly popular in recent years as contemporary seekers, eager to find or adapt alternative modes of religious expression, have become more familiar with the trials endured by early practitioners of Druidic rites.

It is important to bear in mind that the word "Druid" describes not a religion per se, but an elite class of revered and respected Celtic officiants gathered within a powerful network based on common practice and outlook. In their day, Druids appear to have performed the roles today undertaken by members of the clergy, scholars, judges, civic planners, teachers, and even entertainers. Druids also engaged in divination and nature-based worship rituals, leading to later (misleading) dismissals of their work as that of "soothsayers" or "wizards."

It is probably closer to the truth to think of the Druids as an ancient Celtic political and religious network that connected like-minded practitioners within a given region. They were far-sighted, experienced, and highly esteemed members of the community … the "movers and shakers" of their day.

**On the Path**

The available evidence suggests the existence of female Druids, but the record is too sketchy for us to draw any meaningful conclusions about their role or social status within their communities.

## (Conjecture on an) Ancient Druidic Creation Myth

Little is certain of how the Druids explained the origin of the universe, but some scholars have conjectured that the appearance of egglike objects and egg symbols in ancient Druid mysticism reflects a belief in a "hatching myth" involving an egg as the original source of all things. Such a myth would, of course, emphasize a powerful fertility symbol wholly appropriate within a creation account.

While the egg's role in (hypothetical) Druidic creation stories remains a matter of debate, it is certain that the Roman historian Pliny recorded having seen a "Druid's Egg," a diminutive relic purported to have been assembled from the dried expectoration of snakes. According to the Druid from Gaul described by Pliny, the egg was held to have restorative powers.

## Key Concepts from Ancient Druidic Practice

Among the most important points to remember about the religious practices of the Druids are the following:

➤ The title "Druid" (which appears to mean "oak knowledge") was bestowed only on highly regarded members of the community—people who then served as religious officiants and performed a variety of other important social functions.

➤ Druidic practice seems to have focused on a vast array of nature gods (or, to use a modern term coined by Joseph Campbell (noted writer and lecturer in the field of mythology), "living presences"); sacrifice of animals and humans was part of religious practice.

➤ The Celts did have written language, but the Druids seem to have maintained an exclusively oral transmission of their rites. This may be a mark of the secrecy and exclusivity of their practice.

➤ Services took place near lakes and rivers and in tree groves. The oak and the mistletoe were regarded as holy plants.

➤ Suppression of the Druids led to the rise of the "bardic school," which kept Druidic practices alive by means of the relation of myths, quasihistorical heroic stories, and songs.

➤ Druidic practice today is associated strongly with Ireland because Roman authority did not extend as far as the Emerald Isle. Druidic practice thrived in Ireland until the people there were converted to Christianity and the old rites were put down.

Various Neo-Druid movements have gained popularity in the West in recent years.

# Ancient Aztec Worship

The Aztec were the native people who had for centuries enjoyed primacy in central Mexico at the time the Spanish conquered the territory in the sixteenth century C.E. The Aztec priesthood and the religious practices it promulgated served as organizing elements of a centralized and highly developed civilization—one whose achievements in astronomy, engineering, and architecture astonished Europeans.

**On the Path**

A social system comprised of a noble elite, a politically powerful priestly class, and a warrior/mercantile class led the Aztec people to extraordinary accomplishments in the arts, agriculture, mathematics, calendar-making, and many other areas.

## *Aztec Worship: The Cultural/Historical Setting*

The Aztecs were a small and struggling itinerant tribe when they wandered into the Valley of Mexico sometime in the twelfth century C.E. They founded their capital, Tenochtitlan, early in the fourteenth century C.E., and maintained a tenuous sovereignty by making tribute payments to nearby tribes.

Sometime in the fifteenth century C.E., a warrior culture began to flourish—reinforced, no doubt, by the creation myth that appears in the section that follows. Aztec leaders used a skillful combination of religious observance, diplomacy, careful social organization, flexibility in adapting the practices of other tribes, and expert warfare to raise their civilization to a position of supremacy in central Mexico.

Aztec religious tradition assumed a centrality that focused and galvanized the populace—and may well have led to the nation's undoing. When the Spaniard Hernán Cortés led his mission to Mexico in 1519, he and his men were seen by the Aztec ruling class not as European invaders, but as descendants of the ancient Toltec god Quetzalcoatl, long prophesied to return.

Playing upon this belief, Cortés was able to take hostage the emperor Montezuma II (himself regarded by the Aztec people as divine), thus paralyzing the Aztec social system for a time. Later, Cortés mobilized Indian groups that had been chafing under Aztec domination. So it was Cortés that put down the Aztec rebellion that eventually followed his kidnapping of the emperor. The Spanish soon overran Tenochitlan, destroyed it, and assumed control of Mexico.

## The Ancient Aztec Creation Myth

The lord and lady of duality, Ometecuhlti and his wife Omecihauatl, brought into existence all things. The birth of Huitzilopochtli, the great god of the sun and of war, occurred in the following manner: Coatlicue, She Who Wears the Serpent Skirt, was mother of the moon goddess and her 400 brothers. Crisis and universal dissolution loomed, however, when she inadvertently became pregnant again after having tucked a blue feather in her serpent-skirt. The new birth was certain to infuriate her first brood of children, as a goddess was expected to give birth once and only once.

The new god within her, however, assured her that he would protect them both, and Coatlicue took a confident stance at the Serpent Mountain Coatepec as she awaited the onslaught of her own children. Huitzilopochtli came forth from her womb fully armed and slew his brothers and sister, scattering them across the face of the universe. His sister, the cold moon, he beheaded; his dead brothers are the shining stars.

## Key Concepts from Ancient Aztec Observance

Among the most important points to remember about the religious practices of the Aztec people are the following:

➤ Ometecuhlti and his wife Omelcihuatl, who brought about all creation, were regarded as having chosen the Aztec people above others for special favor.

➤ Aztec belief also held that friendly gods required constant appeasement; failure to keep benevolent gods happy would result in the destruction of the earth by malevolent deities.

➤ In order to keep the gods who protected them satisfied, the Aztec maintained a ritual of human sacrifice.

➤ Those sacrificed were generally prisoners of war. Occasionally, however, Aztec warriors would volunteer to be sacrificed.

➤ The Aztec people were closely focused on calendar-making; their intricate calendar combined a 365-day solar year with a 260-day holy period.

➤ Important Aztec deities included Tezcoptipcoca, the sun god, and Tlaloc, the rain god. There were many others.

One final observation on the Aztecs: The collapse of their theocracy in the face of Spanish forces was certainly hastened by their own suppression of neighboring peoples.

---

### The Least You Need to Know

➤ Ancient Egypt boasted an almost incomprehensibly vast and diverse religious tradition, one highlight of which was the remarkably resilient cult of Isis and Osiris.

➤ Elements of ancient Greek mythology and religious practice have pervaded both ancient and modern life.

➤ The Maya of ancient times operated under a complex theocracy that emphasized calendar-making and ties to the earth.

➤ Druids were ancient priests who led nature-based religious ceremonies in Celtic Britain and other European regions.

➤ Aztec leaders used a skillful combination of religious observance, diplomacy, careful social organization, flexibility in adapting the practices of other tribes, and expert warfare to raise their civilization to a position of supremacy in central Mexico.

# Chapter 23

# Nonscriptural Nature Religions

## In This Chapter

➤ Find out about common obstacles awaiting outsiders seeking to understand traditional faiths

➤ Learn about some common elements of traditional Pacific Island, African, and Native American ritual and observance

➤ Discover Huna Kupua, an indigenous Hawaiian worship tradition of great antiquity

➤ Find out about important ideas that guide traditional African and Native American religious practice

In this chapter, you learn about the distinctive features of some important nonscriptural nature-oriented religious traditions, and you find out about some of the obstacles to understanding indigenous faiths.

Before you proceed any further, please understand: There are countless indigenous religious traditions that operate beyond the scope of the regions selected for this chapter. We have chosen to look at some of the specifics associated with Pacific Island, African, and Native American religious practices because these practices have been the subject of keen interest in the United States in recent years. We acknowledge, though, that there are many other traditional patterns of devotion worthy of study in other parts of the world.

Indeed, there are over 100 million practitioners of traditional religions worldwide. It is worth remembering, however, that even the use of the word "religion" must be considered carefully in any discussion of indigenous faiths, since many of these traditions do not draw clear distinctions between everyday life and formal religious practices. All life, in other words, is religious and the systems discussed (in broad terms) in this chapter usually accept that principle.

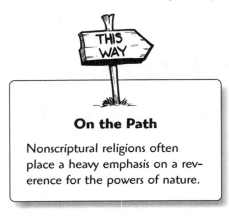

**On the Path**

Nonscriptural religions often place a heavy emphasis on a reverence for the powers of nature.

# Inside, Outside

Most of the faiths described by the word "traditional" are experiential, rather than intellectual. This makes any formulation of "core principles" something of a challenge. All of these patterns of worship demand respect and understanding from the outsiders who wish to learn more about them.

**Bet You Didn't Know**

Unique local traditions usually emphasize familiar cosmologies and the divinity of observable natural processes. Initially, they may not be set in opposition to any other system.

As colonial expansion unfolded over the past 500 years, however, outsiders took on the task of creating labels for religions that remained free from colonial influence, or that somehow managed to survive in spite of that influence. Such labels are for the convenience of the outsiders themselves, and contribute little value to those inside the religions.

It is a common mistake to define traditional religions outside of European or Asian experience by emphasizing the ways in which they differ from that experience. A similar problem arises in the description of traditional faiths by means of what they are not or do not possess.

Traditional religions exist on their own terms. They typically meet the needs of a body of believers who view themselves, not as a tribe or group separate from "dominant" (i.e., external) historical patterns, but simply as "the people."

This is another way of saying that assessing an indigenous set of traditions is a tricky business. Such observations may result in belittling designations such as "savage" or "primitive," or a well-intentioned but equally condescending tendency to romanticize "simpler" pre-technological societies.

Outsiders (like the authors of this book) must always be careful in describing or assessing faiths that present racial, social, or cultural uniqueness. Such outsiders should be aware that in applying labels to these practices, they may be describing only their own preconceptions, not the most important facets of a differing tradition.

## Ideas That Stay

Some traditional religious practices have been carefully preserved by native groups; there are also thousands of active contemporary tribal communities whose members subscribe to traditional religions. Most, but not all, of the practices in these groups are strongly associated with village or tribal settings.

Although it is dangerous to make too many generalizations about these groups and their belief systems, some commonalities are definitely worth exploring.

The following three elements are familiar:

➤ The shaman

➤ The totem

➤ The fetish

## The Shaman

There are many types of shamanistic practice, but a single idea guides those who operate as *shamans* within tribal societies: *The world humans see is occupied by forces that cannot be perceived with the naked eye, forces that may exert positive or negative influence on human affairs.* Unlike priests, for whom religious ritual and observance is a permanent vocation, shamans enter into temporary trances to perform their work as circumstances arise.

Shamans must acquire particular skills. They may inherit their titles from their forebears or be summoned to their calling through dreams, visions, or even possession. They are generally paid for their efforts. They may be either men or women, although male shamans are most common.

### What's It Mean?

A **shaman** is a religious celebrant who is considered to possess more than human powers, including the ability to understand and treat diseases. Shamans may also, in some cases, bring about illness, a consideration that frequently leaves them both feared and respected in the community. Their powers derive from their interaction with, and influence over, certain spirits. Other English terms for the shaman include "medicine man" and "witch doctor."

### On the Path

Traditions and rituals act as a binding force in indigenous African religious practice, just as they do elsewhere in the world. Tribal groups place special emphasis on community ties and values. Village elders and respected spiritual authorities are charged with the important task of handing down expressions of faith and rituals that will encourage harmonious social practices ... and sustain and reinforce the group during times of trial.

### On the Path

For Native Americans, one of the most bitter legacies of the "settlement" of North America by European immigrants and their descendants is the mistreatment of natural forms. The tragedy of modern "development," from the Native American perspective, should be understood not merely as the desecration of particular sacred sites, but as a wide-ranging disrespect for the earth.

Although fetishism expresses itself in traditional practices in distinctive and recognizable ways, traditional religions are certainly not the only systems that promote or reinforce the reverence of objects. An argument can be made that some form of fetishism underlies virtually all religious worship and observance.

## The Totem

A totem is a particular object (generally a plant or animal) held in reverence and regarded as an ancestor or sibling by members of a group. Totemism is prevalent in both North America and Africa. Totems carry important social, ritualistic, and mystical associations, and are today strongly associated with indigenous peoples of the Pacific Northwest in North America. The word "totem" comes from the peoples of that region.

The spirit made manifest by the totem may serve as a powerful unifying element among members of a tribe, familial grouping, or other nonblood related grouping. Given its role as a protector and/or family member, a sacred animal or variety of plant may be declared off-limits by members of the totemic group in its "ordinary" use. (In other words, you can't eat them.) Symbolism associated with a totem may serve as an identifying mark for the group in question. In a number of societies, marriage among members of the same totemic group is prohibited.

## The Fetish

No, we're not talking about psychoanalysis. Before the term "fetish" was appropriated by Western clinicians to describe erotic fixation, it was used by anthropologists to describe inanimate objects held by believers to hold magical powers or even an independent will. Such reverence for and awe of natural or man-made objects is a distinctive feature of many traditional religions, many of which are considered potentially dangerous if mishandled, and so are subjected to rigorous controls.

The term is employed here in a nonjudgmental way, and not as an indictment of "irrationality" or "superstition" among traditional believers.

# Huna Kupua

One particularly long-running example of nature worship can be found in the fifti-eth state.

The system of esoteric wisdom known as Huna Kupua found in the Hawaiian Islands is thought to have existed in Polynesia for many thousands of years. It celebrates na-ture and emphasizes ideas of deep self-perception and an ongoing interrelationship with all existence. Its worship practices were handed down across countless genera-tions as part of an oral tradition. There is one basic commandment within Huna Kupua: "Harm no one and nothing with hate."

Among the core ideas of the Huna tradition are the following:

➤ The **Seven Principles** describe the initial assumptions of the Huna philosophy; they serve as a structural guide to the faith by offering insights on human per-ception of reality. (The first of the Seven Principles is "The World Is What You Think It Is.")

➤ The concept of the **Three Selves** (or the **Four Selves**) explores the Huna view of the self as existing in a multileveled way. From the Huna viewpoint, each qual-ity of "selfness" resides within a distinct realm of perception and contributes a unique aspect of personal experience. The development of the various qualities to be found at each level of the self, and the interaction of these qualities, is held to have a direct relation upon one's connection to and integration with the Higher Self.

➤ The *Huna* understanding of the **Four Levels of Reality** holds all things to be si-multaneously objective (reflecting scientific reality), subjective (reflecting psy-chic reality), symbolic (reflecting shamanic reality), and holistic (reflecting mystical reality). The Kupua (that is, healer or shaman) is able to exist in and move through these various realities in order to effect what-ever changes are deemed necessary.

The practice of what is now known as Huna Kupua only narrowly survived contact with Western mis-sionaries in the nineteenth and twentieth cen-turies. Most of what is now known about this religious practice arose from the research begun in 1920, and carried out over the next five decades, by a remarkable gentleman named Max Freedom Long. Long devoted his life to searching out and interviewing people with firsthand experience of the practice; his invaluable research led to a series of books on the subject. Max Freedom Long, quoted on www.huna.org: "We must be ready with

**What's It Mean?**

**Huna** means "secret." It also re-flects a deeper traditional con-cept that has been defined as follows: "The science of the control of universal life energies through the control of the mind and breath."

understanding to love (through Aloha-Lani) and to welcome with open arms the drawing near of the Mate, our Beloved. We must have learned to give everything, holding back nothing of ourselves. We must be eager to learn and to serve and to love."

### On the Path

"In its simplest form, a Huna prayer works this way: the conscious mind, by conscious breathing and by conscious effort of will, calls mentally for a surcharge of energy to be created and brought up to its level. By continuous breathing and a further effort of the will the energy is stepped up even higher. Then with proper visualizations and words this high energy is sent down to the subconscious and ... to the High Self. When all this is done correctly, miracles happen."

—Dr. Jonathan Parker, Ph.D., *Ancient Huna Secrets*
(article available at www.quantumquests.com)

### Watch It!

The many forms of Native American spirituality are often seen by believers as systems of belief and practice affecting *all* aspects of life, and not as formal or external matters of devotion that are somehow unrelated to other parts of life. Thus, attempts to separate "environmental issues" or "mythological accounts" from "religious matters" may be seen as insensitive and/or ill-informed.

As the twentieth century wound down, more and more Americans and Europeans were, like Long, captivated by the beauty, subtlety, and profundity of this ancient body of belief and practice.

# African Traditions

Traditional African believers pursue many paths and assign many names to the Supreme Being.

## The Names of God

Some of these names emphasize the deity's creative capacity; others call attention to God's role as a great parent or ancestor, either male or female. Some African peoples revere the pervasive universal force as the Source of All Being, the One Who Is Ever Present, the Great Providence Who Determines Destinies, or the One Who Is Never Fully Known. A supreme God who acts as a universal sustainer is a common feature of African traditional observance.

## *Spirits, Good and Bad*

Most groups also acknowledge the influence of spirits and ancestral entities who operate beneath the level of the high God. Practitioners rely on the most benevolent of these to overcome the influence of the wicked forces with which humans must always contend.

As a practical matter, traditional African spiritual groups accept the influences of these spirits as more immediate factors in everyday life than direct contact with the Supreme Being. In other words, immediate encounters with the divine often prove as elusive for an African traditional believer as for her American Catholic counterpart, who might, for instance, appeal to St. Anthony for help in locating a lost article.

### Bet You Didn't Know

Developed by the Yoruba peoples of western Africa many thousands of years ago, the tradition known as Ifa emphasizes internal tranquility and personal autonomy. Its practice was transmitted to the Americas by enslaved African tribespeople; today, it is the subject of renewed interest in America and continued practice in Africa.

Ifa practitioners hold that all things in the universe were created by the ever-constant and unchanging Supreme Head who retains the fullness of all things, known as Olodumare. They also regard Olodumare as the "source being" who imparts rationality, or essential being, to humanity. They believe that Olodumare determines and controls human destiny, and that all of existence operates within the control of Olodumare.

Ifa regards with reverence numerous orisa, or potent messenger spirits, whose energy and support humans may cultivate. For a discussion of a "new religion" that incorporates elements of traditional African and Roman Catholic practice, and that, like Ifa, venerates orisa, see the section on Santeria in Chapter 24, "Modern Times: New Forms".

The Ifa faith emphasizes piety, humility, concern for others, personal strength, tolerance, and a strict moral code that countenances no swindling or double-dealing. It is a joyous, practical system of belief that sets great store by social propriety and moral righteousness.

# Native American Traditions

For all their many tribal and historical differences (and these are not insignificant!) all Native American peoples share a profound and deeply spiritual reverence for the natural world and their land.

Within Native American spirituality, natural forms and processes are seen as containing fundamental creative powers; all processes, human and nonhuman, are seen as inextricably linked. Native American religion does not draw clear lines between natural and supernatural events. It is no wonder that societies that are out of balance with nature are regarded as spiritually deficient by many believers within these traditions.

The twentieth century's systematic desecration and abuse of systems formerly regarded as being in divine balance is seen as having left lasting wounds to the earth and also to Native American spiritual practices.

## All Together, Now

Monotheism in the familiar sense of the word is not a primary feature of Native American religions. Instead, there is an understanding of physical and emotional interconnectedness among all beings. (Many of these groups, for instance, have preserved traditions that carry both spiritual and medical significance.)

All the same, a number of modern Native American groups have developed terminology that employs a single word or phrase for the collection of spiritual forces to be found in the six directions: North, South, East, West, Sky, and Earth.

## Integrity

Although there are many variations and cultural influences within Native American religious practice, an emphasis on balance, completion, and integrity is pervasive. Rituals within the various traditions are meant to promote an appreciation for the cycles of life and death and for harmonious community action.

## Contact!

Many forms of observance involve purification rites, coming-of-age rituals (such as the *Vision Quest*), and mystical ceremonies meant to enable a fuller understanding of human life and the natural world. These rites frequently incorporate some form of direct

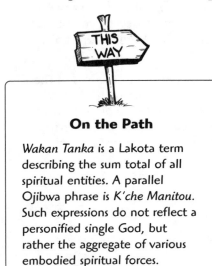

### On the Path

*Wakan Tanka* is a Lakota term describing the sum total of all spiritual entities. A parallel Ojibwa phrase is *K'che Manitou*. Such expressions do not reflect a personified single God, but rather the aggregate of various embodied spiritual forces.

### What's It Mean?

The **Vision Quest,** common in many Native American systems, is a period during which a boy celebrates the onset of puberty by means of solitary meditation, fasting, and tests of physical endurance. (Girls are not generally permitted to engage in the ritual.) The participant's aim: to bring about a vision that will guide him in later life, and to earn the support and protection of a guardian spirit.

208

contact with important spirits, contact that is seen as beneficial not only for the individual but for the community as a whole.

In other words, individuals may bring their own lives—and the day-to-day activities of their social groups—into greater coherence through personal contact and ongoing relationships with particular spiritual forces.

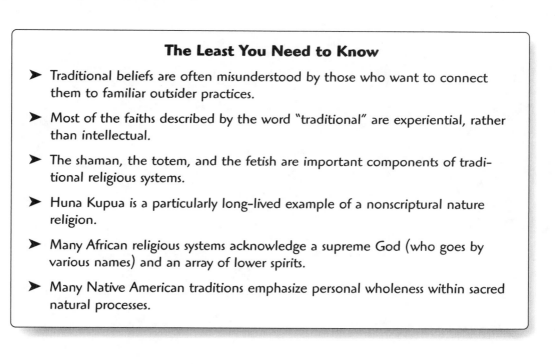

### The Least You Need to Know

➤ Traditional beliefs are often misunderstood by those who want to connect them to familiar outsider practices.

➤ Most of the faiths described by the word "traditional" are experiential, rather than intellectual.

➤ The shaman, the totem, and the fetish are important components of traditional religious systems.

➤ Huna Kupua is a particularly long-lived example of a nonscriptural nature religion.

➤ Many African religious systems acknowledge a supreme God (who goes by various names) and an array of lower spirits.

➤ Many Native American traditions emphasize personal wholeness within sacred natural processes.

# Modern Times: New Forms

Every religion was once a new religion to someone. In this chapter, you will find out about some of the most important new religious movements to surface in the United States over the last hundred years.

## What Is a "New Religion"?

The formal academic definition of a "new religion" is still a matter of scholarly debate, some of it pretty dry. For the (pragmatic!) purposes of this chapter, our working definition of the phrase "new religion" will be accessible, straightforward, and, so far as we can make it, consistent.

All of the new religions discussed within this chapter meet the following criteria:

➤ The movement represents a distinct set of spiritual traditions not widely practiced in the United States before 1900. (Such traditions sometimes, but not always, arise out of variations on or combinations of previously existing faiths.)

➤ The movement clearly emphasizes voluntary membership among newcomers to the system, in practice as well as in theory.

➤ Whether or not the movement features a formal hierarchy or set of doctrines, it has developed a basic structural viability. It is able to provide a continuing focus on fulfilling the spiritual needs of an identifiable body of practitioners. (This chapter does not focus on what appear to the authors to be short-term trends.)

➤ Even though it may embrace certain points of doctrine from an earlier tradition, the movement offers new and alternative patterns of authority, organization, or practice.

# Seven New Faiths ... and a Movement

Using these principles as a yardstick, this chapter will focus on the following new religions:

➤ The Nation of Islam

➤ The International Society for Krishna Consciousness (the ISKCON, or Hare Krishna movement)

➤ Transcendental Meditation

➤ Neo-Paganism

➤ The Baha'i Faith

➤ Santeria

➤ Rastafarianism

➤ The New Age Movement

## Seven? That's It?

The seven faiths examined in depth here are not the only spiritual movements that could be discussed in a chapter like this, and no doubt some practitioners will argue that their tradition has been unfairly overlooked. In part to address this problem, we have also included very short summaries of some other recent traditions and movements at the end of this chapter.

Covering every new religious movement in a book such as this is, however, an impossibility. Each group discussed in this chapter has been chosen simply to illustrate new points of view. Each reflects important trends that have emerged within the American religious experience over the past century. By learning about these, you will be in a much better position to find out more about other traditions that you may encounter.

It's particularly important to bring a spirit of openness to your encounters with new systems of religious belief. After all, these believers are likely (by definition!) to offer perspectives that differ radically from your own experience of religious practice. Remember that fear and skepticism are not the best tools for encountering new systems.

## What About ...?

Many new and well-known religious groups have been passed over here because they appear to many observers to fail an important test: resisting the use of intimidation in recruiting and retaining members.

We take the position that coercion is antithetical to spiritual seeking. However, it should be noted that traditions change, grow, and expand over time. (It's also worth noting that today's "major" religions were the persecuted "minor" faiths of centuries past.)

# The Nation of Islam

The Nation of Islam (or Lost-Found Nation of Islam) was founded in Detroit in 1930 by Wallace Fard, a salesman whose early life remains something of a mystery. Fard claimed a prophetic vision from Allah directed specifically toward black Americans.

He taught that Islam was the only valid faith for African Americans and that blacks were the descendants of the race that had made human civilization possible. His followers considered him to be "Allah in person."

When Fard vanished mysteriously from the scene in 1934, an associate named Elijah Poole, the son of former slaves, changed his name to Elijah Muhammad and assumed control of the church. Muhammad established himself as the "messenger of Allah" and began an economically focused separatist movement that promoted the social power of black communities and rigorous obedience to rules derived from Islam.

### Watch It!

Throwing around terms like "cult," "sect," or "charismatic group" will always close doors more quickly than open them. Avoid labels when you talk about the religious practices of others.

### On the Path

The Nation of Islam is an indigenous (and, frequently, controversial) American movement based on a distinctive brand of Islamic-influenced practice and observance. Debates over racial separatism and doctrinal matters have created two strands within the group. One, led by Wallace D. Muhammad, son of Elijah Muhammad (1897–1975), has changed its name and sought to move closer to traditional Islamic practice; the other, led by Minister Louis Farrakahn, has retained the name "Nation of Islam" and the separatist social vision enunciated by Elijah Muhammad.

## A Distinctive Practice

During Elijah Muhammad's lifetime, however, the movement was never, properly speaking, a branch of mainstream Islamic worship. It developed a distinctively American focus that rejected the civil rights movement's campaign for integration among blacks and whites. It preached rigorous separatism and an unwavering personal moral code. The personal commitment of practitioners was reflected in distinctive dress. At one point Elijah Muhammad called for the establishment of a separate black state.

Muhammad's most important convert to the faith may have been the outspoken and eloquent Malcolm X, a brilliant, vigorous, and effective agitator. Born Malcolm Little, the ex-convict-turned-minister followed established church practice and abandoned his "slave name" when he joined the church.

In 1964, Malcolm broke with the group and established a separate organization. His assassination in 1965 was attributed, in vague terms, to elements within the Nation of Islam, but the event remains a subject of bitter dispute.

## Pride and Action

Despite the criticism and controversy that has swirled around it since the late 1950s, the Nation of Islam remains an instrument of hope, pride, and self-determination for its many practitioners. The impassioned rhetoric of church leaders has occasionally led to cycles of intense media scrutiny of the church and to the unfortunate (and erroneous) assumption among white people that the group promotes racial violence.

The Nation has embraced hard work, piety, and accountability in an unmistakable way. Its practical emphasis on reclaiming drug-ridden urban areas deserves far more attention than it has received. Media coverage of the group's role in the so-called Million Man March on Washington, D.C., in 1996 led to further controversy, this time about the disputed number of attendees and the nature of the church's involvement; nevertheless, the march was a significant achievement.

The Nation of Islam has been among the most visible new religions on the American scene in the second half of the twentieth century, and one that has made a tangible difference in the lives of African Americans.

# The International Society for Krishna Consciousness

"Hare Krishna" devotees, robed and chanting, have become a familiar sight around the world. Founded in 1966 in New York City by A.C. Bhaktivedanta Swami Prabhupada, ISKCON is a distinctive movement that explicitly rejects "the pantheism, polytheism, and caste consciousness that pervades modern Hinduism," according to the group's Internet site.

Outsiders often call the Hare Krishnas a "Hindu sect." Although ISKCON sees itself as continuing important traditions within the Hindu faith, the "sect" designation clearly makes insiders uncomfortable. The group sees itself as a platform for certain important and independent traditions, known as "divine culture."

"Krishna consciousness," the group's statement of purpose explains, "is in no way a faith or religion that seeks to defeat other faiths or religions. Rather, it is an essential cultural movement for the entire human society and does not consider any particular sectarian faith." Despite this cross-cultural emphasis, the group relies on the Bhagavad-Gita as a central text.

**Watch It!**

ISKCON devotees regard Krishna consciousness as transcending narrow sectarian forms. They reject the classification of their movement as representing Hinduism—or as being aligned with any other hierarchically organized religious structure.

## ISKCON's Goals

The group has seven primary objectives:

➤ The propagation of spiritual knowledge ("to society at large") for the overall betterment of the human family.

➤ The encouragement and development of Krishna consciousness, as revealed in holy scriptures.

➤ The union of members of society with each other and "to Krishna, the prime entity, thus developing the idea within the members, and humanity at large, that each soul is part and parcel of the quality of Godhead (Krishna)."

➤ The promotion of the practice of chanting the names of the Deity.

➤ The establishment of places of "transcendental" religious worship and practice—sites devoted to Krishna.

➤ The support and promotion of a simpler way of life more in tune with the patterns of nature than that offered by contemporary society.

➤ The publication and circulation of written works that support the six preceding goals.

### On the Path

The Hare Krishna movement follows the teachings of the Vedas and the Vedic scriptures. It places a special emphasis on the Bhagavad-Gita, and promotes Vaishnavism, a devotional school that inculcates "the essential and universal principle of all religion: loving devotional service to the one Supreme Personality of Godhead." ISKCON regards the chanting of the holy name of Krishna as a primary spiritual practice. It is a nonsectarian, nondenominational movement.

## Core Practices and Beliefs

Beyond "chanting the name(s) of the Lord," members of ISKCON observe strict vegetarianism and accept the formal notion of the guru/disciple role as a component of individual spiritual development. In these respects it shares points of contact with traditional Hinduism.

Significantly, the group has sold over 10 million copies of its vegetarian cookbooks. Its vegetarianism reflects deeply held spiritual principles. ISKCON maintains a vigorous environmental agenda that includes the development of new rural communities; its members see meat-eating as symptomatic of profound environmental, social, and spiritual imbalance. The group considers environmental activism for its own sake to be fundamentally short-sighted, and views the spiritual development of humanity as a whole as the only appropriate response to global social and environmental problems. In particular, any environmental campaign that does not acknowledge the sanctity of all life is seen as fatally flawed.

Although the focus within the ISKCON tradition is on veneration of the Lord Krishna through Hare Krishna mantra meditation, Prabhupada, its late founder, is regarded as the transmitter of truth within an established line of inspired teaching. "He is and will remain always the instructing spiritual master of all devotees in ISKCON," says a group statement.

## Room for All

Dismissed by some observers as overemotional and lacking in theological depth, ISKCON actually represents a sophisticated, albeit direct, revision of familiar Hindu principles. Its unalterable egalitarian stance and its forthright rejection of sectarian conflicts have earned it a passionate following.

ISKCON'S preeminent goal, according to its members, is instructing people in the best and most immediate means of expressing love for God. The exuberance, openness, and complete dedication with which practitioners embrace that objective has become one of the tradition's most distinctive elements.

# Transcendental Meditation

If ISKCON seeks to distance itself from the designation "Hindu sect," the Transcendental Meditation (T.M.) movement appears eager to reject the idea of formal religious observance altogether.

The group prefers to focus on the scientifically verifiable benefits of simple meditation techniques. Nevertheless, it has an identifiable group of practitioners and a discernible spiritual element based on Hindu Vedanta philosophy. It would also appear to have a metaphysical framework, given the group's emphasis on transcending physical boundaries through advanced meditation practice. Some meditators are held by practitioners to be capable of certain forms of levitation.

Remembered by many outsiders as the belief system that served as a spiritual way-station for the Beatles, the Transcendental Meditation movement was introduced to Westerners by Maharishi Mahesh Yogi in 1959. It has attracted many practitioners over the years. It is not seen as exclusive; T.M. practitioners may use their meditation to supplement other faiths, or no faith at all.

## *Simple Meditation*

One learns the T.M. method by means of (paid) introductory sessions with a certified instructor. The techniques are not at all complex, but formal instruction is a prerequisite to participation.

The meditation techniques are practiced twice a day for 15 to 20 minutes while sitting comfortably with closed eyes. Practitioners emphasize the effortlessness of the procedure, and many cite increases in overall health and well-being.

The organization, which promotes its activities via a network of Vedic Schools and affiliates, highlights an impressive number of studies linking Transcendental Meditation to increases in creativity, memory, happiness, energy, and overall stamina. Whether it is a scientifically validated method for personal growth and happiness, a nonscriptural devotional practice, a personal relaxation method, or some combination of all of the above, T.M. has

**On the Path**

For many practitioners, this pragmatic, results-oriented practice is the perfect method for incorporating harmony and integrity into a modern world—a world that may, they argue, need those qualities far more than it needs another organized religious structure. That T.M. has thrived in its current form says much about the limited appeal of traditional religious practice for many today.

emerged as a popular and flexible discipline. It has attracted a number of passionate adherents who are uncomfortable with organized (and perhaps overly dogmatic) religious structures.

## A Non-Faith "Faith"?

T.M. has evolved from an expression of the 1960s youth subculture to a kind of voluntary, open-ended vehicle for nondogmatic meditation principles—a vehicle with apparently benign capitalist overtones. Its insistence on fees for initial instruction has left some wondering at its motives, but the movement is not, to all appearances, an exploitative one.

# Neo-Paganism

This "new" faith, which encompasses many groups, appeals to certain religious practices that are quite ancient in origin. In the distant past, tribal people all over the earth strove to understand the natural world and their place within it. They tended to hold all life in honor, revering the earth as the Mother from whom life springs. Some aspects of the European expression of these faiths have experienced a revival in recent years.

### Bet You Didn't Know

Ancient tribal peoples in pre-Christian Europe saw a profound order in the rhythms and cycles of the seasons, and they celebrated these guiding rhythms in their observances. Today, after centuries of suppression and neglect, many of these mysterious religions are being reanimated and adopted by contemporary followers. Most of these believers fall under the umbrella grouping "Neo-Pagan," and many of them elevate Goddess worship to high importance.

The Neo-Pagan groups in existence today emphasize personal responsibility and see divine force as residing in all things. Worshiping nature and the seasons, they associate particular physical locations with their sacred rites. Most members of these groups openly embrace the formerly derogatory label "pagan," embracing the original sense of its Latin root "country-dweller" while rejecting the negative associations that have accrued to this word over time.

A perception of the giver of life responsible for forming and shaping both earth and heaven has been found in many cultures. Today, among many Neo-Pagans, this figure is called by some variation of the name "Goddess." Her role as all-pervasive Creator of life and of the universe is consistent with the cultural understanding of many indigenous peoples.

## Sun and Moon

The cycles of the sun and moon were among the powers early worshipers sought most fervently to understand. Some scholars suggest that the cycles of the moon were first noticed by women who connected them with another 30-day cycle, the menstrual cycle. It is likely that this initial "noticing" developed into ongoing understandings of important formal responsibilities and the relationship between the tribe, the earth, and the moon whose waxing and waning seemed so clearly to affect the human body.

In this way, many contemporary believers assume women came to perceive the moon itself as Goddess, directly and intimately related to the bringing forth of new life. Women of experience and wisdom eventually became priestesses within their tribes.

## Persecution and Revival

The arrival of the invading Romans signaled the beginning of an assault on the cultures of many ancient tribes of Goddess worshipers. This assault continued throughout the Christian period, and was reinforced by the Muslim conquest in Europe and Asia Minor. Although suppressed (often violently), some of the old ways have, remarkably enough, managed to survive.

In recent years many groups have revived or reconstructed ancient traditions centered on nature and Goddess worship. The belief systems of these gatherings have been eclectic and hard to define. All the same, it is true that the cycles of the year hold important religious meaning for Neo-Pagans.

## The Dance of the Seasons

Seasonal and nature observances play a major role among members of Neo-Pagan groups; accordingly, the following sections will make a modest attempt to look at major calendar observances of importance to these (frequently misunderstood) practitioners. It is important to recognize, though, that this summary is not an exhaustive list of all the holidays and observances of the Neo-Pagan movement. No such list exists! This is a many-layered movement, one that intuitively resists both dogma and centralized structures.

## The Winter Solstice

The winter solstice marks the shortest day of the year in the Northern Hemisphere, the time when the least daylight is in evidence. After a spiraling-down of observable light to this single, shortest day, the year begins its ascent toward the summer solstice, the longest day of the year, six months later. The winter solstice is seen as a time to honor the darkness of night and the womb, and to celebrate emerging life. During this period, the Goddess is recognized as reborn, an infant.

The emphasis on renewal, on rebirth out of darkness, is thousands of years old, and predates the familiar observance of the Christian Nativity festival (Christmas) on December 25, very near to the winter solstice. The burning of candles and logs during the winter solstice is of similarly ancient origin.

### What's It Mean?

**Cross-quarter holidays** are holidays that occur at the points between the four natural solar "quarters" of the calendar (for instance, between the winter solstice and the fall equinox). Neo-Pagan festivals marking these holidays incorporate fire as a central element.

## Imbolc

This *cross-quarter holiday*, also known as Brigid, falls between the winter solstice and the spring equinox. It celebrates the increasing of the light and marks the progression from the newborn moon of winter to the infant moon of spring. This is a fire festival, a time of individual growth and healing, the period of inner power. During Imbolc, the Goddess is revered as a young virgin.

## The Spring Equinox

During the spring equinox, one of the two points in the year at which the daylight and the dark of night are in balance, practitioners honor and celebrate the awakening of plants and animals from the seeming death of winter. Signs of fertility (such as the hare and the egg, familiar symbols in the modern secular Easter) are important parts of this celebration. Signs of returning life are revered; the joyful promise of youth's renewal abounds.

## Beltane

This cross-quarter holiday is after the spring equinox and before the summer solstice. It is a time of flowering for fertile Mother Earth.

During this holiday, young love and sexuality are celebrated with the ancient dance of the Maypole. The Goddess is honored as the maiden whose blood fertilizes the earth, and as the great mother. This is a time to honor personal sexuality and creativity as the source of life.

Celebrants leap across fires to release past injuries, and to warm and open the heart. During Beltane, the pleasure to be found in erotic pursuits is understood as innocent, and is expressed by means of rituals honoring the Goddess.

## The Summer Solstice

This is the time of the longest day of the year in the Northern Hemisphere, and the most light. The Goddess is honored as being at the peak of her fertility, sexuality, and power. The summer solstice is regarded as a time of commitment to one's beloved, and also of the cultivation of healthy self-love.

The hope and promise of new life found in the winter solstice has been brought into existence through the ever-increasing light. Just at this moment of fertility and bounty, the journey back toward darkness begins with the waning half of the yearly cycle.

## Lammas

Lammas is the cross-quarter holiday celebrated at the midpoint between summer and fall. The Goddess revered as the mother at the last cross-quarter holiday is now seen as the matron.

Slowly the days grow shorter and heat intensifies. That which has been planted is ripening but not yet harvested. The Grain Goddesses are celebrated as the bringers of the source of life; this is a time when practitioners honor Mother Earth in her ripeness. It is also a time for focusing on those things one hopes for in the coming harvest of one's own daily efforts.

## The Fall Equinox

This is the second calendar-point of balance between light and dark. The harvest is seen as complete, and the Earth no longer bears fruit. The Goddess is considered as passing into menopause. The fall equinox is a time to give thanks for the rich harvest that will see believers through the coming time of darkness.

## Samhain

This cross-quarter festival celebrates the halfway point between the fall equinox and the winter solstice. It is regarded as the most powerful night of the year, a time when that which separates believers from other worldly forces may be transcended.

The Goddess, last revered as a matron, is now regarded as the crone, the old woman preparing for death. At this time of the year, the old falls to decay, making room, in the fullness of time, for the wonder of rebirth.

At this time, old habits and patterns are ritually burned, and the spirits of those who have passed are considered to be close at hand. Prayers for departed loved ones are offered during this festival.

Samhain (or Hallowmas) marks the Neo-Pagan New Year; it is seen as representing the beginning of the new.

# The Baha'i Faith

Although Baha'i arose in nineteenth-century Persia (the country today known as Iran), it has made its presence felt only in recent years. Its founder, an adherent of the messianic sect of Shiite Islam known as Babism, was a religious leader known to Baha'i practitioners as Baha'u'llah. He was born Mizra Husayn Ali Nuri, the son of a well-to-do government minister. In 1852, while in prison, Baha'u'llah is said to have received a vision concerning God's plan for humanity. Over the following 40 years, he composed a body of scriptures that form the heart of what is now the Baha'i faith. Baha'u'llah, who spent most of his adult life either imprisoned or under watch, died in 1892.

The guiding ideas behind Baha'u'llah's writings are egalitarian, practical, and progressive. In keeping with the central principles of the Baha'i faith, practitioners of this fast-growing tradition regard all previous religions as unified, and accept that God has been revealed to humanity through the influence of various manifestations at various points in history.

**On the Path**

Baha'i believers regard Baha'u'llah as the most recent in a long line of divine messengers that includes Moses, Buddha, Jesus, and Muhammad. These divinely appointed intervening figures are seen as motivating forces in the development of human civilization.

## Unity

Remarkably, the Baha'i tradition survived the death of its founder without encountering discord, internal rifts, controversy, or institutional fragmentation. (If you've been paying attention to the early histories of the other religions discussed in this book, you know that's a pretty impressive feat.) Under the leadership of Abdu'l Baha and Shoghi Effendi, the two men who, successively, headed the movement after 1892, the religion has grown and prospered around the world, notably in Africa and North America. It now boasts communities of believers in 205 countries.

## Equality and Harmony

The Baha'i Faith is the only world religion whose scriptures embrace, without ambiguity or equivocation, the fundamental equality of men and women. Among other principles endorsed in the writings of Baha'u'llah are these:

➤ Humanity as a single race

➤ International government and a single language

➤ The necessity of the elimination of prejudice

➤ The importance of universal education

➤ The negative effects of economic inequality

➤ The necessity of avoiding forbidden activities (such as killing, theft, lying, sexual misbehavior, gambling, abusing drugs and alcohol, and engaging in malicious gossip)

## Rapid Growth

Despite (carefully observed!) scriptural injunctions against proselytizing, the Baha'i Faith has become one of the world's fastest-growing independent religions. In the past century, it has mushroomed from an obscure faith based in the Middle East to a global movement that has attracted believers in virtually every recognized nation. Only Christianity is more widely dispersed—and remember, at a comparable point in its historical development, Christianity, too, was a tiny, suppressed local movement that often appeared to be on the verge of extinction. Followers of the Baha'i faith have also been subjected to persecution in contemporary Iran.

Although its theological structure runs counter to ideas like "dominance," this vigorous, inclusive, and diverse faith may well emerge as one of the most important in the twenty-first century.

# Santeria

Santeria, in contrast to the global reach of the Baha'i faith, is a small and frequently misunderstood religion that combines ancient African and Catholic practice in a remarkable religious synthesis. Although it was almost completely unknown in the United States until very recently, it has been gathering force for over three centuries.

Santeria, which incorporates elements of prayerful animal sacrifice, reached American shores in the wave of immigration that followed the Cuban revolution of 1959. Its American practice is most notable among Afro-Cubans, Puerto Ricans, and African-Americans in sections of New York City, but it has extended elsewhere in the country as well. This (currently) small hybrid religion combines elements of tribal African observance and Roman Catholic terminology and history. Today, Santeria is the subject of increasing devotional and scholarly interest.

## Orisha

Santeria is inspired by the presence of orisha (spirits) known by both African and Spanish names. The strong African elements of the faith can be traced to the slave trade that brought people of the Yoruba nation to lives of forced labor in Cuba for three and a half centuries.

## A New Form

The "conversion" of these slaves to Roman Catholicism resulted not in the eradication of existing African rituals but in their perpetuation in a new and extraordinary form. Santeria combines both indigenous name and ritual with the personifications of acknowledged Roman Catholic saints, a combination that may have been intended to appease religious authorities at first but are now an integral feature of the faith.

Saint Francis of Assisi, for example, is associated in Santeria with the orisha known as Orula, who embodies the principle of wisdom, the number sixteen, the colors green and yellow, and a particular distinctive dance involving the orisha known as Oshun, who in turn is associated with La Caridad del Cobre, the patron saint of Cuba.

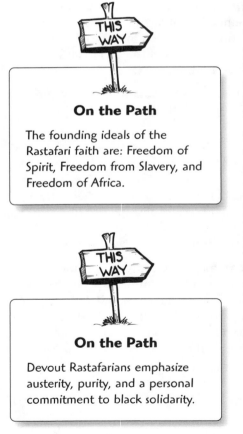

### On the Path

The founding ideals of the Rastafari faith are: Freedom of Spirit, Freedom from Slavery, and Freedom of Africa.

### On the Path

Devout Rastafarians emphasize austerity, purity, and a personal commitment to black solidarity.

## Rastafarianism

The Rastafari movement honors Africa as the birthplace of humankind and issues an unmistakable call for autonomy and self-sufficiency among blacks. This distinctive religious practice was formulated by the descendants of slaves in the slums of Jamaica during the twentieth century.

The origin of Rastafarianism, which is as much a cultural movement as a religion, can be found in the teaching of the Jamaican-born advocate of black nationalism Marcus Garvey, famous for his "Back to Africa" movement. In the 1930s, Garvey's distinctive message of black unity and pride in African heritage found a new expression in Jamaica. News that Haile Salassie had been crowned emperor of Ethiopia was acclaimed not merely as a political development, but as confirmation of a prophecy that a black messiah had been crowned. Many Jamaicans honored Salassie as a living God for the black race. (Salassie's previous name was Ras Tafari, and it is from him that they chose the name of their movement.) Salassie, who died in 1975, was not a Rastafarian.

Rastafarians are perhaps best known for their joyful reggae music and for their use of marijuana in meditation and for health purposes. They believe that the use of this herb is sanctioned by various references in the Bible. It is probably worth noting here that a particularly powerful strain of marijuana, also known as "ganga," grows wild in Jamaica.

True Rastas eat only food that has never been touched by chemical additives, is not canned and is as nearly raw as possible. They use no condiments or preservatives. They drink only herbal drinks, believing that liquor, milk, and coffee are unnatural. They are vegetarians who emphasize the importance of living a peaceful life in study of holy scripture.

As a sign of their beliefs they let their hair grow into dreadlocks, which they see as the image of the lion of Judah. The colors used to represent Rastafarianism are red, gold (or yellow) and green, all adapted from the Garvey movement and associated with new concepts unique to Rasta practice.

Six out of ten Jamaicans are believed to be Rastafarians or allies of the movement. There are said to be hundreds of thousands of practitioners worldwide.

# The New Age Movement

Also worthy of note, but too broadly scaled to fit within the grouping of traditions just named, is the assortment of spiritual movements known as "New Age." This is a broadly inclusive grouping that shows every sign of enriching religious dialogue for decades to come.

This modern spiritual phenomenon has led to a profusion of new sub-movements, the most notable of which combine ancient beliefs about astrology, reincarnation, nature, and Asian medicine with distinctly modern practices.

It is not always easy to make out the line between New Age religious observance and the human-potential movement that began to gain momentum in the 1970s. Some observers use the term "New Age" to describe any hard-to-categorize philosophical system, including the controversial Church of Scientology.

A recent search on the Internet, however, uncovered a broad array of self-described New Age groups whose common trait is open-ended inquiry. Their interests include healing disciplines, new forms of meditation, and environmentally centered spiritual practices inspired by Native American observances.

**On the Path**

For a look at a "new" religion whose practitioners seek to revive and expand a long-dormant series of traditions, refer back to the section on Neo-Paganism.

In the end, the flexible New Age label is probably best understood as an umbrella term for a huge spectrum of beliefs fueled by curiosity and experimentation. New Age enthusiasts are eager to address spiritual questions arising out of the modern world. And this is probably about as far as anyone can go in generalizing about the movement.

# Additional New Religious Practices

Following are brief summaries of some other contemporary practices and movements that may be of interest. To learn more, visit the organization's Web site.

## Aquarian Concepts Religious Order

Summary: Arizona-based order that emphasizes environmental responsibility, interdependence among social groups, and local service. The group holds that the present Aquarian Age represents a period of opportunity for "cooperation, dialogue, and humility," and for fair distribution of resources among all peoples.

Potent quote: "God's perfect will must be each person's goal, as well as an expanded understanding of the Creator's master universe. The laws within our universe can be understood through continued revelation or through 'Aquarian concepts'—spiritual concepts for unity in the new millennium."

The Web site can be found at www.aquarianconcepts.org.

## Eclectic Church

Summary: Group devoted to revising and updating theological tools with an eye toward emphasizing the shared tenets of world religion.

Potent quote: "Where is the 'love of one's neighbor' that has been inspired from the time of Plato to the psychology of C. G. Jung—from the writings of Isaiah to the Gospel of Jesus—from the teachings of Buddha to the faith of Muhammad?

There is a need to reexamine our beliefs in God. People need to rethink the message of the Gospels. Despite the dogma of many religions, until faith becomes meaningful in reality—until men learn to love one another recognizing the Divine quality that is in all human beings—our faith in God is nothing but a proclamation of empty words. Love is not spoken; it is expressed in all we do!"

The Web site can be found at www.eclecticchurch.org.

## Mother Meera

Summary: Indian-born spiritual leader (now headquartered in Germany) whose devotees regard her as Divine Mother. Practice centers around her bestowal of grace to followers who enter her presence physically or spiritually. The group does not emphasize any specific dogma, creed, rituals, or teaching. It is almost completely content-free and attracts followers active within every major religious tradition.

Potent quote: "The Divine Mother has always been worshipped as the sustaining soul and force of the universe. Although some of the faces she wears are well known—Kali, the Virgin Mary, Isis, for example—many of Her embodied forms have chosen to work quietly in the world. In turbulent times such as these, several incarnations of the Divine Mother move among us, each with Her particular task of healing or protection, or transformation. One of the most widely revered and loved of these Avatars of the Divine Mother is Mother Meera."

The Web site can be found at www.mothermeera.com.

## Natural Pantheism

Summary: Contemporary religion embracing and celebrating nature and the cosmos as revealed by various means, including scientific inquiry.

Potent quote: "When you look at the night sky or at the images of the *Hubble Space Telescope,* are you filled with feelings of awe and wonder at the overwhelming beauty and power of the universe? When you are in the midst of nature, in a forest, by the sea, on a mountain peak—do you ever feel a sense of the sacred, like the feeling of being in a vast cathedral? Do you believe that humans should be a part of Nature, rather than set above it? If you can answer yes to all of these questions, then you have pantheistic leanings. Are you skeptical about a God other than Nature and the Universe? Yet do you feel an emotional need for a recognition of something greater than your own self or than the human race? If you answer yes to these additional questions then pantheism is very probably your natural religious home."

The Web site can be found at members.aol.com/Heraklit1.

## Northlight: Pathways to Freedom

Summary: Helpful online summary of contemporary Native American-inspired ritual and practice; includes information on firewalks.

Potent quote: "Here at the Northlight website you will find information on participating and learning about the Native American Culture and Ancient Essene Processes ... Roger Clark, Eaglewolf, is a certified firewalk instructor (with the) FIREWALK INSTITUTE of RESEARCH and EDUCATION. He is also a Sundancer with the Lakota Sioux."

The Web site can be found at members.tripod.com/~northlight.

## Self-Realization Fellowship

Summary: International society founded in 1920 by Parmahansa Yogananda, whose book *Autobiography of a Yogi* has been hailed as a perennial spiritual classic. Promotes ideas related to yoga and yogic practice.

Potent quote: "The universal teachings of Paramahansa Yogananda offer a science of spiritual exploration—one that enables us to create for ourselves spiritually harmonious lives, and to contribute to a more compassionate and peaceful world."

The Web site can be found at www.yogananda-srf.org.

# Synchronicity Contemporary High-Tech Meditation

Summary: Meditation-centered practice that adopts contemporary acoustic and subliminal-message techniques, with the aim of helping practitioners encounter a deeper spiritual experience via the resulting "high-tech" meditation. The Web site features sound excerpts.

Potent quote: "The Synchronicity Paradigm presents a contemporary, scientific perspective in which meditation is directly related to the equilibration of the hemispheres of the brain and deceleration of brain-wave frequencies. Through this balance, the brain's natural opiates are released, opening the meditator to peaceful, blissful, stress-free states and ultimately to the experience of expanded, multidimensional states of Sourceful awareness. Synchronicity technology uses a specific sound patterning to recreate and contemporize the two basic elements of the isolation / cave experience [of classic yogic practice]: the slowing of brain-wave frequencies and the use of subliminal affirmation."

The Web site can be found at www.synchronicity.org.

# World Prayer Chain

Summary: An online interfaith prayer effort proposing specific prayers in a variety of traditions.

Potent quote: "Without God, everything is lacking."

The Web site can be found at www.prayerchain.org.

---

### The Least You Need to Know

➤ Every religion was once a new religion to someone.

➤ In the twentieth century, the Nation of Islam, the Hare Krishna movement, Transcendental Meditation, Neo–Paganism, the Baha'i Faith, Santeria, and Rastafarianism emerged as important new spiritual traditions.

➤ The New Age movement presents a diverse grouping of religious practices with influences both modern and ancient.

➤ Many other new religions exist; the ones discussed in detail in this chapter are only representative traditions.

# Chapter 25

---

# All Down in Black and White

**In This Chapter**

➤ Learn how you can use scriptures from other traditions to build bridges

➤ Find out about the limitations of language (even holy language)

➤ Discover what the world's great religions have to say in response to some of the most important human questions

➤ Learn how even life's great challenges can be seen as "part of the plan"

In this part of the book, you discover important points of contact between familiar religious traditions—ideas that will allow you to find common ground with virtually anyone, of virtually any background, when it's time to address Life's Big Questions.

What do we expect of the world's great religious texts—and how do they overlap?

We're used to thinking of the world's written faith traditions as being in disagreement on specific articles of faith, practice, and outlook. This chapter will show you that this is not always the case!

## Scripture as Meeting-Place

Although some religious systems (such as the Native American and African faiths discussed earlier) manage just fine without them, writings of a spiritual nature are important for most believers. Such writings identify fundamental points of observance and ritual and often lend a sense of permanence and continuity to essential teachings, whether presented as ancient wisdom, timely contemporary instruction, or something in between.

Most important, perhaps, holy scriptures serve as a meeting-point, a common resource and shared spiritual heritage that allows believers within a particular tradition to identify, support, and commune with others. When we encounter someone who treats a sacred text with the same reverence and respect that we do, we can usually, if we choose to, and if we are patient enough, begin to build a bridge with that person.

### Watch It!

So, do "their" scriptures make as much sense as "our" scriptures?

Does it matter? Is the question even worth asking?

"Innocent" criticisms or "objective" analyses of another person's scriptural heritage can feel like direct attacks to the person you're talking to. Your own preconceptions can easily sabotage the conversation, even when you don't mean them to. Try to keep an open mind. Focusing on the "rightness" or "wrongness" of particular points of doctrine or questioning the "logic" of someone else's religious scriptures can undermine the most promising dialogue. Play it safe. Take a neighborly, rather than an intellectual, approach when discussing the scriptural traditions of others.

Early in this book, you saw how the scriptures of the world's great religious traditions addressed knowledge and experience of the divine from very similar vantage points. This chapter aims to offer similar insights on some classic and very human questions of practical spirituality. It is meant to deepen understanding and to help you initiate dialogue, not impassioned debates, with people whose religious practices differ from your own.

### What's It Mean?

A **metaphor** points out how two things are similar without using comparative terms (for example, "like" or "as"). *"All the world's a stage"* is a metaphor. *"My love is like a red, red rose"* is not.

# The Limits of Language (Holy or Not)

What is sacred language? Is it tangible and enduring in and of itself? Is it fundamentally different from other kinds of language? And is it possible to subject it to critical scrutiny without somehow obscuring its message?

## Words, Words, Words

Words—language—reflect our humanness in a fundamental way. They are both our bridge to the holy and also the veil that hides us from the holy. They point us beyond themselves, toward the sacred. They teach of sacred things, but they themselves are not the thing they point to. Words evolve and change as human beings change. It is helpful to keep their limitations in mind as we consider the nature of holy writings.

Every word is really just a *metaphor,* isn't it? It's a name we use to signify something. The word "apple" is not the same thing as our direct experience of an apple. In describing or "naming" anything, we are not defining its essence in any final or unchanging sense. Our endless naming exercise, accomplished through writing or speaking, is the order we bring to our experience: a way of connecting one idea to another. This process feels so natural to us that we may forget that the "real world" exists on its own terms, quite independent of our ways of seeing. By hooking up distinct ideas, language "lies" and "tells the truth" simultaneously.

## "Shall I Compare Thee To ... Wait a Minute ..."

No word exists in a vacuum, not even the words of sacred religious texts. Can anything be a metaphor for the divine?

When we use language, we are making unconscious comparisons based on past experience—our own and other people's. "Sun" comes from an ancient word describing a Mesopotamian deity. "Bias" traces its lineage to a Greek word meaning "oblique," or "on the side;" "fact" comes from the Latin verb meaning "to do." If this is true of our ordinary everyday words, it is equally true of words like "God," "faith," and "divinity."

Language is a tool; it is not the thing it points to.

That having been, er, said ...

### On the Path

Some religious traditions actively encourage the transcendence of written forms. In such traditions, religious observance is incomplete if it focuses too closely on texts. A famous Zen Buddhist story tells of an aging master who reverently passed along to the disciple who was to succeed him a carefully assembled book of their school's most essential teachings. The younger man immediately threw the texts into the fire. In the lineage he was to continue, this was a valid expression of the spiritual heritage.

# A Sense of Purpose

Human beings, the core texts of the world's religions agree, are meant to be happy and to experience fulfillment through the cultivation of love that mirrors perfect divine love.

Most scriptures recognize that the quest for happiness and harmonious interaction among individuals and groups is not without its challenges and obstacles. It involves some kind of spiritual journey, whose completion is an experience of transcendence, homecoming, and contentment beyond the limits of human emotion and ordinary understanding. The fulfillment of this journey is also regarded as concluding all pain, trial, tragedy, distraction, worry, and confusion.

Voices: What Are We Doing Here?

*Buddhism:* Whatever grounds there be for good works undertaken with a view to [auspicious] rebirth, all of them are not worth one-sixteenth part of that goodwill which is the heart's release; goodwill alone, which is the heart's release, shines and burns and flashes forth in surpassing them. (Ittiuttaka 19)

*Judaism:* The Holy Spirit rests only on the one who has a joyous heart. (Jerusalem Talmud, Sukkat 5.1)

*Islam:* The greatest bliss is the good pleasure of God; that is the supreme felicity. (Qur'an 9.72)

*Christianity:* Why take ye thought for raiment? Consider the lilies of the field, how they grow; they toil not, neither do they spin; and yet I say unto you, that even Solomon in all his glory was not arrayed like one of these. Wherefore if God so clothe the grass of the field, which today is, and tomorrow is cast into the oven, shall he not much more clothe you, o ye of little faith? Therefore take no thought, saying, what shall we eat? Or, what shall we drink? Or, wherewithal shall we be clothed?... for your heavenly father knoweth that ye have need of all these things. But seek ye first the kingdom of God, and his righteousness, and all these things shall be added unto you. (Matthew 6:28–33)

*Hinduism:* Giving up all Dharmas (righteous and unrighteous action), come unto me alone for refuge. I shall free thee from all sins. Grieve not. (Bhagavad Gita 18.66)

**On the Path**

A sacred text within the Sikh faith celebrates human purpose as a communion of one's true self with God: "Completely fulfilled is myself, as the Master has granted a vision of the Supreme Being... With Him seated on the throne of eternal justice, ended is all wailing and crying." (Adi Granth, Majh, M.5) Sikhism, from the Punjab region of India, combines Hindu and Islamic Sufi elements. It rejects the caste system of Hinduism, historically emphasizing the ideal of the soldier-saint.

# The Importance of Resolution

In pursuing a spiritual path, the religions of the world place a special emphasis on vigilance and wakefulness, reminding believers that even momentary inattention or disconnection from righteous action and observance can have disastrous consequences.

*Voices:* How Do We Stay on the Path?

*Confucianism:* Flood-like chi [primal energy] ... is, in the highest degree, vast and un-yielding. Nourish it with integrity and place no obstacle in its path, and it will fill the space between heaven and earth....It is born of accumulated rightness and cannot be appropriated by anyone through a sporadic show of rightness. (Mencius II.A.2)

*Christianity:* The day of the Lord so cometh as a thief in the night ... But ye, breth-ren, are not in darkness, that that day should overtake you as a thief. Ye are all the children of the light, and the children of the day. We are not of the night, nor of darkness. Therefore let us not sleep, as do others; but let us watch and be sober. (1 Thessalonians, 5:2–6)

*Hinduism:* Those journeying to heaven do not look back. (Satapatha Brahmana 9.2.3.27)

*Buddhism:* Let me respectfully remind you, life and death are of supreme importance. Time passes swiftly and opportunity is lost. Each of us must strive to wake up, wake up. Take heed. Do not squander your lives. (Traditional reminder issued orally during Zen practice at the conclusion of the day.)

# Loving Others as Ourselves

Is there a single idea that can guide all human behavior and bring it into line with di-vine purpose? For many the answer is yes.

Nearly every religion, regardless of its age or range of geographical influence, empha-sizes the ethical principle known to westerners as the Golden Rule. The world's reli-gions formulate this principle in startlingly similar ways.

Voices: How Should We Act?

*Judaism and Christianity:* Thou shalt not avenge, nor bear any grudge against the children of thy people, but thou shalt love thy neighbor as thyself. I am the Lord. (Leviticus 19:18)

Christianity: Then one of them, which was a lawyer, asked him a question... "Master, which is the great commandment of the law?"

Jesus said unto him, "Thou shalt love the Lord thy God with all thy heart, and with all thy soul, and with all thy mind. This is the first and great commandment, and the second is like unto it: Thou shalt love thy neighbor as thyself. On these two commandments hang all the law and the prophets." (Matthew 22:35–40)

*Confucianism:* Do not do to others what you do not want them to do to you. (Analects 15.23)

Hinduism: One should not behave toward others in a way which is disagreeable to oneself. (Mahabharata, Anusasana Parva 113.8)

**On the Path**

**Jainism** is an Indian religious system that arose in the sixth-century B.C.E. as a protest against certain elements of the Hinduism of its time. It later embraced many notions and practices familiar to Hindu's, but Jainists remain a distinct com-munity of believers who emphasize, in unique ways, charity and respect for all animal life.

# The Almighty as Protector and Sustainer

Even (perhaps especially!) when humans seem least to merit divine grace, it expresses itself. The world's religious scriptures uniformly view divine power as a source of help, support, and unending compassion to the members of the human family. This sustenance is viewed as essential to the completion of life's journeys.

Voices: Who Is Watching Over Us?

*Buddhism:* I appear in the world like unto this great cloud, to pour enrichment on all parched living beings, to free them from their misery to attain the joy of peace, joy of the present world, and joy of Nirvana. (Lotus Sutra 5)

*Judaism and Christianity:* The Lord is my shepherd; I shall not want. He maketh me to lie down in green pastures; he leadeth me beside the still waters. He restoreth my soul; he leadeth me in the paths of righteousness for his name's sake. Yea, thou I walk through the valley of the shadow of death. I will fear no evil, for thou art with me. Thy rod and thy staff, they comfort me. Thou preparest a table before me in the presence of mine enemies: thou anointest my head with oil; my cup runneth over. Surely goodness and mercy shall follow me all the days of my life: and I will dwell in the house of the Lord forever. (Psalm 23)

*Taoism:* Tao never acts, yet nothing is left undone. (Tao Te Ching 37)

# Constant Praise to the Almighty

The faiths of the world agree that the Ultimate is to be openly praised and celebrated. Although praise takes countless forms, the earnestness of spirit and intent guiding this devotion is always recognizable. So, according to the scriptures, are the positive effects upon the individual believer of rendering praise.

Doctrinal and theological disputes aside, the idea of sustained, continual praise to that which is revered as eternal is one of the most exhilarating and dramatic elements unifying human religious practice.

A religion that follows this doctrine is Zoroastrianism. Zoroastrianism is an ancient and influential religion emphasizing the struggle between good and evil forces and predicting the triumph of the supreme spirit, Ahurah Mazdah. Other deities within the system represent supreme righteousness and immortality. The faith is still practiced today in sections of India and Iran.

A holy text within Zoroastrianism summarizes the purifying effect of praising God as follows: "The deeds which I shall do and those which I have done ere now, and the things which are precious to the eye, through Good Mind, the light of the sun, the sparkling dawn of the days, all this is for your praise, O Wise Lord, as righteousness!" (Avesta, Yasna, 50.10)

### On the Path

The *Acarangasutra*, a holy text within Jainism, counsels that "One should not be swept away by the eddies of a mercurial mind."

---

Voices: How Do Human Voices Glorify the Divine Presence?

*The Hare Krishna Movement:* Hare Krishna, Hare Krishna, Krishna Krishna, Hare Hare; Hare Rama, Hare Rama, Rama Rama, Hare Hare.

*Islam:* He is the Living One; there is no God but He: call upon Him, giving Him sincere devotion. Praise be to God, Lord of the Worlds. (Qur'an 40.65)

*Hinduism and Buddhism:* Gate, gate, paragate, parasamgate, bodhi svaha. (Gone, gone, gone beyond, gone beyond—hail the goer!)

*Judaism/Christianity:* Praise ye the Lord! Praise God in his sanctuary! Praise him in the firmament of his power! Praise him for his mighty acts! Praise him according to his excellent greatness!

Praise him with the sound of the trumpet! Praise him with the psaltery and harp! Praise him with the timbrel and dance! Praise him with stringed instruments and organs! Praise him upon the loud cymbals! Praise him upon the high-sounding cymbols! Let everything that hath breath praise the Lord! Praise ye the Lord! Psalm 150)

---

# Suffering and Death

There is no use pretending that the scriptures of the world's religions are in agreement on the answers to fundamental human questions concerning death. They aren't.

As this book nears its end, we appeal not to competing excerpts from ancient religious scriptures, but to a very recent observation from one of today's most influential spiritual writers. The author is the Buddhist monk Thich Nhat Hanh. Although his views do not possess scriptural authority in any tradition, they seem to us to be profound. Perhaps you will agree. Here, then, is one response to what may be the ultimate human question: Why do we suffer and die?

---

Voices: Why Do We Suffer and Die?

When we have a compost bin filled with organic material which is decomposing and smelly, we know that we can transform the waste into beautiful flowers. At first, we may see the compost and the flowers as opposite, but when we look deeply, we see that the flowers already exist in the compost, and the compost already exists in the flowers.

It only takes a couple of weeks for a flower to decompose. When a good organic gardener looks into her compost, she can see that, and she does not feel sad or disgusted. Instead she values the rotting material and does not discriminate against it. It takes only a few months for the compost to give birth to flowers. (Thich Nhat Hanh, "Peace Is Every Step," Parabola, Winter, 1991.)

---

Within the Christian tradition, there is scripture that closely parallels Thich Nhat Han's inspiring words. This saying of Jesus can be found in the Gospel of John.

---

I tell you most solemnly, unless a wheat grain falls on the ground and dies, it remains only a single grain; but if it dies, it yields a rich harvest. (John 12:24–46)

---

As we conclude this work, we acknowledge the enduring power of the force that reconciles all endings and all beginnings, and we look forward to the bountiful harvest that is the birthright of all humankind.

---

### The Least You Need to Know

➤ Scripture can be used to build bridges between people of different religious traditions.

➤ Language, even holy language, is inherently limited because it is based in metaphor and analogy.

➤ Scripture is a tool, not the Goal.

➤ The world's scriptural traditions offer complementary answers to important human questions about human purpose, individual resolve, basic ethical conduct, grace, and the glorification of the divine force.

➤ Even death and suffering can be understood as elements of the divine plan.

---

# Fellow Travelers

## *Thoughts on the sacred, on everyday life, and on the intersection of the two:*

Tell him your future plans.

—Woody Allen, on "how to make God laugh."

The Japanese, concentrating on the abdomen, rid their minds of useless luggage. The Sufi dervishes, using their feet, also rid their minds of useless luggage. The ridding of luggage is more important than the method. What is needed is a method that works, not a philosophy about method, which can be very confusing.

—Sufi Ahmed Murad

Call it Nature, Fate, Fortune; all these are names of the one and selfsame God.

—*Seneca*

All the different religions are only so many religious dialects.

—*G. C. Lichtenberg*

Religion is like the fashion: one man wears his doublet slashed, another laced, another plain, but every man has a doublet; so every man has a religion. We differ about the trimmings.

—John Selden

My reason tells me that God exists, but it also tells me that I can never know what He is.

—*Voltaire*

I feel that there is a God, and I do not feel that there is none. For me that is enough.

—*Jean de la Bruyere*

Every man recognizes within himself a free and rational spirit, independent of his body. This spirit is what we call God.

—*Leo Tolstoy*

"There are quicksands all about you, sucking at your feet, trying to suck you down into fear and self-pity and despair. That's why you must walk so lightly ..."

"The Light," came the hoarse whisper, "the Clear Light. It's here, along with the pain, in spite of the pain."

"And where are you?"

"Over there, in the corner. I can see myself there."

"Brighter," came the barely audible whisper, "brighter." And a smile of happiness intense almost to the point of elation transfigured her face.

—*Aldous Huxley,* Island

I think that the leaf of a tree, the meanest insect on which we trample, are in themselves arguments more conclusive than any which can be adduced that some vast intellect animates Infinity.

—*Percy Bysshe Shelley*

If you can serve a cup of tea right, you can do anything.

—*Gurdjieff*

For the wonderful thing about saints is that they were human. They lost their tempers, got angry, scolded God, were egotistical or testy or impatient in their turns, made mistakes and regretted them. Still they went on doggedly blundering toward heaven.

—Phyllis McGinley

A woman once came to Mahatma Gandhi with her little boy. She asked, "Mahatma-ji, tell my little boy to stop eating sugar."

"Come back in three days," said Gandhi.

In three days the woman and the little boy returned and Mahatma Gandhi said to the little boy, "Stop eating sugar."

The woman asked, "Why was it necessary for us to return after only three days for you to tell my little boy that?"

The Mahatma replied: "Three days ago I had not stopped eating sugar."

—*Ram Dass,* Be Here Now

We trust, sir, that God will be on our side. It is more important to know that we are on God's side.

—*Abraham Lincoln*

All evil vanishes from life for him who keeps the sun in his heart.

—*Ramayana*

Some very humane, simple-minded old lady sees the play King Lear performed, and she is outraged that a poor old man should be so humiliated, made to suffer so. And in the eternal shade she meets Shakespeare, and she says to him, "What a monstrous thing to make that poor man go through all that." And Shakespeare says, "Yes, I quite agree. It was very painful, and I could have arranged for him to take a sedative at the end of Act I, but then, ma'am, there would have been no play."

—Malcolm Muggeridge

When I lay these questions before God I get no answer. But a rather special sort of "No answer." It is not the locked door. It is more like a silent, certainly not uncompassionate, gaze. As though He shook His head not in refusal but waiving the question. Like, "Peace, child; you don't understand."

—*C. S. Lewis*

The essence of civilization consists not in the multiplication of wants but in their deliberate and voluntary renunciation.

—*Mahatma Gandhi*

I have loved to hear my Lord spoken of; and wherever I have seen the print of His shoe in the earth, there I have coveted to set my foot, too.

—*John Bunyan*

As soon as a man is fully disposed to be alone with God, he is alone with God no matter where he may be; in the country, the monastery, the woods, or the city. The lightning flashes from East to West, illuminating the whole horizon and striking where it pleases and at the same instant the infinite liberty of God flashes in the depths of that man's soul, and he is illumined. At that moment he sees that though he seems to be in the middle of his journey, he has already arrived at the end. For the life of Grace on earth is the beginning of the life of Glory. Although he is a traveler in time, he has opened his eyes for a moment in eternity.

—Thomas Merton

God will be present, whether asked or not.

—*Latin proverb*

Lord God of hosts, be with us yet,

Lest we forget, lest we forget.

—*Rudyard Kipling*

He who desires to see the living God face to face should not seek Him in the empty firmament of his mind, but in human love.

—*Fyodor Dostoevsky*

Here is God's purpose—
for God, to me, it seems,
is a verb,
not a noun,
proper or improper.

—*R. Buckminster Fuller*

The soul has the means. Thinking is the means. It is inanimate. When thinking has completed its task of release, it has done what it had to do, and ceases.

—*Vishnu Parana*

To get into the core of God at his greatest, one must first get into the core of himself at his least, for no one can know God who has not first known himself.

—Meister Eckhard

Well, God's a good man.

—*William Shakespeare*

Lord, who art always the same, give that I know myself, give that I know Thee.

—*St. Augustine*

Religion is a way of walking, not a way of talking.

—*Dean William R. Inge*

Religion is doing; a man does not merely think his religion or feel it, he "lives" his religion as much as he is able, otherwise it is not religion but fantasy or philosophy.

—*George Gurdjieff*

We have committed the Golden Rule to memory;
let us now commit it to life.

—Edwin Markham

God is a busy worker, but He loves help.

—*Basque proverb*

Compulsion in religion is distinguished peculiarly from compulsion in every other thing. I may grow rich by an art I am compelled to follow; I may recover health by medicines I am compelled to take against my own judgment; but I cannot be saved by a worship I disbelieve and abhor.

—*Thomas Jefferson*

If you see a child making progress in Bible, but not in Talmud, do not push him by teaching him Talmud, and if he understands Talmud, do not push him by teaching him Bible. Train him in the things which he knows.

—*Anonymous author on Jewish school practices in Germany, circa 1200 C.E.*

If a pickpocket meets a holy man, he sees only his pockets.

—*Hari Dass Baba*

A wise architect observed that you could break the
laws of architectural art provided you had mastered
them first. That would apply to religion as well as to art.
Ignorance of the past does not guarantee freedom
from its imperfections.

—Reinhold Niebuhr

And even in his corrections, let him act with prudence, and not go too far, lest while he seeketh too eagerly to scrape off the rust, the vessel be broken.

—*Time-honored monastery instructions concerning the governance of monks, cited in* Be Here Now, *Ram Dass*

God is a being absolutely infinite; a substance consisting of infinite attributes, each of which expresses His eternal and infinite essence.

—*Baruch Spinoza*


Though the mills of God grind slowly, yet they grind exceeding small;

Though with patience he stands waiting, with exactness grinds he all.

—*Friedrich von Lorgas*


But he learned more from the river than Vasudeva could teach him. He learned from it continually. Above all, he learned from it how to listen with a still heart, with a waiting, open soul, without passion, without desire, without judgment, without opinions.

—Herman Hesse, Siddartha


In the faces of men and women I see God and in my own face in the glass, I find letters from God dropt in the street, and every one is signed by God's name, and I leave them where they are, for I know that wheresoever I go others will punctually come for ever and ever.

—*Walt Whitman*


God is day and night, winter and summer, war and peace, surfeit and hunger.

—*Heraclitus*


Whatever you are, be a good one.

—*Abraham Lincoln*


Hath God obliged himself not to exceed the bounds of our knowledge?

—*Montaigne*


God is subtle, but he is not malicious.

—Albert Einstein

God must not be thought of as a physical being, or as having any kind of body. He is pure mind. He moves and acts without needing any corporeal space, or size, or form, or color, or any other property of matter.

—*Origen (c. 254 C.E.)*

If you have love you will do all things well.

—*Thomas Merton*

Men of sense are really all of one religion. But men of sense never tell what it is.

—*Anthony A. Cooper, Earl of Shaftsbury*

Quit this world, quit the next world, quit quitting.

—*Sufi saying*

The Buddhist doctrine [is] that real riches consist not in the abundance of goods but in the paucity of wants.

—*Alfred Marshall*

You must also own religion in his rags, as well as when in his silver slippers; and stand by him, too, when bound in irons, as well as when he walketh the streets with applause.

—John Bunyan

Imagine the Sanskrit letters in these honey-filled foci of awareness, first as letters, then more subtly as sounds, then as most subtle feeling. Then leaving them aside, be free.

—*Paul Reps, on the use of a mantra*

God is a circle whose center is everywhere and circumference nowhere.

—*Voltaire*

Rain water falling upon the roof of a house flows down
to the ground through spouts shaped grotesquely like a tiger's
head. One gets the impression that the water
comes from the tiger's mouth, but in reality it descends
from the sky. In the same way the holy teachings of godly men
seem to be uttered by those men themselves, while in reality
they proceed from God.

—Ramakrishna

Fear God, yes, but don't be afraid of Him.

—*J. A. Spender*

Talk to me about the truth of religion and I'll listen gladly. Talk to me about the duty of religion and I'll listen submissively. But don't come talking to me about the consolations of religion, or I shall suspect that you don't understand.

—*C. S. Lewis*

...on Sunday go to church. Yes, I know all the excuses.
I know that one can worship the Creator and dedicate
oneself to good living in a grove of trees, or by a running
brook, or in one's own house, just as well as in a church.
But I also know that as a matter of cold fact the average
man does not thus worship or dedicate himself.

—Theodore Roosevelt

It is time now for us to rise from sleep.

—*St. Benedict*

Human endeavor must always remain short of perfection; besides, no one will ever weed out the tendencies innate in his particular nature. The point is to change their force into life power.

—*Ouspensky*

Faith consists in believing when it is beyond the power of reason to believe. It is not enough that a thing be possible for it to be believed.

—*Voltaire*

The finding of God is the coming to oneself.

—*Meher Baba*

It takes place every day.

—*Albert Camus, on the Last Judgment.*

We cannot too often think that there is a never-sleeping eye that reads the heart and registers our thoughts.

—Francis Bacon

To study Buddhism is to study ourselves. To study ourselves is to go beyond ourselves. To go beyond ourselves is to be enlightened by all things. To be enlightened by all things is to free our body and mind, and to free the bodies and minds of others. No trace of enlightenment remains, and this no-trace continues endlessly.

—*Zen Master Dogen*

We live to work out a drama which is God's drama, and therefore anything that happens to us is in some degree God's will. We are participating in the unfolding of God's will. Supposing it's true, for instance, at this moment—which I think it probably is—that what we call Western civilization is guttering out to collapse. If you take that in purely human historical terms this is an unmitigated catastrophe. You and I must beat our breast and say that we lived to see the end of everything, what we love is coming to an end. But the point is, that is a catastrophe only to the extent that you don't see it as part of the realization of God's purposes.

—*Malcolm Muggeridge*

God does not die on the day when we cease to believe in a personal deity, but we die on the day when our lives cease to be illuminated by the steady radiance, renewed daily, of a wonder, the source of which is beyond all reason.

—Dag Hammarskjold

Guru, God, and Self are one.

—*Ramana Maharishi*

The Buddha, the Godhead, resides quite as comfortably in the circuits of a digital computer or the gears of a cycle transmission as he does at the top of a mountain or the petals of a flower.

—*Robert M. Pirsig*

God is over all things; under all things; outside all; within but not enclosed; without but not excluded; above but not raised up; below but not depressed; wholly above, presiding; wholly beneath, embracing; wholly within, fulfilling.

—*Hildebert of Lavardin, Archbishop of Tours*

Time and space are not God, but creations of God; with God, as it is a universal Here, so is it an everlasting Now.

—*Thomas Carlyle*

I have ever been fed by his bounty, clothed by his mercy, comforted and healed when sick, succored when tempted, and everywhere upheld by his hand.

—Jarena Lee, black nineteenth-century evangelist

God shall be my hope, my stay, my guide, and lantern to my feet.

—*William Shakespeare*

God alone is Real.

—*Meher Baba*

God is best known in not knowing Him.

—*St. Augustine*

I consider myself a Hindu, Christian, Moslem, Jew, Buddhist, and Confucian.

—Mahatma Gandhi

# Scriptures to Keep You Company

The following books will offer you a deeper insight into the beliefs and histories of the world's religions.

## The World's Faiths, Old and New

*World Scripture: A Comparative Anthology of Sacred Texts*

International Religious Foundation

Paragon House, New York, 1991

*Readings from World Religions*

Selwyn Gurney Champion and Dorothy Short, compilers

London: Watts & Co., 1951

## Judaism

*The Jerusalem Bible: Reader's Edition*

Alexander Jones, General Editor

Doubleday and Company, Garden City, New York, 1968

*The Mishnah*

Herbert Danby, Translator

London: Oxford University Press, 1933

*The Talmud for Today*

Alexander Feinsilver, Translator

New York, St. Martin's Press, 1980

*A Rabbinic Anthology*

C. G. Montefiore and H. Loewe, Editors

New York: Schocken Books, 1974

*Daily Prayer Book*

Philip Birnbaum, Editor

Rockaway Beach, New York: Hebrew Publishing Company, 1949

# Christianity

*The Holy Bible, Revised Standard Version*

New York: National Council of the Churches of Christ in the USA, 1946, 1971

*The Apocrypha, Revised Standard Version*

New York: National Council of the Churches of Christ in the USA, 1957

*The Complete Gospels: Annotated Scholars Version*

Robert J. Miller, Editor

Sonoma, California: Polebridge Press, 1992

# Islam

*The Meaning of the Glorious Qur'an*

Muhammad Marmaduke Pickthall, Translator

Mecca and New York: World Muslim League, 1977

*Sayings of Muhammad*

Ghazi Ahmad, Translator

Lahore, Pakistan: Sh. Muhammad Ashraf, 1968

*A Manual of Hadith*

Maulana Muhammad Ali, Editor

London: Curzon Press, 1978

*The Translations of the Meanings of Sahih Al-Bukhart*

Muhammad Muhsin Khan, Translator

Chicago: Kazi Publications, 1976–1979 (9 volumes)

*Sayings of Muhammad*

Abdullah Shrawardy, Translator

London: John Murray, 1941)

# Hinduism

*Hymns from the Vedas*

Abinash Chandra Bose, Editor

Asia Publishing House, Bombay, 1966

*The Upanishads*

R. E. Hume, Translator

Nilgiri Press, Petaluma, California, 1985

*The Song of God: Bhagavad-Gita*

Swami Prabhavananda and Christopher Isherwood, Translators

Vedanta Press, Hollywood, California, 1944, 1972

*The Mahabharata, volume 1, The Book of the Beginning*

J. A. B. van Buitenen, Translator

Chicago: University of Chicago Press, 1973

*Vedanta Sutra*

*The Vedanta Sutras of Badarayana*

George Thibault, Translator

New York: Dover Press, 1962

# Buddhism

*Buddhist Texts through the Ages*

Edward Conze, Editor

New York: Philosophical Library, 1954

*Buddhist Wisdom Books: Concerning the Diamond Sutra and the Heart Sutra*

Edward Conze, Editor

London: Allen & Unwin, 1958

*Perfection of Wisdom in Eight Thousand Lines and Its Verse Summary*

Edward Conze, Editor

San Francisco: Four Seasons Foundation, 1983

*The Tibetan Book of the Dead, or: The After-Death Experiences on the Bardo Plane, According to Lama Kazi Dawa-Samdup's English Rendering*

W. Y. Evans-Wentz, Editor

London, Oxford University Press, 1960

*The Dhammapada*

Irving Babbitt, Translator

New York: New Directions, 1965

*A Guide to the Bodhisattva's Way of Life Shantideva*

Stephen Batchelor, Translator

Dharamsala, India: Library of Tibetan Works and Archives, 1979

*The Zen Teachings of Huang Po*

John Blofield, Translator

New York: Grove Press, 1959

# Confucianism

*The Analects of Confucius*

Arthur Waley, Translator

London: Allen & Unwin, 1938

*Book of History (Shuh Ching): A Modernized Edition of the Translations of James Legge*

Clae Waltham, Translator

Chicago: Henry Regnery, 1971

*Book of Ritual (Li Chi): A Collection of Treatises on the Rules of Propriety of Ceremonial Usages*

James Legge, Translator

Oxford, Clarendon Press, 1885

*Book of Songs (Shih Ching)*

James Legge, Translator

Oxford: Clarendon Press, 1895

*Classic of Filial Piety (Hsiao Ching)*

James Legge, Translator

Oxford: Clarendon Press, 1879

*Doctrine of the Mean (Chung Yung)*

James Legge, Translator

Oxford, Clarendon Press, 1893

*The I Ching, or Book of Changes*

Richard Wilhelm and C. F. Baynes, Translators

Princeton: Princeton University Press, 1977

*Mencius*

D. C. Lau, Translator

London, Penguin Books, 1979

# Taoism

*Tao te Ching: The Classic Book of Integrity and the Way Lao Tzu*

Victor Mair, Translator

New York: Bantam Books, 1990

*The Complete Works of Chuang Tzu*

Burton Watson, Editor and Translator

New York: Columbia University Press, 1968

*The Texts of Taoism: The T'ai Sahng Tractate of Actions and their Retributions*

James Legge, Translator

Oxford: Clarendon Press, 1891

# Shinto

*Shinto: The Way of the Gods*

W. G. Aston

London: Longmans, Green & Co. 1905

*Kojiki*

Donald L. Philippi, Translator

Tokyo: University of Tokyo Press, 1959

*The World of Shinto*

Norman Havens, Translator

Tokyo: Bukkyo Dendo Kyokai, 1985

# Native American Religions

*American Indian Myths and Legends*

Richard Erdoes and Alfonso Ortiz, Editors

New York: Pantheon, 1984

# Traditional African Religions

*Comparative Studies of African Traditional Religions*

Emefie Ikenga-Metuh

Onitsha, Nigeria: IMICO Publishers, 1987

# The Baha'i Faith

*Kitab-i-Iqan: The Book of Certitude*

Baha'u'llah

Wilmette, Illinois: National Spiritual Assembly of the Baha'is of the United States, 1931

*Epistle to the Son of the Wolf*

Baha'u'llah

Wilmette, Illinois: National Spiritual Assembly of the Baha'is of the United States, 1941

*The Seven Valleys and the Four Valleys*

Baha'u'llah

Wilmette, Illinois: National Spiritual Assembly of the Baha'is of the United States, 1945

*The Hidden Words of Baha'u'lla*

Baha'u'llah

Wilmette, Illinois: National Spiritual Assembly of the Baha'is of the United States, 1985

# Timelines of Major World Religions

Following are condensed timelines, drawn from a variety of sources, for five of the world's major religious traditions. Many of the dates are subject to disagreement among the best scholars; we have tried to present the most generally accepted chronologies.

## Hinduism

Pre-2000 B.C.E.: Harrapa culture exists in Indus Valley.

Circa 2000 B.C.E. Aryans migrate into region now known as India. Interplay of cultures and religious practices takes place.

Circa 1500 B.C.E.: Compilation and development of the Vedas is thought to have begun at around this time.

Circa 800 B.C.E.: Compilation and development of the Upanishads is thought to have begun at around this time.

Pre-sixth century B.C.E.: Development of Samkhya (classical school of thought and practice).

Circa sixth century B.C.E.: Development of Nyaya (classical school of thought and practice).

Circa sixth century B.C.E.: Development of Vaisheshika (classical school of thought and practice).

Circa second century B.C.E.: Development of Yoga (classical school of thought and practice).

Circa second century B.C.E.: Development of Purva Mimamsa (classical school of thought and practice).

Circa 200 B.C.E.–200 C.E.: Bhagavad-Gita refined.

Circa first century C.E.: Development of Vedanta (classical school of thought and practice).

C.E. 711: Muslim incursions into India.

C.E. 1498: Portuguese incursions into India.

C.E. 1750–1947: Period of British control over India.

C.E. 1869: Mohandas Gandhi (later known as Mahatma Gandhi) is born.

C.E. 1947: India wins independence.

# Judaism

Circa 2085 B.C.E.: Accounts of Abraham's life reflective of events in this period. Hebrew peoples leave Mesopotamia for Canaan.

Eighteenth century–circa 1500 B.C.E.: A portion of the Hebrews who end up on the outer edge of Egypt are enslaved.

Circa thirteenth century B.C.E.: Moses leads the Hebrews out of Egypt. Scriptures relate a divine encounter and the transmission of the Ten Commandments during this period.

Circa 1000–circa 900 B.C.E.: Palestine conquered, Judea united; David reigns in Jerusalem. Solomon succeeds him. On Solomon's death, chaos and secession within David's kingdom turn Judah, to the south, into the only remaining tribe within the house of David.

Ninth–eighth centuries B.C.E.: Under the sway of the Assyrians, the northern kingdom (Israel) enters a period of decline and corruption. Prophets foresee doom. Assyrian kings eventually carve Israel into subjugated provinces, but leave Judah intact.

Sixth–fifth centuries B.C.E.: Jerusalem falls to Nebuchadnezzar; period of exile to Babylon is marked by retention of religious traditions, and terminates in a return to the holy city. Restoration of the Temple, originally constructed by Solomon, also occurs during this period.

Circa 440–430 B.C.E.: Formulation of legal code under Ezra. First public reading of the Torah.

Fourth–third centuries B.C.E.: Egypt emerges as the dominant force in Palestine and permits a significant measure of autonomy to the Hebrews.

Second century B.C.E.: Syrian power is ascendant in Palestine, resulting in the desecration of the Temple.

165 B.C.E.: The Maccabee family leads a revolt against the Syrians that culminates in the restoration of the Temple.

C.E. 63: Rome's period of tolerance of Judean social institutions comes to an end as Pompey subjugates Jerusalem.

C.E. 66–70 Period of revolt culminates in the destruction of the Temple by the Romans.

Circa C.E. 90: Canon of Hebrew scriptures is completed.

Circa C.E. 200: Mishnah is completed.

Circa C.E. 400: Palestinian Talmud is completed.

Circa C.E. 600: Babylonian Talmud is completed.

Circa C.E. 1135–1204: Life of the scholar and philosopher Moses Maimonedes, probably the most gifted Jewish thinker of the Middle Ages.

C.E. 1492: Jews are expelled from Spain; the event is representative of a long period of segregation, abuse, legal persecution, and expulsion of Jews in many European nations.

Eighteenth century C.E.: Founding of Hasidic movement in Poland.

C.E. 1810: Beginning of the Reform movement in Germany.

Late nineteenth century C.E.: Huge numbers of Jews emigrate to the United States, fleeing persecution in Russia and Eastern Europe.

C.E. 1896: Founding of Zionist movement.

C.E. 1937–1945: Nazis systematically murder six million Jews during World War II.

C.E. 1948: State of Israel is born.

# Buddhism

Circa 560 B.C.E.: Birth of Gatauma Buddha. (Note: Buddha's birth is placed at various points in time by various sects. This is the most commonly accepted dating.)

483 B.C.E.: Council at Rajagrha.

Circa 440 B.C.E.: King Kolasoka's Council.

250 B.C.E.: Council of Asoka.

Circa C.E. 30: Council at Sri Lanka.

Circa C.E. 100: Mahayana ("Greater Vehicle") Buddhism emerges, focusing on goals of compassion and service to others. The new school's approach contrasts with the previous emphasis on solitary practice, which comes to be known as Hinayana ("Lesser Vehicle") Buddhism.

Second century C.E: Life and ministry of Nagarjuna.

Second–sixth centuries C.E.: Refinement of scriptures known as pitakas (baskets) after centuries of oral transmission.

C.E. 470–534: Period attributed to the life and teachings of Bodhidharma.

Sixth century C.E.: In China, mahayana practice combines with the teaching of Bodhidharma. The result is Ch'an, or sitting meditation practice.

C.E. 817: Great Council (Tibet).

Twelfth century C.E.: Ch'an practice spreads to Japan, where it takes the name by which it is best known today, Zen.

C.E. 1160: Council of Anarahapura, Ceylon.

C.E. 1870: Council at Mandalay.

C.E. 1893: First World Parliament of Religion takes place; based in the United States, it exposes many Westerners to Zen Buddhism for the first time.

C.E. 1930: Founding of Japanese Soka Gakkai school.

C.E. 1950: Council at Rangoon.

# Christianity

Circa C.E. 30: Ministry and crucifixion of Jesus of Nazareth.

Circa C.E. 33: The Apostle Peter (the first pope) leads the new church. Stephen, early deacon of the Christian Church, is stoned to death.

Circa C.E. 36–67: Saul of Tarsus suppresses Christians in Jerusalem; later, he experiences a powerful conversion, changes his name to Paul, and becomes apostle to the Gentiles, author of many epistles, and the foremost early Christian theologian. During this period, early Christians spread through Judea; time of oral transmission of Jesus' sayings and life story.

Circa C.E. 65–125: Period of composition of the four Gospels: Matthew, Mark, Luke, and John.

Circa C.E. 66–70: Period of the Roman-Jewish war; destruction of Herod's Temple.

C.E. 125–300: Christians vigorously persecuted in Rome.

C.E. 300–400: Formal Christian doctrine set forth; unorthodox practices branded heretical.

C.E. 313: Constantine I and Licinius issue the Edict of Milan, making toleration of Christianity official Roman policy.

C.E. 325: First Council of Nicaea. Attended by major bishops and papal legates, this Ecumenical Council addressed doctrinal and theological issues and standardized the observance of Easter. Other councils included those of Arles (314), Constantinople (381), Ephesus (431), and Chalcedon (451), and the second council of Nicaea (787), which addressed the vexing issue of the role of religious imagery.

C.E. 800: Pope Leo III crowns Charlemagne emperor on Christmas Day in Rome. The event marks the inauguration of the political entity that would become the Holy Roman Empire, and helps to legitimize Charlemagne's position as ruler over Western European lands once controlled by the Roman Empire.

Eleventh and twelfth centuries C.E.: Rifts between secular and ecclesiastical authorities common.

C.E. 1054: Formal split between Eastern Orthodox and Roman Catholic churches; Eastern Orthodox authorities reject the jurisdiction of the pope, but accept the pronouncements of the first seven Ecumenical Councils.

C.E. 1096–1291: The Crusades.

C.E. 1233: Inquisition founded to counter heretical practices.

Fourteenth century C.E.: Excesses in Rome lead to calls for reform and the foundation of the Franciscan and Dominican orders.

C.E. 1517: Martin Luther initiates the Protestant Reformations; John Calvin follows suit in later years.

C.E. 1529: Henry VIII defies the Pope and declares himself head of the Church of England.

C.E. 1545: Council of Trent. This, the nineteenth Ecumenical Council of the Roman Catholic Church, addressed issues raised by the Protestant Reformations and produced significant internal reforms. It took place between 1545–1547, 1551–1552, and 1562–1563.

Sixteenth and seventeenth centuries C.E.: Missionary activity in Asia; many Christian groups emigrate to North America.

Eighteenth century C.E.: Secular understanding of social groupings becomes more pronounced after European Age of Reason; powerful "revival" movements reinvigorate specific Christian practices in England and the United States. Missionary activity vigorous, particularly in Africa and Asia.

C.E. 1869: First Vatican Council proclaims that the Pope is infallible when he speaks *ex cathedra,* that is, when he, in the exercise of his office of his supreme apostolic authority, decides that a doctrine concerning faith or morals is to be held by the entire Church.

C.E. 1948: World Council of Churches founded to promote dialogue and cohesion among Protestant churches and to acknowledge areas of agreement between Protestant and Catholic practice.

C.E. 1962–1965: Second Vatican Council incorporates observers from Protestant and Eastern Orthodox faiths; promotes diversity, liturgical reform, and involvement of lay people in Catholic worship.

# Islam

C.E. 571: Birth of the prophet Muhammad in Mecca. The city will be the destination of countless pilgrimages in the centuries to follow.

C.E. 610: Muhammad receives his first revelation in the cave at Mt. Hira; this event regarded as holy initiation of the Qur'an.

C.E. 622: Muhammad organizes a Hegira (exodus) of his followers at Mecca to go to Medina.

C.E. 632: Death of Muhammad.

C.E. 656–661: Caliphate of Ali. Bitter division over his legitimacy as leader of the faith causes a split resulting in two divisions of Islam. Shite and Sunni. Shiites regard Ali as the first Imam (leader).

C.E. 661: Founding of the Ummad dynasty under Muawiya.

C.E. 750: Umayyad dynasty overthrown by Abbasid family, which is descended from the uncle of Muhammad. (Abbasid dynasty endures until C.E. 1258)

C.E. 780–1031: Period of the Western caliphate (based in Spain), founded by a surviving member of the Umayyad family.

C.E. 909–1171: Period of the Fatimid caliphate (based in Africa).

C.E. 1258: Baghdad falls to the Mongols; Abassids flee.

C.E. 1517: Capture of Egypt by the Ottomans; Selim I is proclaimed caliph. A long period follows during which Ottoman sultans retain the title of caliph.

C.E. 1924: Title of caliph abolished.

C.E. 1968: Enlargement of Haram in Mecca is completed.

C.E. 1979: A group of extremists led by Theological University of Medina students occupy the Haram in Mecca and hold out against military forces for two weeks before they are overcome by superior power. The holy mosque, revered by millions of Muslims, is recovered.

# Glossary

**Advent**  Season of preparation for Christmas; begins on the Sunday nearest November 30, and lasts until Christmas itself. (Christianity)

**Agnostic**  A person who believes that the existence of God, or a primal cause, can be neither proven nor disproven.

**Ahimsa**  Hindu principle of reverence for life.

**Akikah**  Birth or welcoming ceremony. (Islam)

**Al-Isra Wal Miraj**  Holiday marking Muhammad's divinely supported journey from Mecca to Jerusalem, where he is said to have ascended to meet with God. (Islam)

**Apostolic succession**  Doctrine that, in transmitting authority to the Apostles, Jesus initiated a chain of authority that has extended in an unbroken line to current Christian bishops. (Christianity)

**Arhat**  In the Theravada Buddhist tradition, one who attains enlightenment through solitude and ascetic practices.

**Asceticism**  A practice or set of practices such as fasting, going without sleep, and putting up with rough conditions, that disciplines the body and helps the practitioner concentrate on achieving spiritual perfection and union with God.

**Ash Wednesday**  The seventh Wednesday before Easter. The first day of Lent, marked by the imposition of ashes onto the foreheads of worshipers. (Christianity)

**Atheist**  A person who believes that there is no such reality as God or a primal cause.

**Atman**  In Hinduism, the essential, unending self or soul.

**Bardo Thodol**  Tibetan Buddhist text that sets out instructions for the dying and for their spiritual guides. Popularly known as *The Tibetan Book of the Dead.*

**Bhagavad Gita**  Epic poem relating the dialogue between the human Prince Arjuna and the beloved Lord Krishna, one of the most important Hindu deities. A hugely influential religious text. (Hinduism)

**Bodhisattva**  In the Mahayana school of Buddhism, one who deserves Nirvana but postpones entry to it until all sentient beings are rescued from rebirth and suffering.

**Bodhi Day** Day celebrating Gautama's decision to sit beneath the bodhi tree until he attained enlightenment. (Buddhism)

**Bodhi tree** Sacred fig tree under which Gautama is believed to have received the supreme enlightenment that marked his emergence as the Buddha. (Buddhism)

**Brahma** Personification of the Absolute, the creator of the world, which is perpetually destined to last for 2,160,000,000 years before it falls to ruin, at which time Brahma recreates it. One of the three supreme gods in the Hindu triad. *See also:* **Vishnu, Shiva.**

**Brahman** Ultimate reality. (Hinduism)

**Brahmin** Member of a priestly Indian social caste. (Hinduism)

**Buddha** A fully enlightened being. Siddhartha Gautama became known as Buddha Tathagata ("he who has gone through completely"). Other names for this revered figure include Bhagavat (Lord) and, simply, the Buddha.

**Buddha Day** Day on which the Buddha's birth is celebrated.

**Caliph** Title bestowed on the designated successor to Muhammad in leading the Islamic faith. (The office is now abolished.)

**Chanukah** Festival of Lights celebrating the victory of the Maccabees over the Syrians in the second century B.C.E. (Judaism)

**Christmas** The feast of the Nativity, celebrating the birth of Jesus. (Christianity)

**Chun-tzu** Noble individual. (Confucianism)

**Chung** "Faithfulness to oneself." (Confucianism)

**Conservative Judaism** Branch of Judaism between Reform and Orthodox, willing to accommodate some contemporary social trends. *See also:* **Reform Judaism, Orthodox Judaism, Reconctructionist School.**

**Covenant** Agreement; specifically, the agreement between God and the ancient Israelites, under which God promised protection in return for obedience and faithfulness. (Judaism, Christianity)

**Decalogue** The Ten Commandments that appear in the Hebrew Bible. (Judaism, Christianity)

**Dharma** In Buddhism, sublime religious truth; also, any particular facet of experience or existence. In Hinduism, a religious obligation, social convention, or individual virtue.

**Dualism** The attempt to explain phenomena by means of opposing poles: good and evil, black and white, old and new, "I" and "other," God and creation, and so on.

**Duhsehra/Durga Puja** Hindu holiday celebrating the triumph of good over evil.

**Easter** The central Christian festival, celebrating the resurrection of Jesus after his crucifixion and proclaiming the spiritual rebirth of believers through their union with the risen Christ.

**Ecumenism** Gathering of initiatives promoting greater understanding and tolerance among the various branches of the Christian churches. (The words *ecumenical* and *ecumenicism* are also sometimes used to refer to the process of attaining greater cooperation and understanding among widely differing faiths.)

**Eightfold Path** The path that leads to the cessation of craving and attachment; marked by right understanding, right purpose, right speech, right conduct, right livelihood, right effort, right alertness, and right concentration. (Buddhism)

**Epiphany** Holiday commemorating: the visit of the Wise Men to the newborn Jesus; Jesus' baptism; and Jesus' first miracle, the changing of water into wine; as recounted in the Gospels. (An Epiphany may also be a manifestation of the divine in one's own experience, through a vision, for example.)

**The Five Classics** The *Book of Changes (I Ching)*, the *Book of History (Shu Ching)*, the *Book of Poetry (Shih Ching)*, the *Book of Rites (Li Chi)*, and the *Spring and Autumn Annals (Ch'un Chi)*, which chronicle major historical events. (Confucianism)

**Five Pillars** Five obligations, outlined in the Qur'an, essential to the lives of Muslims. They include: confession of one's faith of God and in his prophet Muhammad, ritual worship, almsgiving, fasting, and pilgrimage. (Islam)

**The Four Books** Confucian texts incorporating the works of Confucius and Mencius (372–289 B.C.E.) and the commentaries of their followers, considered the fundamental teachings of early Confucianism. They include the *Analects (Lun Yu)*, the *Great Learning (Ta Hsueh)*, the *Doctrine of the Mean (Chung Yung)*, and the *Book of Mencius (Meng-tzu)*. Together with the Five Classics, the Four Books make up the basic texts of Confucianism.

**Four Noble Truths** The most important principles of the Buddhist faith; they hold that life is suffering, that suffering is caused by craving and attachment, that craving and attachment can be overcome, and that the means of overcoming craving and attachment is the Eightfold Path. (*See also:* **Eightfold Path**.)

**Godhead** The essential being of God.

**Good Friday** The Friday before Easter, when believers recall the death of Jesus on the cross. (Christianity)

**Guru** Personal spiritual guide, typically one who develops an important personal relationship with a disciple or practitioner. (Hinduism)

**Hajj** A pilgrimage to the holy city of Mecca, required at least once in the lifetime of every Muslim who is of sound body, sane, and able to afford the journey. (Islam)

**Hinayana** Another name for the Theravada school of Buddhism. *See also:* **Theravada**.

**Id al-Fitr** A feast period that takes place at the end of Ramadan and lasts for three days. (Islam)

**Jananzah** Islamic funeral service.

**Jen** The compassion and humanity arising from genuine love. (Confucianism)

**K'che Manitou** An Ojibwa (Native American) term describing the sum total of all spiritual entities; the aggregate of various embodied spiritual forces. *See also:* **Wakan Tanka**.

**Kami** Japanese word for "spirit" or "one residing above." (Shinto)

**Kami-dana** Shelf of the Spirits in the home of a Shinto believer; a miniature depiction of the holy central section of a shrine.

**Karma** Doctrine embodying an impartial principle of moral cause and effect, under which actions have unavoidable implications and even affect one's future incarnations. Only those who escape the cycle of birth and death may be said to go beyond the reach of karma. (Hinduism, Buddhism, and other faiths, in different forms)

**Koan** Zen Buddhist riddle that invites the responding student to overcome potential barriers to enlightenment.

**Krishna** Popular Hindu deity; an incarnation of Vishnu. (Hinduism)

**Krishna Janmashtami** Holiday celebrating the birthday of Krishna. (Hinduism)

**Lailat ul-Qadr** The final 10 days of Ramadan, when Muslims celebrate Muhammad's first experience of divine revelation. (Islam)

**Law** In the Jewish tradition, the written account of the revelation of God.

**Lent** A season of repentance and fasting that serves as a spiritual preparation for the joy of the Easter festival. (Christianity)

**Li** Correct ritualistic and etiquette-based behavior between individuals. (Confucianism)

**Liturgy** Public worship or ritual.

**Mahayana** Younger of the two major schools of Buddhism; venerates the **bodhisattva** (*see separate listing*) and emphasizes the necessity of helping all living beings attain liberation. *See also:* **Theravada**.

**Mantra** Word or phrase repeated in meditation and religious ritual. (Hinduism, Buddhism, other systems)

**Maulid al-Nabi** Holiday celebrating the birth of Muhammad. (Islam)

**Monotheism** Belief in a single personal God, usually a figure seen as unifying the entire universe.

**Mosque**  Building used by Muslims for worship and prayer. (Islam)

**Muslim**  Literally, "one who submits." A follower of Islam.

**Mysticism**  Pursuit of a direct, often ecstatic, inner experience of the Ultimate.

**Nichiren Buddhism**  Term describing a number of Japanese Buddhist schools.

**Nirvana**  State of final liberation from the cycle of birth and death. (Hinduism, Buddhism)

**Nirvana Day**  Day on which the Buddha's passing is observed.

**Nukhagni**  Hindu cremation ritual.

**Orthodox Eastern Church**  The dominant form of Christian worship in Greece, a large region of eastern Europe, and parts of the Middle East, within which individual national churches share liturgical traditions but operate independently of their counterparts. (Christianity)

**Orthodox Judaism**  Branch of Judaism notable for its emphasis on the supreme authority of the Torah, and for followers' scrupulous adherence to tradition. *See also:* **Reform Judaism, Conservative Judaism, Reconctructionist School.**

**Palm Sunday**  The final Sunday of Lent and the last Sunday before Easter; the first day of Holy Week. (Christianity)

**Passover**  Major holiday honoring the delivery of the Jewish people from slavery in Egypt.

**Pauline Epistles**  Ancient letters, attributed to the Apostle Paul, offering guidance to particular congregations and to the Christian church as a whole. (Christianity)

**Pentecost**  Feast commemorating the gift to the disciples of the Holy Spirit following Jesus' resurrection and ascension. (Christianity)

**Pesach**  *See* **Passover.**

**Proselytize**  To make an effort to convince another to convert, typically to another faith or sect.

**Protestant Reformations**  Series of religious and political upheavals in sixteenth-century Europe, leading to the formation of Protestant denominations that rejected the authority of the pope. (Christianity)

**Protestant**  Umbrella term for a diverse set of Christian traditions that came into existence following the Protestant Reformations, and that deny the authority of the pope. (Christianity)

**Puja**  Ritualized worship of a particular deity or holy figure. (Hinduism)

**Pure Land School**  Buddhist movement emphasizing absolute reliance on the Buddha's grace and unwavering faith in the Buddha Amitabha (Amida), who is held to have vowed, in the second century B.C.E., to save all sentient beings.

**Purim**  A festival celebration commemorating the deliverance of Persian Jews from destruction. (Judaism)

**Qibla wall**  In a mosque, the wall that faces Mecca. (Islam)

**Qur'an**  Sacred text held by Muslims to consolidate and fulfill all past revelations from God; regarded by the faithful as the Word of God, whose instrument was the Prophet Muhammad. (Islam)

**Rabbi**  A respected teacher and leader of worship, usually connected to a particular synagogue.

**Rama**  In the epic *Ramayana*, deity whose story celebrates the commitments of family life and the virtue of right living; an incarnation of Vishnu. (Hinduism)

**Rama Navami**  Important holiday centered on the god Rama. (Hinduism)

**Ramadan**  The name of both a month of the year and a period of religious observance. During the holy festival, which occupies the entire month, adults embark on a rigidly observed period of abstinence, reflection, and purification. (Islam)

**Reconstructionist School of Judaism**  Movement holding that Judaism is a fundamentally social (rather than God-centered) religious civilization.

**Reform Judaism**  Wing of Judaism notable for its attempts to adapt the faith to the demands of the modern world, and for its liberal approach to matters of criticism and interpretation of the Law. *See also:* **Orthodox Judaism, Conservative Judaism, Reconstructionist School.**

**Rig Veda**  Earliest and among the most revered of the holy scriptures of Hinduism.

**Roman Catholic Church**  Those Christians worldwide who identify themselves as being in communion with the bishop of Rome, the pope. (Christianity)

**Rosh Hashanah**  The Jewish New Year (observed in September/October).

**Samadhi**  In Buddhism, a state of single-minded concentration; an important tool for pursuing a path of self-awakening. In Hinduism, the point at which an individual's consciousness merges with the Godhead.

**Samsara**  The process of accumulated, karma-driven birth, in which the thoughts and deeds of past lives are addressed. *See also:* **Karma.** (Hinduism, other faiths)

**Sangha**  A monastic community, much like a Western monastery. (Buddhism)

**Second Vatican Council**  Roman Catholic gathering convened in 1962 that eventually led to dramatic reforms in church practice. (Christianity)

**Shabbat**  Sabbath, day of rest. (Judaism)

**Shahada**  Ritual marking a young Muslim's formal entry to the Islamic faith.

**Shaman**  Religious celebrant who is considered to possess more than human powers, including the ability to understand and treat diseases—and sometimes bring them about. (Traditional religions)

**Shavout**  Holiday celebrating the spring harvest season and God's gift of the Torah. (Judaism)

**Shiite sect**  Smaller of the two dominant sects of Islam; emphasizes the authoritative role of religious leaders and their teachings. *See also:* **Sunni sect.**

**Shiva**  Deity symbolizing the various potent forms of the energy of the Ultimate; usually depicted with four arms and surrounded by fire. One of the three supreme gods in the Hindu triad. *See also:* **Vishnu, Brahma.** (Hinduism)

**Shiva Ratri**  All-night celebration of the Divine as manifested in the god Shiva. (Hinduism)

**Sufism**  A variety of movements within Islam that stress **mysticism** and **asceticism** *(see separate entries).*

**Sunni sect**  Larger of the two dominant sects of Islam, often according more authority to the sacred writings of Islam than to human religious authorities. *See also:* **Shiite sect.**

**Sunyata**  (Sanskrit: "emptiness") Principle that all ultimate entities including the Buddha and the state of Nirvana are empty, that is, completely undivided from the rest of the Supreme Reality. (Buddhism)

**Tao**  Literally "path" or "way." According to the scriptures of this faith, the "eternal Tao" cannot actually be named. However, it has been described as a sublime "Natural Order" marked by the effortless alternation of cycles (night and day, growth and decline). The Tao may best be described as "the way the universe works."

**Talmud**  Extensive compilation of rabbinical discussions, commentaries, and clarifications; the Oral Law and its commentaries. (Judaism)

**Te**  Controlling power, virtue, or magical energy; also, integrity or moral rectitude. (Taoism)

**Theravada**  Older of the two major schools of Buddhism; historically one that re-emphasizes the spiritual progress of the individual. *See also:* **Mahayana.**

**Torah**  The scroll containing the Five Books of Moses; also, in a broader sense, the accumulated sacred Jewish writings of the centuries.

**Tori**  Gateway identifying the entrance to a Shinto shrine.

**Totem**  Particular object (generally a plant or animal) held in reverence and regarded as an ancestor or sibling by members of a group. (Traditional religions)

**Upanishads** (Sanskrit: "sitting near") Texts that mark the final phase of the sacred Vedas and contain direct accounts of advice from spiritually advanced mystics. (Hinduism)

**Vajrayana** A Tibetan strand of Buddhist tradition emphasizing yogic discipline.

**Veda** (Sanskrit: "knowledge") The great collection of early Hindu religious scriptures. The Vedas outline spiritual principles accepted by Hindus as fundamental to their religion.

**Vedanta** Classical school of Indian philosophy that gave rise to disciplines emphasizing the transcendent messages of the **Upanishads** *(see separate entry)*. (Hinduism)

**Vishnu** Deity who is seen as a force of transcendent love and whose many incarnations include Krishna and Rama. One of the three supreme gods in the Hindu triad. *See also:* **Brahma, Shiva.** (Hinduism)

**The Vision Quest** Period during which a boy celebrates the onset of puberty by means of solitary meditation, fasting, and tests of physical endurance. The participant seeks a vision that will guide him in later life, and the support and protection of a guardian spirit. (Native American systems)

**Wadu** Ritual washing before prayer. (Islam)

**Wakan Tanka** A Lakota (Native American) term describing the sum total of all spiritual entities—the aggregate of various embodied spiritual forces. *See also:* **K'che Manitou.**

**Waleemah** Wedding reception. (Islam)

**Wu-wei** Taoist concept of an inaction that is really a kind of sublime efficiency.

**Yoga** Classical school of Indian philosophy meant to help instill personal, physical, and spiritual discipline. (Hinduism)

**Yom Kippur** A Day of Atonement marked by fasting and prayer. (Judaism)

**Yorozu-yomi** Doctrine of flexibility that allows Shinto to be adapted easily to the lives of many people.

**Zen** Influential school of Buddhism originally known as "Chan." Bodhidharma is acknowledged as the founder of Zen.

# Index

# C

# I

**279**